Women's Activist Theatre in Jamaica and South Africa

NATIONAL WOMEN'S STUDIES ASSOCIATION /
UNIVERSITY OF ILLINOIS PRESS FIRST BOOK PRIZE

A list of books in the series appears at the end of this book.

Women's Activist Theatre in Jamaica and South Africa

Gender, Race, and Performance Space

NICOSIA SHAKES

© 2023 by the Board of Trustees
of the University of Illinois
All rights reserved
Manufactured in the United States of America
1 2 3 4 5 C P 5 4 3 2 1
♾ This book is printed on acid-free paper.

Library of Congress Cataloging-in-Publication Data
Names: Shakes, Nicosia, 1978– author.
Title: Women's activist theatre in Jamaica and South Africa :
   gender, race, and performance space / Nicosia Shakes.
Description: Urbana : University of Illinois Press, [2023] |
   Series: National women's studies association / university
   of illinois press first book prize | Includes bibliographical
   references and index.
Identifiers: LCCN 2023007281 (print) | LCCN 2023007282
   (ebook) | ISBN 9780252045233 (cloth ; acid-free paper) |
   ISBN 9780252087370 (paperback ; acid-free paper) |
   ISBN 9780252054754 (ebook)
Subjects: LCSH: Feminist theater—Jamaica—History—21st
   century. | Feminist theater—South Africa—History—21st
   century. | Theater and society—Jamaica—History—21st
   century. | Theater and society—South Africa—History—
   21st century.
Classification: LCC PN1590.W64 S43 2023 (print) | LCC
   PN1590.W64 (ebook) | DDC 792.082—dc23/eng/20230227
LC record available at https://lccn.loc.gov/2023007281
LC ebook record available at https://lccn.loc.go v/2023007282

*For my beloveds who have passed on:
My sister, Gail Marie Clarke,
and father, Edward Roy Shakes*

Contents

Acknowledgments   ix

A Note on Terms and Concepts   xiii

Introduction: Race, Gender, Space   1

1 "Mek Wi Choose fi Wiself": Performing a Discourse of Justice in *A Slice of Reality*   21

2 "The Wound Is Still There": *Walk: South Africa* and the Ontological Violence of Rape   59

3 "Mi a go try release yu": Mourning, Memory, and Violence in *A Vigil for Roxie*   91

4 Alternative Spaces: Black Self-Making, Space-Making, and the Work of Olive Tree Theatre   127

Coda: Performing Activism across Space and Time   157

Notes   167

References   181

Index   201

Acknowledgments

This book would not exist had it not been for the warm welcome and cooperation I received from the members, founders, and affiliates of Sistren Theatre Collective, the Mothertongue Project, Letters from the Dead project, and Olive Tree Theatre, as well as other activists and artists. I must single out Honor Ford-Smith, former artistic director of Sistren and associate professor emerita in the Faculty of Environmental and Urban Change at York University, who became a collaborator and colleague over the last nine years; Lana Finikin, executive director of Sistren; Sara Matchett, artistic director of Mothertongue and senior lecturer in the Centre for Theatre, Dance and Performance Studies at the University of Cape Town; and Ntshieng Mokgoro, founder of Olive Tree Theatre. They were my first points of contact and continue to be my go-to persons for more information. The other participants in this project are Rehane Abrahams, Afolashadé, Carolyn Allen, Althea Blackwood, Pauline Blake, Sonia Britton (who passed away in 2021), Lorna Burrell, Nina Callaghan, Amba Chevannes, Karlene Campbell, Chantelle de Nobrega, Gcebile Dlamini, Lihle Dlomo, Beverly Hanson, Joan French, Genna Gardini, Marvin George, Cinderella Green, Brian Heap, Taitu Heron, Siphumeze Khundayi, Carol Lawes, Hertencer Lindsay-Sheppard, Chuma Mapoma, Mbala Mbogo, Patricia McCrae, Makgathi Mokwena, Marlon Moore, Malika Ndlovu, Hilary Nicholson, Rosa Postlethwaite, Koleka Putuma, Cammille Quamina, Patricia Riley, Jean Small, Joan Stewart, Marlon Thompson, Danielle Toppin, and Eugene Williams. I am grateful to the Jamaica Information Service, the Mothertongue Project, Shasta-Lee Smith, and Marlon Thompson for granting me permission to reproduce photos in their ownership, and persons other than my interviewees who agreed to have their images featured in the book: Neila Ebanks, Nipho Hurd, and Beverly Qwabe. I must also mention Sherie Cox, who agreed to let me reproduce screenshots from a video she captured, though I was unable to use the images due to their low resolution. My work in managing this large volume of information, images, and documents was facilitated by my diligent research assistants, Lesley Chinery and Chantel DaCosta.

Another large group of people provided me with feedback on my research and writing as well as mentored me throughout the process. Keisha-Khan Perry, formerly at Brown University and now Presidential Penn Compact Associate Professor of Africana Studies at the University of Pennsylvania, guided me excellently and continues to be a valuable mentor, reviewer of my writing, and friend. Also at Brown, Anthony Bogues, Paget Henry, and Patricia Ybarra provided thorough comments, wrote numerous reference letters, and helped with research resources. I must likewise acknowledge Brian Meeks, Tricia Rose, and Corey Walker, who are former chairs of the Department of Africana Studies at Brown; the late Anani Dzidzienyo; and other Africana studies faculty members who showed an active interest in my research.

Ethnographic research needs substantial funding, and several institutions provided me with grants and fellowships. These are the Inter-American Foundation, the Cogut Center for the Humanities, the Pembroke Center for Teaching and Research on Women, the Watson Institute for International and Public Affairs, the Brown University Graduate School, the Brown University Graduate Student Council, and the Heimark Fund, administrated by Anani Dzidzienyo. While conducting research, I also needed facilitation from academic institutions in Jamaica and South Africa. I thank Verene Shepherd, former university director of the Institute for Gender and Development Studies Regional Coordinating Unit at the University of the West Indies (UWI), Mona; the late Harry Garuba, former interim chair of the African Studies Centre at the University of Cape Town; and their colleagues for hosting me in 2014 and 2015.

Some of the best advice I received came from my peers in graduate school at Brown. Shamara Wyllie-Alhassan, now an assistant professor at Arizona State University, read parts of the book and conversed with me for hours about the writing process. Her first book, for which she won the 2019 National Women's Studies Association (NWSA)/University of Illinois Press (UIP) First Book Prize, is under contract with UIP. Amanda Boston, now an assistant professor at the University of Pittsburgh, was one of my writing companions and offered valuable feedback on sections of the book manuscript. Brandeise Monk-Payton (now at Fordham) and Sachelle Ford (now at Duke) were my co-conveners on the colloquium Mobilizing Performance: Identity and Self-Making in Black Women's Aesthetic Practices, which was held at Brown in 2013–14. It was the first event I co-organized to assist with my research. I also received feedback on my writing from participants in the Brown University Mellon graduate student workshop Performing Dissent, convened by Esther Kurtz and Stefanie Miller. External to Brown University, I received assistance from scholars with whom I have worked on multiple projects. Kanika Batra, professor in the Department of English at Texas Tech University, whose scholarship I draw on, served as a reference for my Joukowsky Family Foundation award from Brown in 2017. Maziki Thame, senior lecturer at the Institute for Gender and Development Studies at UWI Mona, was my co-convener on a major conference panel and has commented on my research; and Shani Roper, curator of the UWI Museum at Mona, is currently planning to co-edit a publication on Sistren with me. I have to also acknowledge Rupert Lewis, professor emeritus in government at UWI Mona. He is my former professor and colleague, and has been a consistent mentor for more than two decades.

Alongside the individuals who have served as collaborators, reviewers, and mentors, I received significant assistance from institutions that organized short-term writing, research, and presentation workshops. Among these are the Brown University Writing Center and its associate director, Stacy Kastner; and Pamela Gaddi and Vanessa Ryan of the Brown University Graduate School and their colleagues who organized Research Matters! in 2016, one of my most memorable professional experiences. Between 2020 and 2022 I also participated in two programs for tenure-track faculty members at the University of California, Merced, which included intensive writing workshops. These were the Mellon Faculty Summer Institute (2020) and the Mellon Pathways to a Diverse Faculty yearlong program (2021–22), facilitated by Tanya Golash-Boza, Christina Lux, Dalia Magaña and Jeff Yoshimi, with administrative support from Jen Quiralte.

Over the past six years I have worked full time at the College of Wooster (2017–20) and the University of California (UC), Merced (2020 to present). Though I am grateful for the generally collegial atmosphere at both institutions, I can only name persons with whom I have worked closely on research or who provided specific personal and professional support. At the College of Wooster these are Ahmet Atay, Christa Craven, Shannon King, Olivia Navarro-Farr, Jimmy Noriega, Helis Sikk, Santha Schuch, Dheepa Sundaram, and Barbara Thelamour. My close friendships with some of these colleagues helped me adjust to a difficult first year on the tenure track. Additionally, I am grateful to Wooster's Department of Africana Studies, including Boubacar N'Diaye and former chair Josephine Wright, who selected me for my first job out of graduate school. At UC Merced, I have received tremendous support, understanding, and encouragement from David Rouff, chair of the Department of History and Critical Race and Ethnic Studies (CRES); and Sapana Doshi, chair of CRES. Ma Vang and Kit Myers, my colleagues in CRES, have provided close personal support throughout the previous difficult two years. By extension, the entire faculty body of the department have been excellent colleagues and inspired me with their commitment to research and student mentorship, as well as their generosity toward me and one another.

I will be forever grateful to the National Women's Studies Association and University of Illinois Press for awarding me the 2017 NWSA/UIP First Book Prize, which came with my first book contract. In addition to winning the prize I received valuable feedback on the first draft of the manuscript from the NWSA/UIP 2017 First Book Prize committee members: Ruth Nicole Brown, Dia DaCosta, Treva Lindsey, and Richa Nagar (with whom I stayed in touch). Over the past six years the editors I have worked with long term at UIP, including Alison Syring Bassford, Megan Donnan, Dawn Durante, and Dominique Moore, have guided me patiently throughout the process, and the editorial team, art department, and public relations team at UIP have all worked assiduously to produce this book. I appreciate their skills, energy, and commitment.

My family and nonacademic friends have made as much impact on my career as my colleagues and, in some cases, even more of an impact. They have my unrelenting gratitude. My father, Edward Roy Shakes, did not live past 2021 to physically be present when the book was completed. However, he was my most enthusiastic cheerleader in life and in my academic work, and still encourages me every day. I'm thankful to the rest of my immediate family for their support: my mother, Elaine Shakes; Gail Clarke, my sister who passed on in 2011; my other sister, Tracey Clarke; and my brother, Edward Jnr. I am grateful as well to my partner and occasional research assistant, Marlon Moore, and my many friends for their love and encouragement. My son, Ayotunde, was born in 2022 while I was preparing the final version of the manuscript. He is my main inspiration, and caring for him has taught me new ways of prioritizing and making the most of limited time. If there is anyone I have forgotten given how long this process has been, I beg your understanding for the oversight and extend my gratitude to you.

And finally, to the Creator and the ancestors: thank you so much. Àse.

A Note on Terms and Concepts

Given some of the misunderstandings around racial, ethnic, gender, and other terminologies, I define here how I apply them in this book. I use the terms *Africana, African, African Diasporic,* and *people of African descent* to refer to people with unambiguous sociohistorical and racial origins in Africa. I often use these terms interchangeably with *Black*, except when it is necessary to underscore geographic distinctions over racial ones. *People of color* is an umbrella term for those who belong to the majority of the racial groups in the world and are not phenotypically European, particularly in the North American context, in which the term was popularized. *Coloured* is a racial-ethnic category that emerged under apartheid in South Africa to classify mixed-race and some South Asian–descended people. It is still used today, though many who formerly would have been categorized as coloured self-identify as Black or mixed. It should not be confused with the archaic word *colored*, employed to describe Black people in North America during the late nineteenth and early twentieth centuries, and I retain the *u* in *coloured* to indicate this distinction. With regard to regional-cultural designations, the terms *Global South* and *Global Majority* refer to Africa, Asia, the Caribbean and Latin America, and the Pacific, the Indigenous and Aboriginal nations of the Americas and Oceania, and their descendants. Depending on the context of the discussion, the terms *Western* and *Global North* may refer broadly to the relatively wealthy countries of Europe, Australasia, and North America, or more precisely to their white populations and academic knowledge systems.

With regard to words that define one's gender and sexual orientation, I apply the term *queer* as an open identifier for anyone who does not fit the conventions of cisgender heterosexual identities or binary gender identities. I often use the abbreviation LGBTQ since the term *queer* is not utilized by many people in Africa and the Caribbean. Cisgender women of various sexualities are the main focus of the book, because the organizations and projects I study overwhelmingly represent them. Whenever a more gender-fluid approach is needed, I apply it.

Aspects of the Jamaican orthography I apply might be unfamiliar to readers who do not know much about the Jamaican language. For instance, I use the term *Patwa* and not *patois* when referring to Jamaica's popular idiom to acknowledge that it is a language in its own right, much like Haitians utilize *Kreyól* and not *creole* to refer to their language (Braithwaite 1984; Devonish 2007). For the Patwa sentences and phrases I quote from unwritten works, I use a spelling system that is close to the one developed at Di Jamiekan Langwij Yuunit (the Jamaican Language Unit) at the University of the West Indies, drawing on the Frederic G. Cassidy system. For excerpts from written works that are in Jamaican, but not standardized Patwa, I reproduce the script verbatim.

Women's Activist Theatre in Jamaica and South Africa

Introduction
Race, Gender, Space

Why This Study? A Self-Reflexive Account

My interest in the link between theatre and social change began in Jamaica, where I had my earliest exposure as a child to conversations about gender and sexuality through plays and skits. The first of these was created by my mother. For many years, she taught family life education at the local vocational training school where my father was the principal. One year, as part of her goal of finding creative ways of engaging the community, she wrote, directed, and acted in a play about how pregnancy affects the lives of girls and women. I was too young then to now recall most of the details of this play, which was staged on a cool evening in the tightly packed canteen of the training center in front of an audience of mainly people from the community. I do remember that it featured a series of vignettes depicting different stories. The one that stuck with me the most was about a teenage girl who was forced to drop out of school because she became pregnant. This story may have resonated with me because my mother played the girl, and seeing her in such a vulnerable role was equal parts entertaining, fascinating, and unusual. There was, however, nothing unusual or unfamiliar about the play as a whole when placed in the larger context of teachers and community leaders using performance as a method of education and public discourse. And it certainly was commonplace to see talented people who had never been trained formally in the performing arts putting their skills on display. This is because in my rural community of Seaford Town, where there were no cinemas, nightclubs, or dine-in restaurants, much of the public entertainment involved our own innovations. These ranged from skits at school, church, and community concerts, to street performances such as a lively military parade by men and boys armed with wooden rifles during Christmastime.[1]

With the knowledge of how integral these types of performances were to our social bonding and sharing of ideas, my mother focused her play on speaking with people at the grassroots level. She was among many teachers who were specially trained by the Jamaica Family Planning Board to address high birth rates among teenage girls and other economically vulnerable populations, and the effects of multiple unplanned pregnancies on women disproportionate to the effects on their male partners. Her play—and similar ventures by other teachers—can be classified as *theatre for development*, theatre aimed at poverty alleviation, population control, and a reduction in sexually transmitted infections, in accordance with guidelines established by the Jamaican government and the World Health Organization. According to such official measures, the sex education projects were successful in Seaford Town: community members frequented the health center to collect free contraceptives, and young women in particular made a connection between their education and their ability to plan their families and ultimately, their lives. However, these projects also generated more impactful conversations. They created a space to critique unequal gender norms that placed more childbearing responsibilities on women, while men, by and large, "continued to have their own social lives" (Elaine Shakes, pers. comm., 2022). Thus, plays and skits like the one my mother wrote allowed for incisive conversations through the talent, bodies, and language of community members. In this respect, they were influenced by Jamaican traditions of community theatre—performances that are mostly created by practitioners who are not formally trained, and staged for relatively localized audiences, sometimes with the help of professional artists (see Van Erven 2001). The 1980s to early 1990s was a particularly prolific period for community theatre in Jamaica.

My mother's untitled play was the first of three theatre pieces centering girls and women that my family created and performed in. Years later, at a similar community concert organized by our youth club, my sister played the boyfriend of a girl who was rejected by her family and expelled from school after becoming pregnant. And I wrote a play inspired by that one, which I performed at the Montego Bay High School (for Girls) annual cultural competition when I was in tenth grade. Although my sister and I definitely reproduced stereotypes to get laughs from the audiences, our cross-dressing performances of macho older men who exploited teenage girls showed that we understood the notion of reproductive freedom in relation to women's sexuality. I did not yet have the language to define the projects that I, my mother, my sister, and others produced, but they influenced my notions of theatre as pedagogy.

Even with my early introduction to conversations about sex and reproduction through performance, I did not learn about the history of the Jamaican women's movement until I watched the TV film *Miss Amy and Miss May* (1990), produced by Sistren Theatre Collective. The film depicts the lives of Amy Bailey and May Farquharson, two Jamaican women who were instrumental in activism around contraception in the 1930s and in the history of Jamaican feminist and women-focused activism. In sharp contrast to the often classist representations found in mainstream discussions about women and sex, Sistren's pedagogy was rooted in the perspectives of working-class Black Jamaican women and girls. For this reason and others, Sistren occupies a significant place in my and others' education about women's lives. Therefore, by the time I entered graduate school in the United States decades later, Sistren was already firmly placed as one of the most influential groups in the history of Jamaica's women's movement and contemporary Jamaican theatre. My research on Sistren allowed me to place my mother's and other family life education teachers' work into broader context. They were Sistren's counterparts in the use of theatre for education in the 1980s, the decade in which the organization was arguably most active and influential. Additionally, I realized that many of the theatre artists with whom I had worked or whose paths had crossed with mine over the years—particularly when I attended the University of the West Indies (UWI), Mona—had collaborated with Sistren or were participants in the movement to develop Jamaica's theatre scene and emphasize its role in pedagogy and social change.[2]

After deciding to make Sistren the focus of my early research in Africana studies, I aimed to find a women's theatre collective on the African continent that I could also write about, but I was unsuccessful in this search for over a year. Then, in 2013, while attending the theatre colloquium of the Brown International Advanced Research Institutes, I met Sara Matchett, artistic director of the Mothertongue Project, who presented on her organization's work. I was struck by the similarities between Sistren and Mothertongue, including their founding in the early decades following their countries' official transition to democracy, their use of the collective model of devising and composing, and their important work in marginalized Black communities. I also acknowledged the differences, such as the range of performance forms used by Mothertongue in contrast with Sistren's primary focus on drama and film, and the inclusion of queer South Africans' stories in Mothertongue's work in contrast to Sistren's heteronormative bent. (The latter tendency is partly explained by the fact that Mothertongue is a much younger organization that benefited from global LGBTQ-rights movements in the 1980s and 1990s, as well as the fact that South African theatre is more inclusive toward LGBTQ experiences than Jamaican theatre is).

Conducting the first phase of my ethnographic research in Jamaica and South Africa on Sistren and Mothertongue, from 2014 to 2015, I became interested in the Letters from the Dead project and Olive Tree Theatre. Although Letters is not a Sistren project, it has connections to Sistren because the principal researcher is Honor Ford-Smith, who is also Sistren's founding artistic director. Letters emerged from Ford-Smith's research project titled "Memory, Urban Violence and Performance in Jamaican Communities," and is a transnational undertaking that focuses on how marginalized urban communities memorialize people who have died violently. In June 2015 I coordinated Letters from the Dead's interactive exhibition and performance *Song for the Beloved: Memory and Renewal at the Margins of Justice*, which opened with the play *A Vigil for Roxie*. Also in 2015, I learned about Olive Tree Theatre, a company founded in the township of Alexandra a few miles from the Johannesburg city center, by a young Black woman named Ntshieng Mokgoro. Olive Tree's most well-known event while it operated was the Women's Theatre Festival, which I attended in November that year.

Because of time constraints I could not include Letters from the Dead and Olive Tree in my initial research project. However, years later, I have been able to expand my analysis through this book. In sum, what began as a case study of two theatre collectives founded by women in different African and African Diasporic countries has evolved into a work that seeks to critically engage with questions around how race, gender, and sexuality interlock with other social identifiers such as class and geographic positioning; and the ways in which spatial politics as manifested in the use and control of physical spaces is interrogated and redefined through activism in theatre.

In the public imagination and global mass media, theatre-based activisms usually take a back seat to other more broadly circulated forms of advocacy. This is understandable. Certainly, social media hashtags, massive street marches, and passionate speeches from leaders of civil groups appear far more spectacular and wide reaching than do grassroots-based performances. However, these forms of activism, though distinct, are certainly not disconnected from theatre. They all exist in the same continuum, influencing and drawing on one another's work while exercising varied imperatives. For example, the play *A Vigil for Roxie*, produced by the Letters from the Dead project, is part of a transnational movement against gang and state violence that also encompasses peace demonstrations, memorial art, and global movements like Black Lives Matter. Similarly, Maya Krishna Rao's *Walk* is situated within the conversations that took place in tandem with the 2012 uprising in India and neighboring countries following the sexual assault and murder of Jyoti Singh Pandey. It influenced the creation of the Mothertongue Project's *Walk: South Africa* in response to the similar murder of Anene Booysen, a seventeen-year-old Black girl, in 2013. As these and other performances demonstrate, theatre is located in the subjective sphere, embodying the lives of society's most marginalized people and facilitating interactions with audiences that enable them to absorb, question, and join in critical conversations.

My analysis centers productions that fit within a definition of theatre as a genre of performed storytelling mostly for a live audience, constructed through written and unwritten processes, and involving costuming, props, sets, or other physical accessories. Certainly, many aspects of activism can be analyzed as performative or performatic (see D. Taylor 2003). Marches, demonstrations, rituals, and other forms of expression utilized by activists share with theatre the use of creative expression, bodies, and humanmade instruments to portray a narrative. In parts of this book I show how these work alongside theatre in social justice advocacy. However, with the intention of highlighting how Africana women have innovated artistic and pedagogic practices within the genre of theatre, I have chosen as the subjects of this book self-defined theatre practitioners, many of them with years of experience in the art form.

Sistren, Mothertongue, Letters from the Dead, and Olive Tree connect with traditions and modern iterations of activism in the public sphere and with theatre's capacity to create as well as claim stories that seek to influence the public imagination. They demonstrate that women are using theatre and performance to define and redefine the racial and gendered bounds of geographic space in their countries. This practice is necessarily decolonial, challenging their societies to not reinscribe systems of power that have defined centuries of European colonization and white supremacy, including, racism, classism, economic oppression, and patriarchy. They disrupt the colonial and imperialist tendency to universalize European and white American interpretations of the world by grounding their practices in the artistic and intellectual innovations of Black women and other women of the Global Majority. Thus, they exemplify theatre's integral role in the ongoing project by Black/Africana people to decolonize knowledge of the world. It is in this respect that theatre forges theory. To understand this fact we must accept that cerebral processes of formulating knowledge are integrally connected to physical and experiential ones (Boyce Davies 1994; Christian 1988; Jones 1997, 2015; Nagar 2014). Intertwined with their decolonial practice are their contributions to feminist and womanist thought and organizing in their societies. While not all of the key participants in the four organizations and projects self-identify primarily as feminist or womanist, their work converses with these paradigms. Black, African, Caribbean, Global South, and transnational feminist theories have made major academic and popular impacts on how we understand the connections among gender, racial, and economic oppression over the last several decades. The womanist paradigm is not as ubiquitous in scholarship and popular discourse as feminism is. Yet, its emphasis on social justice perspectives rooted in Black and African women's creativity, centering of Black and African women as knowledge-makers, and focus on the interconnectedness of people of various genders, the spiritual world, and the environment, encapsulates the vital labor carried out by women throughout Africa and the African Diaspora (Hudson-Weems 2000; Maparyan 2008; Ogunyemi 1985; Walker 1983). These groups and projects—two theatre collectives, one performance project, and one commercial theatre with a social justice orientation—theorize the link between gender, racial, and economic hierarchies and the ways in which the multiple manifestations of these hierarchies can be transgressed.

Sistren Theatre Collective is the oldest organization featured in the book. It was founded in 1977 during the early postcolonial period in Jamaica, with the goal of representing the perspectives and lives of mainly working-class Black Jamaican women. It has been the most influential women's theatre group in the Anglophone Caribbean and a major participant in contemporary Caribbean women's movements. The Mothertongue Project was established in 2000, during the decade of South Africa's democratic transition from apartheid, with a similar goal to center South African women's stories through theatre. And throughout its twenty-three years, Mothertongue has expanded its definitions to generate discussions around gender and sexuality through a more gender-fluid approach that includes nonbinary perspectives. Over the decades the two collectives have also designed community-based projects involving people of different genders in marginalized Black communities. These include Sistren's Tek It to Dem and Rise Up Wi Community project and its work with the Citizen Security and Justice Programme, and Mothertongue's Langeberg Youth Arts Project. Even so, they maintain their major emphasis on gender and sexual justice activism for women. While Sistren and Mothertongue were established with woman-focused imperatives, Letters from the Dead, the performance arm of the "Memory, Urban Violence and Performance" project, which began in 2007, has a more general focus on the impact of civilian and state violence on urban communities in Jamaica and beyond. Its aesthetic relies on memorial rituals and urban art in order to interrogate how marginalized communities forge their own ideas about social justice and healing amid violence. Sistren's, Mothertongue's, and Letters from the Dead's performance repertoires involve a blend of plays in theatre institutions, community-based projects in working-class Black communities, and site-specific performances in which the setting of the performance serves as an integral part of its messaging and structure. Olive Tree Theatre, founded by Ntshieng Mokgoro in 2013, differs from the others in that it was a commercial company. However, its Women's Theatre Festival was a not-for-profit social justice initiative that provided mentorship for mostly Black South African women theatre-makers and created the space for them to hone their crafts. Mokgoro established this economic and artistic venture in the heart of Alexandra, one of South Africa's largest, poorest, and most volatile townships and also one of its most central locales in the anti-apartheid movement. Olive Tree closed in 2020 after it relocated to Marlboro, a peri-urban community close to Alexandra.

The most obvious parallels among Sistren, Mothertongue, Letters from the Dead, and Olive Tree are their formation by women and their use of theatre as the primary mode of performance. Central to their work is their reliance on performance forms primarily innovated by Black women, other women of color, and women of the Global Majority in general, even though a few members and affiliates are white. Additionally, these organizations engage in the practice of placemaking with their emphasis on creating theatre for public performance and in Black-majority urban and peri-urban communities. They are activist in the sense that they seek to interrogate and confront oppressive social structures such as racism, gender-based violence, gang and state violence, and economic injustice. Intersecting with their preoccupation with these structures is an awareness of the significance of geography and place specificity in the lives of Africana people.

My major focus in this book is on the possibilities for a transnational Africana understanding of racial and gender justice advocacy through theatre and performance. I do not seek to prove the similarities between Jamaica and South Africa or minimize their differences. While the organizations and projects do not resist the country specificity of their work, they consider themselves through transnational lenses and continue to form networks with activists in various countries. For example, Ntshieng Mokgoro repeatedly emphasized her goal to broaden the global reach of the Olive Tree Women's Theatre Festival through a Pan-African lens (Mokgoro, pers. comm., 2015, 2018). Likewise, as I learned from Sara Matchett on the day that we met at Brown University in 2013, Mothertongue members have long been aware of the work of Sistren. In fact, Sistren was discussed briefly by Mothertongue member Awino Okech (2007) as a model of women's theatre collectives, in her thesis about Mothertongue's *Rite of Being* (2005). Thus, the idea of a transnational, transcontinental viewpoint through which to consider their work already exists in their own outlook as well as in published works that examine theatre and other art produced by Africana women in different countries (see, e.g., Coly 2019; Marzette 2013; Migraine-George 2008; Plastow et al., 2015). For instance, poet, playwright, and Mothertongue collaborator, Malika Ndlovu stated in her 2015 interview with me, "It's refreshing to be hearing about women who are doing work in Jamaica."

Essentially then, their initiatives fit within frameworks of Africana activisms and movements that think in local, national, and global terms, meaning they are attuned to national concerns directly tied to local and national organizing, but also engage in conversations that have global resonances in Africa and the African Diaspora.[3] With respect to the national specificities of Jamaica and South Africa, this book offers a lens to consider how race, gender, and space operate in two Black-majority contexts in which the specters of slavery and colonialism loom alongside current imperialism and neoliberal inequalities. One major preoccupation among feminists, womanists, and other gender-justice advocates in these countries is with how their governments shortchange women in official conceptualizations of national development. Mothertongue member Nina Callaghan summed up her feeling about this dissonance in her country when she stated, "Women's liberation has not been on course with the nation's liberation in South Africa" (pers. comm., 2015). Callaghan's statement is consistent with a viewpoint that citizenship and national belonging are not just natal or residential conditions, they are affected by racial and gender hierarchies. Thus, space-making is not just a physical phenomenon as seen in Africana women's presence in positions of economic and political power, and in places that are associated with relative freedom and progress. Space-making involves confronting gender, sexual, and racial power structures embedded in society through historical and contemporary processes.

Space, Place, and Black Women's Geographies

Africana women's experiences are an intricate milieu of differences and intersections of time, space, place, and physicality, defined by race, sexuality, gender, class, and geographic boundaries. These have been mediated by the experiences of racialized slavery, colonial subjugation, segregation, and modern spatial (trans)figurations such as gentrification and the ghettoization of Black communities globally. As Katherine McKittrick (2006, 45) writes in *Demonic Grounds: Black Women and the Cartographies of Struggle*, "Black women's own experiential and material geographies indicate a very complex and difficult relationship with space, place, and dispossession."

McKittrick's book was inspired by Sylvia Wynter's (1993) canonical essay "Beyond Miranda's Meanings: Un/Silencing the 'Demonic Grounds' of Caliban's 'Woman.'" In it Wynter theorizes a separate unknowable domain for Black women, which is disregarded in men-centered postcolonial narratives of Black and Indigenous subjugation in the Americas. She argues that the textual nonexistence of the mate of Caliban—a trope for the colonized Caribbean man—in William Shakespeare's *The Tempest* and in anticolonial Caribbean criticism indicates an ontological absence in which the only model of a desired partner for the colonized man is presented as a white woman who is part of the colonial project (Miranda). Therefore, to discern the ground on which the colonized woman stands, one has to devise a separate way of knowing that moves beyond physical differences. The demonic is this ground, a site that holds within it the sum total of unexplored knowledge. Black and feminist geographers have over the last five decades challenged androcentrism and imperialism in conventional geography as well as the epistemological approach that treats physical spaces as static and passive with purportedly homogenous inhabitants (Brown 2005; Duncan 1996; Oberhauser et al., 2017; Woods and McKittrick 2007). Geographic theories of race and gender have elaborated on how these identity categories determine how human beings experience the world, including through the organization and definition of physical space. Spatial difference also indicates temporal difference, particularly as it relates to access to the amenities that define a modern life.

For instance, writing on the failures of cosmopolitanism in Cape Town, South Africa, as reflected in the lives of women in the community of Mannenberg, Elaine Salo (2009, 13) argues that younger generations experience different temporalities within urban and peri-urban spaces. Based on this research, she exposes the flaws in mainstream neoliberal postapartheid narratives: "the gendered meanings of post-Apartheid cosmopolitanism in South Africa, so often celebrated as the non-violent peaceful achievement of harmonious relations across socio-economic and racial divides, are differently reflected in younger women's local experiences due to vulnerability to sexual violence, especially in the urban peripheries." Thus, divergent experiences overlap in physical spaces that appear homogenous on a mainstream map. In the city of Kingston, Jamaica, the life of an upper-middle-class woman in Graham Heights is markedly different than the life of a woman in Standpipe, a poor urban community located barely one mile (two kilometers) away. And while rich Jamaicans and foreigners purchase overpriced luxury apartments in rapidly gentrifying areas, poor urban and rural communities remain largely neglected in successive governments' plans to make Jamaica the ideal place to "live, work, raise families and do business" (Planning Institute of Jamaica, n.d.). Likewise, in Johannesburg, South Africa, upper-middle-class and wealthy women can shop at one of the high-end stores in the luxurious Sandton City Mall, while their housekeepers, who probably live four or five miles (seven kilometers) away in Alexandra, may be more inclined to shop at PEP, a retail chain designed for low-income people. The residents of these urban and peri-urban communities in both countries also exist in different temporalities because their lives may be defined by labels such as "developed" and "underdeveloped" based on the technological resources available to them. Thus, notwithstanding their Black-majority populations and majority-Black middle classes, African and Caribbean countries continue to display the legacies of colonialism and slavery through class distinctions. In Jamaica and South Africa, the racial element of classism is illustrated by the fact that most of the poor are Black, and most of the wealthy are white or otherwise non-Black.

The public space is the main site of these various interactions, differences, intersections, and conflicts, which are differently experienced across social hierarchies. This space has different meanings based on notions about who should have the freedom to move undisturbed through it. As can be seen in the experiences of sexual harassment and assault of mostly women and girls on the streets globally, navigating the public realm can be fraught with problems. Contemporary cases of inordinate police brutality and the monitoring of Black people by white civilians in white-majority countries on public streets and other common areas further illustrate how social power determines even quotidian activities such as simply walking or driving from one point to another. These forms of suppression and scrutiny have their genealogies within the spectacular violence of colonialism, apartheid, and African enslavement, which relied on what Saidiya V. Hartman (1997) refers to as "scenes of subjection." Included in these scenes are the punishments that were enacted against rebel women during transatlantic slavery. Afua Cooper (2007) has documented the case of Marie-Joseph Angélique, the enslaved Black woman who was accused of setting fire to most of Montreal, New France (Canada), in the eighteenth century. She was hanged and then burned, and her ashes were scattered throughout Montreal. Angélique's punishment bears a striking, though by no means exceptional, resemblance to that of the Khoekhoe woman servant Zara, one of the subjects of the Mothertongue Project's production *Womb of Fire* (2018). I first learned of Zara through my interviews with Mothertongue co-founders Rehane Abrahams and Sara Matchett (who wrote/performed in and directed the play, respectively; see De Beer 2018). In 1671, after twenty-four-year-old Zara committed suicide, her body was posthumously publicly punished by being dragged through the streets of Cape Town via a donkey, then hung and mutilated by the Vereenigde Oostindische Compagnie (Dutch East India Company). This was the penalty for the crime of taking her own life (Upham 2022). In both Angélique's and Zara's cases, the scattering or dragging of the women's remains throughout the city means that their bodies are permanently physically enlaced in the geographies of these spaces.

In addition to the historical and contemporary realities of racist violence in which Black people have had to exercise caution in public spaces or be subject to public humiliation, protests can be risky. There is always the possibility of arrest, harassment, and other forms of containment from bigoted vigilantes and people in positions of authority.[4] This holds true even for small-scale, silent, controlled demonstrations. For instance, in 2016 four young Black women carried out a silent protest against sexual violence in South Africa, invoking the name of Fezekile Ntsukela Kuzwayo (known as Khwezi).[5] One decade earlier, in 2005–6, Khwezi had accused future president Jacob Zuma of rape in a highly controversial trial. Zuma was acquitted, and three years later he was elected president. The 2016 protest happened at the election center in Pretoria, where President Zuma was delivering a live-broadcast speech on the municipal elections. The women stood silently at the front of the room, dressed in black and holding handwritten placards. Security guards pushed them onto the stage, ripped the signs from their hands, and then removed them from the room, with one woman falling in the process. Zuma appeared to chuckle briefly while they were being removed. The women were heavily condemned by members of the African National Congress political party, including, most notably, women ministers Lindiwe Zulu, Nomvula Mokonyane, and Bathabile Dlamini, who reportedly supported their removal by security. The protestors—Simamkele Dlakavu, Tinyiko Shikwambane, Naledi Chirwa, and Amanda Mavuso—had expected that their demonstration would draw criticism, but not the kind of aggression with which they were met (Britton 2020; Nicholson 2016). This incident shows that there are always risks involved when activists make the decision to publicly assert their position, especially when they challenge powerful people.

Notwithstanding the prominence of policing and punishment in public, this space offers enormous possibilities for activism, mobilizing, and organizing. The public space exists in the vernacular sphere, with all of its excitement, contradictions, and potential (Duncan 1996; McDowell 1996, 1999). This of course does not mean that open debate necessarily works in the interest of marginalized people. Often powerful interest groups are able to exploit the exposure they receive in public debates, in addition to their political power in governmental institutions, to implement laws and policies that mostly disadvantage women (see Walsh 2010). The debate around legalizing abortion in Jamaica's constitution is a good example of this. Anti-choice religious groups have exercised far more power in the debates given their connections in Parliament, funding, and social impact on the population through churches. A relatively weak opposition party with a disproportionately small number of parliamentary seats, which also seems to not have a consensus on the issue, also works against the push for legalization.

Nevertheless, the public arena is the site in which democracy continues to be defined. As D. Soyini Madison (2010, 6) notes, "a public space is a promise of a democratic space. And a public performance becomes an open invitation to participate and (or) witness how democracy can be variously conjured and re-imagined." As with marches and other demonstrations, theatre in widely accessible community spaces mobilizes and informs beyond the immediate audience, reaching any passerby or person watching on social media or otherwise throughout the world. Moreover, theatre has the capacity to provide avenues for stories that are usually marginalized and policed. When relayed through narratives in public, experiences that are traditionally considered private (such as people's reproductive and sexual lives) transgress the conceptual and political line between the private/domestic sphere and the public arena. Moreover, the creation of a space of performance in a setting that is not designed for one, for the purposes of reaching a broad audience, is a primary feature of activist performance. This engagement with audiences outside of conventional or elite theatre spaces is a main connecting thread for the projects I focus on in this book.

Defining Activist Theatre and Place Specificity

Most of the events analyzed in this book can be classified in theatre scholarship as site-specific performances, or as performances that display strong elements of site specificity. As a term, *site-specific theatre* became prevalent during the latter part of the twentieth century, contemporaneous with the development of theatre and performance studies as a discipline (see Birch and Tompkins 2012). It generally describes theatre events that are held outside of conventional theatre spaces, that is, institutions that are dedicated to theatre performance with the infrastructure in place to accommodate them. Site-specific theatre events do not simply travel to other spaces to accommodate audiences, like when a commercial play is temporarily staged at a high school auditorium. Rather, the performance space is an integral part of the story, the creators' message, and the overall intent of the project. Thus, the place in which the performance is held is not simply a passive physical container but rather an essential component. The definition offered by Mike Pearson and Michael Shanks (2001, 23) in *Theatre/Archaeology* is instructive. They state that site-specific performances are "inseparable from their sites, the only contexts within which they are intelligible." Moreover, "the multiple meanings and readings of performance and site intermingle, amending and compromising one another." The performance I examine in chapter 1, Sistren and Hannah Town Cultural Group's *A Slice of Reality* (2009), is an archetypical piece of site-specific theatre. It was a pro-choice skit performed in the Jamaican Houses of Parliament as part of the debates to repeal the country's anti-choice laws. Its location affirms its distinctly political aims as well as the skit's function as a transgressive work that interrupts the elitism, male-centered sexual politics, and patriarchy in the Jamaican government. Mothertongue's *Walk: South Africa*, a 2014 performance of which is discussed in chapter 2, also displayed strong elements of site specificity, as do many performances in the Letters from the Dead project.

Whether classified as site-specific performances or not, all the productions I analyze are integrally engaged in conversations about the centrality of geography to the stories they tell and the imperatives their creators abide by. Olive Tree Theatre, for example, was established in two of South Africa's most volatile townships (Alexandra and Marlboro) as part of founder Ntshieng Mokgoro's commitment to these townships' development. This consciousness of how people affect and are affected by the social spaces that they live in and traverse intersects with the wider goals of these projects to confront racism, gender-based violence, gang and state violence, and economic injustice, and to envision more just societies. The term activist theatre embraces their use of the art form as a method of discourse, pedagogy, and practice. It relates to activist aesthetics, a concept that I have also applied heuristically to their work (Shakes 2018, 2021). Jaime Harker and Cecilia Konchar Farr (2015) utilize activist aesthetics to define the work of feminist and womanist authors and printing presses that emerged within the women's liberation movement of the 1960s–80s in North America (see also Rosenberg 2009). Other recent texts on the aesthetics of Africana women theatre artists have analyzed the political ideologies in the work of playwrights, based on their artistic approaches (Jones, Moore, and Bridgforth 2010; Marzette 2013; Okagbue 2009; Plastow et al., 2015).[6] Thérèse Migraine-George's (2008, 46) scholarship on African women playwrights is particularly useful for her conceptualization of the link between art and politics. She argues, "Because aesthetic productions in Africa convey the complexity of lived relations, they are often endowed not only with social functions but also with specific ideological and political purposes . . . art and performances have been used to express and re-activate collective relations, but also to achieve certain political goals through the conscious transformation or manipulation of the representative process."

There is a need for more scholarship on how Africana women practice theatre as activism and social commentary, particularly in the Caribbean and Africa.[7] Also, there remains a necessity to complement the mostly literary emphasis and focus on individual playwrights in the existing transnational scholarship, with more attention to groups and to performances. In my conversations with the theatre artists featured in this book, the question emerged as to how feasible it is for theatre artists—especially women—to write about their own work, including the methods that they have created while practicing their art. A common response was that it is extremely difficult to do both. For example, Joan French, who served as a resource person for Sistren in the 1980s and 1990s, stated that at the height of the collective's activities, they were so busy "doing the work" that it was difficult to also theorize about it (French, pers. comm., 2014). Nevertheless, Mothertongue's Sara Matchett and Sistren's Honor Ford-Smith, who are also scholars and university professors, have been prolific in writing essays on their collectives' methods and activism (Ford-Smith 1986, 1989, 1995, 1997; Matchett 2009, 2012; Matchett and Cloete 2015; Matchett and Mokwena 2014). In 1990, reflecting on her work in Sistren and at the Jamaica School of Drama, Ford-Smith published an essay in which she called for a "new aesthetic" that affirms the role of the artist as a social change maker. She emphasizes the importance of enabling the actor's agency and challenges the norm of theatre production in which actors must serve as vessels for the playwright and submit to the authority of the director. Accordingly, she uses the term *cultural worker* to highlight the role of the arts and culture in social change:

> The cultural worker wants to break with some of the forces that constrain the life of the artist in the west and north. S/he wants to break out of that particular notion of sensitive passivity, intelligent and inquiring powerlessness . . . the task of the cultural worker is an attempt to re-create life so

that the realms of thought, feeling and action are no longer kept separate and distinct. That [sic] this work is not seen as something separated from economic or political activity, but as part and parcel of the attempt to reveal experience in an integrated way. (Ford-Smith 1990, 27)[8]

Ford-Smith further underscores the importance of artists developing works that fit their social contexts. Her emphasis on context, like mine and that of several of the persons I have spoken with, acknowledges that artists should have international dialogues while questioning the automatic universalizing of performance forms and aesthetic standpoints developed in European and white American societies to fit their sociohistorical contexts. Ford-Smith's essay is a rare published articulation of methods and techniques forged by Jamaican theatre practitioners. It also documents how Sistren members and other theatre activists operating during the 1970s and 1980s defined themselves.

In theatre scholarship as well as scholarship on activism, several terms have emerged to describe performances that serve a social function, particularly with regard to pedagogy. Earlier, I mentioned *theatre for development* as a term that describes theatre used in school or community settings to convey information about a subject with a view to creating positive social change, often based on the standards set by a development agency (Epskamp 2006). Another concept is *applied theatre*. This is an umbrella description for a set of small-scale community-based theatre practices, most commonly involving theatre as therapy or education in communities that have experienced some form of trauma or that face a current social problem. It was formulated as a means of distinguishing theatre directed at educating and engaging communities from theatre that exists for a commercial purpose. Some artist-scholars have critiqued the term for being redundant. For example, Victor Ukaegbu (2004) argues that historically, the entertainment function of theatre has never been separate from its social purpose. Others, like Judith Ackroyd (2007), have wondered whether applied theatre is an exclusionary category that creates criteria that socially conscious theatre artists must ascribe to, and argued that the label is overused and has replaced other paradigms such as theatre in education. Sara Matchett used the more recent and now popular terms *artivist* and *artivism* to describe Mothertongue's work (pers. comm., 2015). This designation pointedly underscores Mothertongue's aim to inspire its audiences to act toward resolving a social problem. My use of the term *activist theatre* envelopes these various definitions and terms, with a pointed focus on how theatre informs social change.

The settings and scope of Sistren's, Mothertongue's, Letters from the Dead's, and Olive Tree's performances have varied over the years. Sistren and Mothertongue have created work in and external to conventional theatre spaces for a range of audiences, and Olive Tree and Ntshieng Mokgoro only create plays within spaces dedicated to theatre production. Letters from the Dead has shifted its performance forms and spaces more than the others in its travels to small communities, staging of street performances, and curation of exhibitions that are aligned with the places in which they are mounted. Notwithstanding these variations, many methods of play creation emerge commonly in their work: the application of people's personal stories, including real-life incidents; an emphasis on collectivity in the creation process; an appreciation for orality as well as written text; the centrality of movement and dance; minimalism in costume and set design; and the incorporation of rituals. *Ritual performance* involves the employment of ceremonial practices that are rooted in religious and other traditions, for the purposes of memorialization, celebration, assertion of a political perspective, and the forging of communal bonds (see Harrison, Walker, and Edwards 2002; V. Turner [1969] 1995). It is ubiquitous in the productions featured in this book and is an indicator of the extent to which Sistren, Mothertongue, Letters from the Dead, and Ntshieng Mokgoro draw on their communities' performance traditions and knowledge systems. Essentially, their aesthetics emerged from their experiences of organizing; research; studies of African, Caribbean, and global theatre techniques; and innovations linked to what they have learned from the audiences, networks, and communities in which they work. I have sought to reflect these multiple influences, priorities, and resonances in this book.

Approach and Structure of the Book

Women's Activist Theatre in Jamaica and South Africa is the product of nine years of ethnographic research. The first phase consisted of preliminary research in 2013, followed by extensive ethnographic information-gathering in 2014–15, when I spent sixteen months living in Jamaica and South Africa. Subsequently, I traveled to both countries multiple times from 2016 to 2021, as well as maintained communication with the main leaders and artistic creators of the four organizations and projects. I also made a one-week trip to Toronto, Canada, in 2015 to examine a section of Sistren's archives housed by Honor Ford-Smith, making use of the Jamaican Diaspora as a research resource. I conducted fifty in-depth interviews with forty-four persons, both those involved in the creation and performance of the theatre projects, and activists and theatre artists affiliated with them. Additionally, I had brief conversations with others who share their goals.

Drawing on the framework articulated by critical performance ethnographer Dwight Conquergood (2002, 149), I describe my ethnographic method as *co-performative witnessing* as opposed to participant observation.[9] Co-performative witnessing moves beyond seeing the ethnographer solely as an observer (see also Madison 2007, 2010). By describing myself as a co-performer I emphasize the performative or action-oriented nature of my work, in which I take on various roles as researcher, writer, interlocutor, traveler, and reporter. I maintain relationships with the participants in my research that sometimes blur the line between researcher and subject. For instance, as stated, I have participated in the Letters from the Dead project, in which Sistren, too, is a collaborator. In 2015, I coordinated the event I analyze in chapter 3, and in 2016 I was a performer at one of Letters from the Dead's events at the Hemispheric Institute's biennial conference in Chile. While I was attending Olive Tree's Women's Theatre Festival in October 2015, I enrolled in, and learned a lot from, a workshop on scriptwriting. Also, though I was not involved in Sistren and Hannah Town Cultural Group's pro-choice play *A Slice of Reality*, in 2019 I joined the movement to repeal Jamaica's anti-choice laws. Kim Tallbear's (2014, 2) suggestion to see research as a "relationship-building process . . . as an opportunity for conversation and sharing of knowledge, not simply data gathering" corresponds with my approach. As a Jamaican I am more physically and emotionally associated with theatre and activism there than in South Africa, and at times I write authoritatively on the sociopolitical landscape in Jamaica. However, I share palpable African Diasporic connections with Black South Africans, connections that emerge in the analysis in this book as well as in my continuing interest in Black/African Diasporic cultural similarities despite linguistic, geographic, political, and other cultural distinctions.

One challenge of multisited transnational ethnography is the need to have a balanced analysis of the subjects under study. Thus, I was concerned with maintaining the same level of interdisciplinary analysis across chapters. While these four organizations and projects are similar in their commitments, their structures and ages vary and so do the performances I analyze. The first chapter focuses on *A Slice of Reality* (2009), which was created and performed by the Sistren affiliate Hannah Town Cultural Group and which was the performance with which I began this study. My analysis of the performance is largely a work of excavation because *A Slice of Reality* is the oldest and shortest theatre production featured in the book, and, unlike the others, it is not recorded in a clear format. It was difficult for me and my research assistant to decipher the content of the skit, and the performers themselves were challenged to remember it when I interviewed them in 2015. They therefore did not go into detail about their artistic process. Rather, their focus was on their positioning within the Jamaican pro-choice movement. Commensurate with my aim to reflect the opinions of the artists and activists in my research and the spaces and social contexts in which the performances occurred, I treat *A Slice of Reality* as a catalyst in the more recent focus on women's lived experiences, race, and class in debates about reproductive justice. The piece was part of a political and legal process to introduce the proposed Termination of Pregnancy Act; therefore, it is crucial to examine its emergence and influences within those contexts. This approach is different from the one I take in chapters 2–4, in which the performances—while spurred by contemporaneous events—are not tied to a specific process of legislative change. *Walk: South Africa*, *A Vigil for Roxie*, Ntshieng Mokgoro's plays, and those of the participants in the 2015 Olive Tree Women's Theatre Festival are full-length theatre productions that can be performed independent of the times and spaces I researched, while maintaining their pedagogic meanings. For example, *Walk: South Africa* was performed eleven times from 2014 to 2020 and evolved with different casts. There are other analytical differences as well. While chapters 1–3 each focus on one theatre event, for example, chapter 4 treats Olive Tree Theatre as an institution alongside the work of Ntshieng Mokgoro and three young Black women playwrights featured at the Women's Theatre Festival. *Women's Activist Theatre in Jamaica and South Africa* therefore reflects the range of form, content, and intentions of Africana people's theatre-based activism in these two countries and globally.

In chapter 1, I place Sistren and Hannah Town Cultural Group's *A Slice of Reality* (2009) into conversation with the scholarship on gender justice in the Caribbean and a decades-long process to repeal Jamaica's anti-choice laws. Not only did the skit make history as the first to ever be performed in the Houses of Parliament, it broke with class-based and gender conventions in its casting, language, and content. It was performed by eight working-class and unemployed Black women from Hannah Town, a poor urban community. Their presence in Parliament, use of Jamaican language in a space where English is celebrated, application of popular Jamaican/African Diasporic performance forms, and representation of actual women's experiences enabled their viewpoints on the relationship between gender and class justice in a process dominated by middle-class people.

In chapter 2, I continue with an analysis of the Mothertongue Project's *Walk: South Africa*, which asserts female bodily autonomy with a focus on sexual violence. The chapter examines a 2014 performance of *Walk: South Africa* that was staged in an unconventional performance space with a concluding walk into the city streets. The piece centers the emotive, psychic, and physical trauma of rape and therefore critiques the normalization of sexual violence by representing rape as horrific. Its major pedagogical value emerges from its no-holds-barred approach to the subject, its resistance to a resolution, and its aim of moving its audiences to action by nonverbally spurring them to take to the streets.

In chapter 3, the focus broadens to the general theme of violence writ large and its effects on marginalized Black communities, through an examination of the play *A Vigil for Roxie* (2015). Produced by the Letters from the Dead project, *Vigil* tells the story of a mother who holds an annual event to memorialize her son, Roxie, a gang leader who was murdered by soldiers. Through Roxie's family and other characters, the play de-individualizes gang and state violence and treats them as interconnected with oppressive social hierarchies in Jamaica and the wider Americas. Furthermore, by depicting the story mostly through the voices of women, using a woman actor to embody nine characters of different genders and ages, it enables an understanding of how children and women are affected by violence, even while the victims and perpetrators of killings are mostly men.

The subject of how Black people shape the spaces in which they live amid historical and contemporary racial violence and economic precarity informs chapter 4. This chapter analyzes the playwriting of Olive Tree's founder, Ntshieng Mokgoro, as well as the fourth Olive Tree Women's Theatre Festival (2015). The festival displayed Olive Tree's existence as a social justice project insofar as it created a unique opportunity to address the gender inequities in theatre directing as a professional field, particularly for the benefit of Black South African women. My conversations with the directors in the festival and with Mokgoro focused on their ideas of gender equity in relation to Black women's representation and storytelling. Although the theatre closed in 2020 due to financial problems made worse by the COVID-19 pandemic, I place Olive Tree within a long history of Black space-making, survival, and resistance in Alexandra, the township in which it was initially established.

In conclusion, my coda provides an account of the recent work of Sistren, Mothertongue, Letters from the Dead, and Olive Tree, and it acknowledges Africana women's organizing from a transnational perspective. I then restate my mission to center theatre performance as womanist, feminist, and decolonial knowledge-making in Africa and the African Diaspora, using as my point of departure an impactful street performance against sexual violence in Jamaica in 2017.

CHAPTER 1

"Mek Wi Choose fi Wiself"

Performing a Discourse of Justice in *A Slice of Reality*

It is March 12, 2009, in Kingston, Jamaica. I am watching the evening news half-attentively as most of us do, when I get captivated by a story about the day's proceedings in Parliament. For the past year, I had been following media reports about the government's review of the country's anti-choice laws, which criminalize abortion. These reports mostly featured excessive moral proclamations from church leaders, as well as statements from overworked but determined activists insisting on the urgency of changing the law. But this news report is different from the others: it focuses on a performance produced by Sistren Theatre Collective. A group of Sistren-affiliated activists had decided that they wanted to make their pro-choice submission to Parliament in the form of a skit; and so, I watch a set of suit-wearing, middle-class, straight-faced politicians looking at eight working-class Black women dancing, singing, and chanting to the sound of a booming drum, and I am profoundly impressed. I am fascinated by Sistren's resourcefulness in placing reproductive justice on the government's agenda through theatre, and enthused that a group of performers had invented another way to explore art's pedagogic possibilities. What better way to achieve a public conversation on women's empowerment and prove the importance of theatre as a mode of political inquiry than to have performers debate a law in the legislative space in which it is being reviewed?

The performance remained largely unnamed in the media after this news broadcast. However, I found out many years later that its title was *A Slice of Reality* and that Sistren had produced it in collaboration with the Hannah Town Cultural Group (HTCG), a troupe of artists from the community of the same name on the periphery of downtown Kingston,

Jamaica's capital city. In true Sistren fashion, the skit drew on the knowledge, voices, and bodies of working-class Black women to make a statement about the importance of women as decision-making agents in the national conversation about pregnancy, child-rearing, and family planning; and it discussed in frank terms the disastrous effects of Jamaica's ongoing regulation of women's bodies and sexualities. Thus, throughout the performance, Sistren/HTCG spoke directly to the members of Parliament (MPs), physically and vocally engaging them, but did not involve them in the narrative. After all, these lawmakers and the lobby groups they met with had already spent the past several months speaking of and not with poor Black women, whose lives anti-choice laws affect most adversely. At one point, the women all faced the MPs and performed a dub poem in which they categorically stated their opinion on women's right to reproductive choice.

The title phrase of this chapter, "mek wi choose fi wiself" (let us choose for ourselves), is taken from a line in this dub poem, which was spoken in the middle of the skit. The phrase encapsulates *A Slice of Reality*'s function as a performed assertion of bodily autonomy and the importance of women's knowledge in the process of constitutional change.

Consistent with how the members of HTCG view *A Slice of Reality*, I treat the skit as a political submission and research-driven theatre presentation. In situating it within the pro-choice movement in Jamaica, I concentrate mostly on 2007–9, the time period in which the Termination of Pregnancy Act was proposed, and the skit was developed. Additionally, I reflect on the skit's resonances in the contemporary pro-choice activism in which I am involved, and the five-decade process to decrease legal restrictions on abortion in Jamaica. I begin my analysis of the performances in this book with *A Slice of Reality* because it is the main inspiration behind my research into how Africana women utilize unconventional performance spaces in order to advance social justice activism. However, unlike the other productions I analyze, it remains without a script or adequate records, and given its short length of thirteen and a half minutes, it does not invite lengthy textual examination.

The performers/creators use the term *skit* rather than *play* to describe *A Slice of Reality* due to its fluidity, use as an educational resource, short length, and oral structure. Because of these characteristics, my research was as much a process of excavation as of analysis. The performance was in 2009, six years before my ethnographic study began, and the only existing recording of it is a mobile phone video uploaded to YouTube by Taitu Heron (2009a, 2009b), a member of the 2009 pro-choice coalition. Consistent with the mobile phone technology of that time, this video is partly inaudible, with unclear visuals. But thankfully it exists: no one other than videographers from the Public Broadcasting Corporation of Jamaica (PBCJ) were allowed to record the performance; Heron's recording subverted the rules. I spent two years trying to get a copy of the clearly recorded, high-definition footage I had seen in 2009, reaching out to the PBCJ, several television stations, and the government-owned Jamaica Information Service to no avail. Eventually, with Heron's video and help from HTCG members who shared memories of the performance, I pieced together the poetry, dialogues, and singing.

One lesson we can learn from the performance is to pay attention to the art produced by people who have limited access to literary resources and recording technologies but who nevertheless participate in wide-reaching, impactful, and high-stakes conversations. Theatre, like other art forms, has hierarchies rooted in differential access to recording technology, funding, formal training, and publishing. Therefore, in order to incisively analyze the roles of women artists from all backgrounds, we must attend to myriad forms of performance, including those that usually remain at the grassroots and community-based levels.

A Slice of Reality made history as the first skit to ever be produced in the Jamaican Parliament as part of a debate around legislative change. To date, I have found no other example in the world of the same type of performance being presented as a political submission in the highest governmental space in a country for the purpose of instituting a law. Hence, even beyond Jamaica it is unique, though it tracks with forms of protest in which marginalized groups confront their elected officials using a performance-based or embodied method, momentarily interjecting their discourses and bodies into spaces that routinely neglect them. The 1990 Capitol Crawl, in which more than a thousand physically disabled people crawled up the steps of the US Capitol in order to influence the passing of the Americans with Disabilities Act, is an example of this type of protest (Little 2020). Another example, as it relates to bodily autonomy, is a silent protest that took place in South Africa in 2016 against sexual violence. Four young Black women stood during a speech at the Pretoria election center that was being delivered by President Jacob Zuma, who was accused and acquitted of rape in 2006 (see my introduction; Giokos and Vilakazi 2016). Amid these forms of protest, *A Slice of Reality* functions as a model for the use of devised theatre, originally designed for community audiences, to engage government officials. Although the skit is somewhat ephemeral due to its blurred existence in the archives and its rare acknowledgment today, it helped usher in no-holds-barred public conversations on women's bodies, patriarchy, and sex, which would become characteristic of organizing around gender and sexual justice in the 2010s.

With the phrase "a discourse of justice" in my chapter title, I place *A Slice of Reality* into conversation with Eudine Barriteau's (2004) essay "Constructing Feminist Knowledge in the Commonwealth Caribbean in the Era of Globalization." In this essay, she asserts that there are fundamental faults in the official discussion of women's issues under a development framework informed by neoliberalism. She implicates Caribbean policymakers and international organizations such as the United Nations in this framing. According to her, "From its inception, examining women in Caribbean societies has been a discourse on utility. It has never been about women's freedom, but more about what needs to be done to reduce the obvious inequalities between women and men in the public" (441). This "discourse of utility" characterizes governments' approach to gender issues; by achieving prescribed minimums on gender equity (such as celebrating International Women's Day and providing minimal funding for centers that cater to women), governments can avoid more profound questions about women's rights. While Barriteau discusses the conflict between a discourse of utility and a more meaningful discourse of rights, she cautions against framing the conversation in such binary terms. Instead, she calls for a discourse of justice, an ideal that she defines as "a societal condition in which there are no asymmetries of access to, or allocations of, status, power, and material resources in a society" (439). There are many instances in which a rights-based discourse overlaps with a discourse of utility. For example, over the years, some pro-choice individuals and groups have called for the repeal of laws against abortion, with the reasoning that it will help control crime and violence. This was one argument made by the People's National Party Women's Movement in its July 2019 presentation to Parliament (PBC Jamaica 2019a).[1] The rationale is that many young men who become involved in violent crime were beaten by their mothers, and thus decriminalizing abortion would in the long run lead to a decrease in instances of child abuse by overstressed women who were forced to have children they did not want, thus reducing future crime. Arguments emphasizing the societal good of abortion are usually meant to be politically expedient, given the power of anti-choice advocacy to override arguments grounded in calls for gender and sexual autonomy. Yet, once the conversation veers toward men, we risk obscuring the oppressive nature of anti-choice legislation on women. A discourse of justice tackles gender and sex oppression and makes a claim for viewing women and girls as always already deserving of attention by governments. In Jamaica, with regard to abortion, the major obstacle to forging this discourse of justice is the political influence of religious and moral codes.

Activisms around gender justice involve significant political maneuvering around moralistic and religious dictates about sex, reproduction, and national well-being. Throughout this chapter I use the terms *anti-choice* and *pro-choice* to characterize the opposing activisms in this process. I reject the term *pro-life* as it reinforces the notion that those who argue for a woman's right to an abortion are somehow pro-death. Essentially, the debates concern whether someone should have the right to choose to get an abortion. These disagreements manifest in two major opposing coalitions, but by delineating anti- and pro-choice positions I am not arguing that the activists on each side are homogeneous. Particularly on the pro-choice side, there are varied opinions about the circumstances in which terminating a pregnancy should be legal. For example, most pro-choice activists in Jamaica agree with abortion only in extenuating circumstances, such as situations in which the woman's health and life are at risk, teenage pregnancy, and pregnancies resulting from rape.

Anti-choice activism is based on a religious philosophical perspective around fetal personhood, the belief that the fetus at every stage of development has human rights, including the right to life (see Orentlicher 2015). However, speeches, marches, and sermons against abortion also heavily rely on what I refer to as *morality posturing*: they lean on deeply held prejudices around gender, sexuality, and culture that carry potent propagandistic power. Morality posturing consists of four major tendencies: the framing of abortion as something pathological and exceptional, as opposed to a common though secretive practice; an anti-imperialist and culturalist argument that posits that abortion is out of place in Jamaica; the assertion that abortion is harmful to respectable family life and the building of a sexually pure society; and a refusal to engage with the argument that policies against abortion are patriarchal, which overstates the extent of girls' and women's sexual agency. These approaches to the issue lead many anti-choice activists to make statements that reject abortion outright, even in cases where the pregnancy is a risk to the pregnant person's life and health. For example, as reported in the *Gleaner*, Jamaica's most famous advocate against abortion, Catholic priest and Missionaries of the Poor founder Richard Ho Lung, stated in an interview that "the beautiful people are those who suffer on behalf of the life of others. In other words, it would be terrible if a mother intentionally sacrifices the life of a child for herself" (Cunningham 2014). Pro-choice activists put forward a moral position of their own—that it is unconscionable to force women to carry a pregnancy to term regardless of their circumstances—but they do not have the vastly influential support of religious doctrine or conservative notions of sexuality and patriarchy.

Given the dominance of anti-choice moralism in the conversations about abortion and the social stigma, it is difficult to have honest public conversations about abortion. In fact, even members of the government themselves usually shy away from the subject, and it is rare for individual politicians to publicly or passionately express support for it. Yet, as with all issues considered taboo, people's thoughts on abortion vary widely. Public opinion polls have resulted in conflicting findings, though several show majority approval in exceptional circumstances such as teenage pregnancy and pregnancies resulting from rape (Cunningham 2014; Hall 2018; Hope Enterprises 2006; Radio Jamaica News 2019). In 2006, the government-appointed Abortion Policy Review Advisory Group (APRAG) conducted a survey that found that 54 percent of Jamaicans supported abortion in cases of rape, teenage pregnancy, or life-threatening pregnancy. Only 4.3 percent supported the right to terminate a pregnancy under "all conditions" (Jamaica Ministry of Health 2007, 5). Moreover, people's acceptance also depended on the use of the phrase *termination of pregnancy* instead of the word *abortion*. In fact, the APRAG and pro-choice groups such as Women's Media Watch of Jamaica have both pointed out that the word *abortion* has a negative connotation in Jamaica because of its association with murder, making people more likely to use other words to refer to the same thing.[2] For example, a study conducted in 1988–89 in rural Jamaica by Elisa J. Sobo (1996) found that respondents were more tolerant of termination of pregnancies in the early stage and euphemistically referred to pregnancies terminated with pharmaceuticals and "bush" (herbal) medicines as "washouts." These abortifacients were commonly used and prescribed by traditional healers, even amid the presence of social stigmas. Thus, it is vital that conversations on the subject apply nuanced language, center the difficult circumstances in which pregnant women and girls often find themselves, and focus on the frequency of abortion rather than public moral condemnations of it. Here, community-based theatre with its focus on education and reliance on audience feedback serves a crucial purpose. As Sistren/HTCG members recount, when they performed *A Slice of Reality* in different communities in 2009 they received only limited resistance from their audiences, including from a former anti-choice protestor who later, after the performance, confessed to having had an abortion (HTCG interview, 2015). That incident and others show that much of the anti-choice advocacy is highly performative, involving a presentation of propriety that people may not practice in their daily lives.

Within this context, the most valuable contribution that Sistren/HTCG made to the pro-choice movement in 2009 was to expose the defects in anti-choice arguments by embodying the stories of real girls and women in the content of their skit. *A Slice of Reality* rejects the notion of abortion as a shameful practice and frames unregulated illegal abortions as an option that women in desperate situations pursue, despite the health risks. Furthermore, it critiques anti-choice laws as out of touch with reality and detrimental to women's well-being. Thus, it provides a counterdiscourse that does not simply engage in rhetoric about women's autonomy, but also embodies a pro-choice commitment. By centering the voices, artistry, and bodies of working-class Black women, Sistren/HTCG rejected the societal tendency to depict these women as a blank slate on which ideas about national well-being are imposed.

Gender, Race, Class, and Black Women's Sexuality

In Jamaica as throughout the African Diaspora, Black women are usually celebrated for their strength, reviled for their exercising of sexual agency, sexually objectified, blamed for societal problems, or portrayed as existential victims without agency by well-meaning people. These expectations and labels affect how mothering and motherhood are inscribed. Mothering figures prominently in discourses about ideal citizenship in Jamaica and the rest of the African Diaspora. Notwithstanding the validity in feminist critiques about how expectations of childbearing burden women, it is important to recognize the nuanced cultural interpretations about motherhood among Black people. There are ideas about the queen mother and the warrior queen that find resonance to an extent in respect for elder women, celebration of motherhood, and the political uplifting of mothering. Additionally, Black people have our own pronatal tendencies, which emerge from a focus on family and community—especially given the long history of Black family life being undermined and destroyed under slavery, colonialism, and racial segregation. However, these tendencies often combine with a gender expectation of women's identity as being inextricably tied to motherhood as a biological process, beyond the sociopolitical symbolism of mothering (Rowley 2011). Furthermore, as in every discussion around gender and sexuality in the country, working-class Black women are hypervisible in the celebrations of a self-sacrificing motherhood and female propriety, though their voices are rarely centered in the media.

The racial dimension of the subject of abortion has not generally been at the forefront of pro-choice campaigning, given Jamaica's demographics as an overwhelmingly Black-majority country where racism has not been overtly institutionalized since the colonial period. Rather, in the justice system, racism is usually slipped under classism because the majority of the poor are unambiguously Black, while the wealthiest tend to be white, mixed race, or of another lighter-skinned, straighter-haired racial group. Some pro-choice activists and opinion makers in the media have included race in critiques of anti-choice laws. For example, academic and cultural critic Carolyn Cooper (2009), in a column in the *Gleaner*, pointed out that enslaved Black women practiced abortion and thus, ironically, had more control over whether to go through with a pregnancy than do their descendants in contemporary Jamaica. She also asserted that anti-choice laws in the postslavery period functioned as part of a colonial plan to increase the labor force. As I discuss later, Cooper's and others' arguments draw on the work of historians who have studied the links among racism, patriarchy, and colonialism.

Racial analyses are more prevalent among pro-choice groups today, in 2023, than they were in 2009. Thus, in keeping with the emphasis on gender and class (and less on race) in the 2009 debates, *A Slice of Reality* did not make explicitly racial statements. However, by the performers' presence in Parliament and the use of an aesthetic that relies on African/Black Diasporic performance forms, Sistren/HTCG emphasized the inextricability of race and class in Jamaica and demonstrated the importance of poor Black people as repositories of African-based, decidedly Black resources of knowledge in the country. Of course, Sistren and HTCG cannot reflect the opinions of all working-class Jamaican women about abortion, nor do they claim to. However, the performance marked the first time a group of working-class Black women spoke for themselves and in their own language in the Jamaican Parliament.

The legislative process does not generally accord priority to emotion, affect, lived experiences, testimony, or other human phenomena, which are thought to be out of place in government. Within the European Enlightenment theories of the state on which the governmental structures of Anglophone Caribbean countries are based, gendered categories define the domestic/private space and the public space. The domestic space is usually considered female, artistic, and irrational in contrast to the public space, which is framed as male and therefore rational and scientific (see Pateman 1988).[3] The geographic elements in these categories are of course not fixed, and as Richa Nagar (2002, 69) posits in her study of women's theatre in northern India, "the meanings of spaces as well as of the discourses produced/challenged therein are embedded in gendered materialities, and are negotiated through the politics of publicization and privatization." Despite a woman-centered environment in certain public spaces, such as food and craft markets, where women vendors dominate, the apex of public life and careers is still governance, and the government continues to be a space under the control of upper-middle-class, heterosexual-presenting, and cisgender men. Further, given Jamaica's history of colonization by the British and the adoption of British systems of governance, the legislative process reflects colonial legacies, especially with respect to language, dress, and parliamentary procedures. Its elitism derives directly from these colonial retentions in combination with the dominance of middle-class people in political debates. Therefore, alongside exposing the deficiencies in morality posturing in the conversations about abortion, Sistren/HTCG transgressed a discursive and physical space in which patriarchy, classism, and elitism are enforced and preserved in Jamaica through legislation and policies. For over 150 years, among the most restrictive pieces of legislation have been the two clauses in the Constitution that prohibit abortion.

The Context: The Debates to Amend Jamaica's Anti-Choice Laws

Interrogating the Law

In its Constitution, Jamaica has retained the archaic provisions of sections 72–73 of the Offences against the Person Act (OAPA) of 1864, which criminalize abortion. Like most sections of the Constitution, they were written under British colonialism and therefore replicate provisions of the 1861 English act of the same name. These sections of the Jamaican OAPA state,

> Every woman, being with child, who with intent to procure her own miscarriage, shall unlawfully administer to herself any poison or other noxious thing, or shall unlawfully use any instrument or other means whatsoever with the like intent; and whosoever, with intent to procure the miscarriage of any woman, whether she be or be not with child, shall unlawfully administer to her, or cause to be taken by her, any poison or other noxious thing, or shall unlawfully use any instrument or other means whatsoever with the like intent, shall be guilty of a felony, and, being convicted thereof, shall be liable to be imprisoned for life, with or without hard labour. Whosoever shall unlawfully supply or procure any poison or other noxious thing, or any instrument or thing whatsoever, knowing that the same is intended to be unlawfully used or employed with intent to procure the miscarriage of any woman, whether she be or be not with child, shall be guilty of a

misdemeanor, and, being convicted thereof, shall be liable to be imprisoned for a term not exceeding three years, with or without hard labour.

Thus, these sections heavily criminalize women seeking an abortion, practitioners of abortion, and anyone who assists with an abortion, while not stating any instances in which it would be legal to terminate a pregnancy. The lack of nuance continues in section 74, which criminalizes the concealment of a stillbirth or newborn's death, and section 75, which addresses infanticide, with a sole focus on new mothers as perpetrators. The only relief from the overbearing legislation on abortion is a common-law (i.e., based on custom, not statute) exception that may be made in cases where the pregnant person's physical or mental health is at stake. This exception is based on the English case *R. v. Bourne*, which occurred in 1938 while Jamaica was still a colony of Britain.[4] I have not found a record of any Jamaican cases where *R v. Bourne* set the precedent for an acquittal, but it is often referenced in conversations about abortion in Jamaica, including in the report of the APRAG (Jamaica Ministry of Health 2007).

Although the OAPA establishes penalties for both pregnant women who seek an abortion and those who assist them, I have not found a record of any case in which a woman was arrested or charged in Jamaica according to the stipulations of the act, even though many admit to an abortion after having to seek medical help.[5] In actuality, practitioners and facilitators of abortion appear to be the main targets for enforcement, and this makes the process of analyzing the law's impact convoluted. For example, in 2012–14 the physicians Lloyd Goldson and Lloyd Cole faced charges under the OAPA for performing abortions on a twelve-year-old and a sixteen-year-old, respectively.[6] In both cases the law against performing abortions was applied alongside child protection laws.[7] The mother of the twelve-year-old girl was also arrested and charged not only with procuring an abortion, but also with failing to make a report to the Office of the Children's Registry—ostensibly regarding the pregnancy of a minor. The lawyers in both cases argued that the physicians carried out the abortions in order to preserve their patients' health. Furthermore, in one instance, the girl on whom the abortion was performed expressed that she did not want the court to move forward with the trial, and in the other no witnesses showed up. Ultimately, the two physicians and the twelve-year-old's mother were acquitted when the cases went to trial years later (Gabbatt 2012; *Jamaica Observer* 2014; *McKoy's News* 2017; Radio Jamaica News 2012). These cases illustrate how haphazardly the anti-choice laws are applied. Gynecologists do frequently perform abortions in instances when carrying the pregnancy to term would threaten the patient's life, and hospital records show that women often admit to having had an abortion when they have to seek post-abortion medical help at public hospitals (Jamaica Ministry of Health 2007). It seems that charges are brought against practitioners or facilitators only if the abortion was done on a minor, if someone decides to inform the police, or if there are health complications (ABC13 2010). There has also been at least one case in which the pregnant girl who had an abortion had been raped by an older man who forced her to end the pregnancy; in this case, too, the police were more preoccupied with the girl's age and the rape than the abortion itself.[8]

In all these cases reported to the media, the law has been applied with the rationale of protecting the patient, not with an intention to punish her. Even so, the possibility of arrest and conviction means that anti-choice legislation has had a chilling effect on women, medical practitioners, and others who support abortion. And as with the similarly outdated colonial antibuggery law, which prohibits anal sex and is seemingly only enforceable in cases of sexual assault against men by men, a strong moralistic element is at work here.[9] As a colonial-era law that dates back to the 1800s, the prohibition on abortion also undermines Jamaica's self-assertion as a modern, independent nation-state and specifically indicates a disregard for women's autonomy in the democratic process. In contrast with Jamaica, Barbados and Guyana (also previously colonized by Britain) have long moved past the criminal law, legalizing abortion in cases of rape, incest, fetal deformity, teenage pregnancy, risk to the health and welfare of the mother, and difficult socioeconomic conditions—as well as, in Guyana, simply on the woman's request up to eight weeks. On the other side, Jamaica is joined by countries such as Antigua and Barbuda, Dominica, Saint Kitts and Nevis, and Trinidad and Tobago, which have essentially retained the law. The remaining Caribbean countries that are former British colonies have made amendments to it or introduced new laws that legalize abortion in extenuating circumstances.

The fact that most of these countries have chosen to keep this colonial-era law in some form, including with slight amendments, seems bizarre, given that even the four territories of Britain (England, Northern Ireland, Scotland, and Wales) have now decriminalized abortion in most circumstances. However, as M. Jacqui Alexander (2005, 24) notes, heteropatriarchy—as manifested in laws and policies—is "useful in continuing to perpetuate a colonial inheritance." Colonial-era laws and new laws that are based on those written under colonization continue to serve contemporary oppressive purposes, such as the maintenance of patriarchal codes despite women's economic and political mobility over the decades, and they also illustrate how Christian churches operate as unofficial power brokers in governance. The only time the Jamaican government changed its position on abortion was in the 1970s, when it acted to make abortion legal in practice, despite a lack of constitutional change.

In 1976, the government, prompted by then minister of health Ken McNeill, established a fertility management unit at the Glen Vincent Health Centre, a low-cost public clinic in Kingston. This move was spurred by the strength of the Jamaican/Caribbean women's movements at the time and the relatively progressive system of democratic socialism in the 1970s. The fertility management unit operated for two decades, guided by policy documents that clearly laid out the criteria under which a patient could access an abortion, including teenage pregnancy, sexual assault, economic destitution, and cases referred by the Family Court (Jamaica Ministry of Health 2007). The facility closed in 1995 due to both the retirement of key staff members and defunding by the government (Heron, Toppin, and Finikin 2009; Maxwell 2012). While the subject of abortion has always been a part of public discussions, it would not reemerge as a policy issue until a decade after this closure.

In 2004, the government convened the aforementioned APRAG to assess the law and make amendments to it. Following three years of research and consultation with medical practitioners, the APRAG presented a report in February 2007, in which it identified unregulated abortion as a serious public health problem and urged the government to repeal the anti-choice law and replace it with a civil law called the Termination of Pregnancy Act, which would state the conditions under which abortion would be legal. Referencing policies in other countries in and outside of the Caribbean, including South Africa and Guyana, the APRAG recommended that abortion be decriminalized, that a system of registration, training, and monitoring of medical practitioners be put in place, and that facilities be established to provide "therapeutic" abortions in each health region. It also recommended resources be put aside to provide for pre- and post-abortion counseling (Jamaica Ministry of Health 2007). It posited a trimester system differentiating the conditions under which an abortion would be performed and monitored. Under this system, abortions up to twelve weeks (the first trimester) would be allowed at private doctors' offices and could be performed by a registered medical practitioner, while those after twelve weeks needed to be performed at hospitals by an obstetrician/gynecologist. For pregnancies that had advanced beyond twenty-two weeks, the report stated that abortions should only be allowed in "exceptional circumstances agreed upon by the woman" and should be performed by two practitioners in an "appropriate facility authorized by the Ministry [of Health]" (6). More vaguely, the report recommended "special provisions" for minors, persons with a mental disability, and those under the age of eighteen. And, as a concession to medical practitioners who disagree with abortions, it stated that "the right to conscientious objection is recognized" (6).

The APRAG report also commented on the role of classism in Jamaica's retention of anti-choice laws. One of its strongest arguments is that these laws affect mainly poor women, who end up seeking dangerous abortions from cheap but unqualified practitioners, while middle-class and rich women can access less-risky medical attention from private, expensive gynecologists. Thus, the report states, "the law persists because the middle and upper classes live above the law and enjoy access to professional medical services" (Jamaica Ministry of Health 2007, 20). The APRAG report laid the groundwork for the 2008 formation of the parliamentary Joint Select Committee on Abortion, which received submissions from individuals, feminist and women's organizations, academics, health practitioners, lawyers, and churches. As of 2022, there is still no draft legislation that would eventually develop into a Termination of Pregnancy Act (though the APRAG report refers to one being drafted) and still no consensus on the circumstances under which abortion should be legalized, other than the trimester system outlined in the report. Thus, the debates about abortion continue to be framed around whether the law should be repealed, what purpose it serves in modern-day Jamaica, and under what circumstances termination should be permitted.

Against Choice: Moralism and Morality Posturing

Moral arguments dominate the public discussions around abortion, and Christian groups led the anti-choice efforts in 2009, just as they continue to do today. While two Christian groups—Catholics for Choice and United Church of Jamaica—have shown support for repealing the anti-choice laws, they do not exercise the immense political power that anti-choice groups like Missionaries of the Poor, the Ecumenical Pro-Life Council, Lawyers' Christian Fellowship, and the Coalition of Lawyers for the Defence of the Unborn (CLDU) do. And while men's voices have been the loudest in opposition to changing the law (because of the dominance of the church in these efforts), these groups, including the CLDU, are led by people of different genders—many of them high-profile women like Shirley Richards, coauthor of the CLDU submission and member of the Love March Movement.[10]

The CLDU's submission to Parliament, authored in 2008, is a comprehensive, well-written anti-choice document that encapsulates the major arguments that emerged from the anti-choice coalition—arguments that are still pervasive today and that *A Slice of Reality* directly challenged. It began by obscuring the colonial origin of anti-choice laws with an anti-imperialist statement that urged Jamaicans not to follow the path taken by other countries because, "it is not the first time in history that these developed countries have demonstrated lack of conscience where human life is concerned" (CLDU 2008, 2). Thus, laws against abortion were portrayed as nationalistic, and a moral rift was imagined between Jamaica and those other Caribbean or Global Majority countries that had instituted progressive laws on abortion. The CLDU tackled the question of class disparities with regard to unsafe abortions by focusing on trite analyses of the cultural norms and behaviors of poor people. This was in reaction to statistics about women who sought assistance at public hospitals following complications from abortion. The APRAG and the pro-choice coalition had called on these statistics to underscore the point that by making abortions illegal, the government was creating an underground market of dangerous abortions and harmful abortifacients. For example, the APRAG report quoted statistics from public hospitals revealing that most women who sought assistance there for abortion-related complications were poor or unemployed (Jamaica Ministry of Health 2007, 5).

When manipulated through a classist lens, such statistics can create the perception that women who seek abortions are mostly from poor, urban communities. Thus, disregarding the arguments that the APRAG and other pro-choice groups were making—that the illegality of abortion endangers mostly poor women's lives—the CLDU instead used these statistics and others to further its moralistic agenda.[11] The submission posed the question, "Could it be that if these women were employed that they would not have fallen victims to sexual allurement? For surely it is no coincidence that all of them were unemployed!" (CLDU 2008, 3). Alongside its disparaging language around class, the CLDU's submission contained disconcerting racial references. Drawing on controversial statistics used by anti-choice lobbyists in the United States, it posited, "Abortion has been made to appear by some as the road to improvement in our social conditions. We note that abortion has not helped the black race in the United States" (6). It went on to quote statistics on high rates of abortion, incarceration, and HIV/AIDS among Black people in the United States. This statement responds to pro-choice arguments that abortion has a utilitarian function—particularly in the realm of poverty and crime control—a position that can be problematic, as already mentioned. Most disingenuously, though, it employs an analysis rooted in respectability politics, without any thought to systemic racism and its impact on Black people's social condition and Black women's reproductive lives.

The legacies of slavery, colonialism, and imperialism in Jamaica ensure that the majority of the poor and unemployed are Black; and that women are disproportionately more likely to be unemployed than men (McIntosh 2021). Furthermore, households in which a woman is the sole parent are poorer than those in which a man is the sole parent or those that have a nuclear family structure (Planning Institute of Jamaica 2019, xviii). Thus, conversations around poverty, unemployment, single-parent households, and irresponsible sexual behavior have distinct racial and gendered implications. The CLDU's moral arguments and those of other Christian-based anti-choice groups fall in line with rhetoric that focuses on Black women's shortcomings as mothers, sexual agents/victims, citizens, and human beings in general—discourses grounded in what Veronica Marie Gregg (2005, 59) refers to as the "generative belly of the Negro woman."[12]

Enslaved Black women generally had low birth rates, a result of malnutrition and their physical mistreatment under slavery, as well as abortions. After the end of the slave trade in 1807 and the introduction of amelioration policies by Britain, the plantocracy and the British government stressed the importance of reproduction in sustaining the enslaved workforce, to which end white male doctors were hired to take charge of reproductive health care and circumvent the Black women midwives who had attended to pregnant women for centuries prior. This concern with increasing the birth rate was shared by white abolitionists, even while the two sides may have disagreed about the continuation of slavery. As Sasha Turner (2019, 42) points out, during the final decades of slavery in Jamaica, British abolitionists connected reproduction to the economic benefits of colonialism: "Women were expected to birth a great number of children who would then be trained from their infancy to become loyal and industrious free people." We can surmise from these facts that anti-choice laws in England and its colonies were therefore introduced in the postslavery period, which corresponded with the Industrial Revolution and the Victorian era, as well as with the rise of the (male-dominated) fields of gynecology and obstetrics (see also Morgan 1989).

The arguments of anti-choice lobbyists continually sidestep analysis of racial, economic, and gender hierarchies. Over the years, anti-choice groups have recommended many alternatives to abortion, including construction of more orphanages. For example, in a 2009 interview during the debates, Catholic cleric Kenneth Richards emphasized that abortion should not be legal in any circumstance. He spoke positively about Mary's Child, a Catholic facility for pregnant women and girls who are contemplating adoption, noting that "100 percent" of them end up keeping the child (*Gleaner* 2009). Other recommendations from anti-choice activists have included greater enforcement of laws against sexual violence, job creation to resolve the problem of unemployment among poor women, and the institution of more mechanisms to hold accountable men who abandon the women they get pregnant. When considered on their own, these solutions are positive. However, they are usually steeped in moralistic language and disregard the physical and psychological effects of pregnancy. For example, alongside a call for greater enforcement of laws to punish sexual predators, the CLDU (2008, 20) suggested measures to "unashamedly promote abstinence and purity and promote the restoration of communities and families," which is similar to Richard Ho Lung's (2008) calls for the government to "join with the churches in stating that extra-marital [sexual] activities are evil, against both natural law and the law of God."

In sum, Sistren and HTCG had to tackle negative public perceptions and the moral and propagandistic power of anti-choice lobbyists. Up until the point at which they performed in Parliament, women and girls who had had abortions existed merely as statistics. And statements published in the media about women who had pursued an abortion tended to have an anti-choice angle: anecdotes from Christians about women who regretted an abortion or who chose to keep the pregnancy after receiving Christian counseling. Because of the limited enforcement of the law and the secrecy and shame attached to abortion, no woman or girl has ever become the face of the pro-choice movement in Jamaica. This differs from the situation in countries where pro-choice activists have recourse to high-profile cases to give face to their efforts. In Kenya, for example, the High Court ruled in 2019 in favor of the family of a teenager who died after a botched abortion, in effect ruling in favor of abortion when a pregnancy results from rape (Bhalla and Malalo 2019). In Mexico, which recently changed its legislation, pro-choice activists have pointed to the many cases in which women who have had abortions have been convicted and sent to prison (Gottesdiener 2021). *A Slice of Reality* therefore sought to embody the lived realities of actual Jamaican girls and women whose experiences had not previously been reflected in the activism. In so doing the skit bridged distinct spaces both private and public: the private material and experiential space in which people contemplate reproductive decisions and exercise degrees of sexual agency; the community or grassroots sphere in which Jamaicans share information and converse; and the sphere of government, in which laws are made by a select group of elites who purportedly represent the interest of the masses.

Making *A Slice of Reality*: From Community Spaces to Parliament

Sistren formed the Hannah Town Cultural Group in 2002 as part of its work with the Citizen Security and Justice Programme (CSJP), an initiative of the Jamaica Ministry of National Security. CSJP mobilized residents of communities with high rates of crime and violence through various strategies, such as encouraging collaboration between them and the police and finding avenues for community members to express themselves creatively.[13] In the case of HTCG, members joined the group because they saw it as an opportunity to put into practice their interest in performing, as well as to help their community. They all had a lifelong interest in theatre, which they could not pursue as a career because of more pressing economic demands that required them to find work at very young ages or to find more financially feasible employment to support their families. Althea Blackwood stated, "I used to do drama in clubs at school, but after a time, having the children and things like that, I kinda just stop doing drama. But I was thankful when Sistren came along, and I just grab on to it" (pers. comm., 2015). Other members, such as Pauline Blake, remarked on getting involved in drama again after a lifetime of being interested in it: "When Sistren come in and mi hear 'bout the drama mi glad fi it because mi get back part of mi life" (pers. comm., 2015). Members' training in theatre has mostly been through Sistren due to the inaccessibility of training at theatre education institutions.

HTCG has tried to move beyond its initial role as Sistren's protégé in CSJP, becoming involved in a number of public education initiatives around gender, and programs that focus on gang and state violence. The group is often conflated with Sistren because Sistren has produced most of its well-known projects, and its performances have occurred under the funding and auspices of Sistren. For Sistren, which was founded in 1977, the absence of a core membership following the migration, retirement, or death of most of its original members means that HTCG has functioned as its performance arm. Sistren and HTCG developed *A Slice of Reality* as part of a collaborative process with other advocacy groups who formed the Working Group for Reproductive Health in 2009.[14] The skit began as part of Sistren's ongoing projects of research and public education. HTCG had over the years devised several street theatre projects geared at addressing gender-based, gang, and state violence and inviting feedback from audiences. Therefore, once Sistren became involved in the 2008–9 activism around abortion, HTCG began to incorporate that topic into the conversations its members had in communities. Wherever they went, people kept approaching them with their own and others' stories about botched abortions or lives that had been affected by the illegality of abortion. They decided to collect these stories and build the skit around them: "All the characters came out of real-life situations. And I think that . . . was one of the reasons that it got the kind of attention that it got, because we had explained to them [audiences] that these are actual persons' stories. It's not no make believe situation. These are the stories of real-life Jamaican women" (Marlon Thompson, pers. comm., 2015).

HTCG devised *A Slice of Reality* using Sistren's method of collective creation based on research, a technique that the organization became known for in the 1970s and 1980s. HTCG members did not produce a script for the skit after they completed its first version. Within the orality-based tradition of storytelling in Jamaica, this allowed *A Slice of Reality* to retain a high level of fluidity and respond to audience reception, even while it made the process of archiving difficult. After finishing the first version, they traveled to different communities, performed it for free, and incorporated audience feedback and discussion into later versions. The discussions were lively, and HTCG members stated that they received mostly positive feedback from their community audiences. This is another indication of the nuances involved in discussing public approval or disapproval of abortion in Jamaica. According to Sonia Britton, one of the performers, "Most people were in agreement. They say it's your right and your body and you free to do what you want with your body" (pers. comm., 2015). They only received opposition once, when they went to do a performance in collaboration with the Ministry of Health at a town hall meeting in the city of Montego Bay. When they got to the venue, they were confronted by Christian protestors who bore anti-choice placards and denounced them. However, as it turned out, these protestors came inside and sat and watched the performance without interrupting. Then, afterward, one of them approached the group, apologized for the way she had treated them, and disclosed that she had had an abortion: "She said that her mother had to get her one so she could finish her studies at university" (Britton, pers. comm.). This incident raises the larger issue of how moral rhetoric against abortion relies on an appearance of propriety that many people do not practice in their daily lives—much like how the anti-choice law itself is rarely enforced but still maintains its control on Jamaicans. The woman's confession and apology underscore the importance of audience feedback and engagement in community-based performances, which created the environment for her to feel comfortable discussing her personal conflict with Sistren/HTCG members.

Given the success of *A Slice of Reality* in connecting with community audiences, and its ethnographic foundations, when the time came to make a formal submission to Parliament in favor of the Termination of Pregnancy Act, Sistren/HTCG members decided that they would honor their niche in using the medium of theatre for advocacy and consciousness-raising. Importantly, they also decided (in contrast with the community performances of *A Slice of Reality* but in keeping with Sistren's practice in its early years) to feature only women in the cast. Originally, Sistren had featured women actors even in male roles, although the collective often worked with male directors and technicians. The inclusion of men in performances and educational work marked one of the organization's evolutions in its later years to respond to calls from local communities for a more holistic approach to addressing sexual rights and gender-based violence.[15] Sistren expanded its educational focus by hiring male development specialists and male artists to engage men in urban communities. Thus, HTCG contains men and women, though most of the members are women (in 2015 HTCG comprised ten women and three men).[16] In keeping with the group's communal approach, community performances of *A Slice of Reality* featured a sympathetic male character played by a man in the group, consonant with the group's intentions to engage across gender lines around subjects that are often perceived as female or women's issues. For the performance in Parliament, HTCG was accompanied by a male drummer, Julian Hardie, who has worked with Sistren over the years. However, the skit itself featured only female characters, played by eight women in the group: Althea Blackwood, Pauline Blake, Sonia Britton, Karlene Campbell, Cinderella Green, Patricia McCrae, Patricia Riley, and Joan Stewart. They felt that the play's message of empowerment and women's agency would be more effective without any male characters in the already male-dominated space of Parliament.

Like most national government buildings throughout the world, the George William Gordon House—the meeting place of Parliament—is an elite site. It is not closed off from the public, though certain styles of clothing are prohibited, including flip-flops, shorts, tights, and revealing shirts and blouses. As long as people adhere to the dress code and other standard rules of behavior and sign their names in a register, they can enter and watch committee meetings; people are not generally searched by the police or security guards when they enter.[17] Nevertheless, the space reflects and preserves the gender and class hierarchies in Jamaica. The fact that Jamaica once had a woman prime minister, Portia Simpson-Miller, has not yet significantly transformed the gender composition of Parliament.[18] As of 2022, the total percentage of women MPs is 28 percent, and at the time of the performance it was 21 percent. This has implications for policymaking on abortion because, as many researchers have indicated, women's representation in global legislatures largely determines the priority given to issues that primarily affect women, including reproductive rights (Berkman and O'Connor 1993; Ogmundson 2005; Paxton 2014; Sawer, Tremblay, and Trimble 2006; Taylor-Robinson and Heath 2003).

In addition to Parliament's being the most powerful patriarchal institution in Jamaica, its policies and procedures are veritable indicators of the Westminster system of governance and thus of British cultural hegemony. Among the features of this hegemony are: (1) the type of dress expected of parliamentarians, which is usually a three-piece suit for men, tailored suit or dress with sleeves for women, and white wig and black robe for the Speaker of the House of Representatives; (2) the dominance of the English language, which is Jamaica's official language, though politicians sometimes switch to Jamaican Patwa in heightened emotion; and (3) Christian prayer, which opens the parliamentary sittings.

Although Sistren/HTCG had to get approval to perform a skit instead of the standard presentation of a reading from a previously submitted paper, the performance still subverts the norms: when the realms of state and theatre meet, it is usually government officials who enter performance spaces

Figure 1. The site of the performance. A sitting of the Jamaican Parliament in 2016. Photo courtesy of the Jamaica Information Service.

(either physically or legislatively) to exercise control. There are various examples of this globally (Larasati 2012; Ngũgĩ wa Thiong'o 1997; Ongiri 2010, 109). The Jamaican examples include the expulsion of Sistren Theatre Collective from the auspices of the Jamaica School of Drama in 1980 following a violent election, and the bulldozing of the Bellevue Garden Theatre in 1982 (Ford-Smith 1997; Hickling 2004). In addition to its unusual and transgressive use of Parliament as a site of performance, the skit interrupted the cultural norms of this elite governmental space through its reliance on popular Jamaican and African Diasporic language, aesthetics, and content.

Caribbean theatre artists have a history of utilizing popular performance forms rooted in African Diasporic techniques and rituals in order to make social commentary. Elaine Savory Fido (2005, 245) refers to this practice as "rehabilitating popular traditions as anti-imperialist forms." Consistent with this tendency—and with Sistren/HTCG's larger body of work—*A Slice of Reality*'s speech, singing, and poetry were delivered mostly in Jamaican Patwa, with English reserved only for middle-class characters. This adherence to Jamaican Patwa in Sistren's repertoire and in HTCG's work emerges from the anticolonial grassroots commitments made by them and other artists connected to the Jamaican theatre movement of the 1970s, from which Sistren emerged. The collective's use of Patwa has not escaped controversy, particularly with regard to the translatability of their plays for international audiences, but Sistren has resisted the pressure to edit their language and context for the benefit of these audiences. For example, Hertencer Lindsay-Sheppard, director of Sistren's hit play *QPH* (1981), recounted to me that they refused to translate the Patwa dialogues for the play's 1982 international run (pers. comm., 2014).[19]

Sistren's decision to make the women "speak with their own voice" (Lindsay-Sheppard) finds its musical equivalent in the use of Black/Jamaican music forms in the collective's work, including popular music as well as traditional and still-evolving forms like drumming, which was central to *A Slice of Reality*. Various drums that originated in West and Central Africa, such as the kete, djembe, and gumbeh, have a history of defiance in Jamaica, dating back to the slavery era, when they were used for communication, resistance, and recreation. As Errol Hill (1992, 248–49) notes, in the early postslavery period colonial authorities and white property owners continued to be preoccupied with drums and drumming during recreational activities like the Jonkonnu and other Christmas performances; and there were several confrontations with the police and soldiers in which drums were seized and civilians assaulted and killed.[20] The postcolonial majority-Black Jamaican government has advanced beyond the colonial aversion to African Diasporic drums, and government agencies like the Ministry of Culture even show acceptance of them during Black celebratory events like the annual national Emancipation Day vigil. Nonetheless, drums are definitely not embraced as respectable instruments in the highest official ceremonies. Given the absence of African Diasporic art forms and Jamaican popular language from formal governmental procedures, the skit's music, dialogues, poetry, and movement enabled Black cultural affirmation and commentaries on race, class, and gender that form the substance of Sistren/HTCG's pro-choice arguments.

A Slice of Reality had only one scene, with a plot structured around a fictional community meeting in an unnamed community in which women spoke about their life experiences. There was neither a set nor props. Eight unnamed characters related scenarios created from the life stories that HTCG and Sistren had gathered in different communities. The actors'

Figure 2. The performers of *A Slice of Reality* with Lana Finikin, executive director of Sistren, at the Abortion Public Forum, University of the West Indies, Mona, April 2009. *From left, front row:* Pauline Blake, Sonia Britton (deceased 2021). *Middle row:* Patricia Riley, Julian Hardie (drummer), Karlene Campbell, Joan Stewart, Lana Finikin, Althea Blackwood. *Back row:* Marlon Thompson, Patricia McCrae. Missing: Cinderella Green. Photo courtesy of Marlon Thompson.

costuming varied but was generally based on the casual clothing worn by women every day in communities across Jamaica. The skit utilized three main performance techniques: dialogues, dub poetry, and dance. The women employed these techniques to perform/argue the importance of actual women's experiences, the combined sexism and classism of anti-choice laws, and women's bodily autonomy.

Dialogues, Testimony, and Safe Spaces

A Slice of Reality stressed the need for nonjudgmental spaces for women and girls considering an abortion. The setting of the skit itself was an informal community meeting in which women could speak candidly about their experiences. This technique of testimony is useful in therapeutic, educational, and other forms of community theatre to articulate experiences garnered through research. Testimony can lessen the risk of retraumatizing an audience, by reenacting a character's or community's memories, and in theatre that addresses sexual matters it can avoid unintentionally objectifying the actors' bodies through a dramatized reenactment. Unlike what transpires in a court of law, in which the story is heavily mediated through questioning from lawyers and the strictures of the court proceedings, dramatic testimony is monologue based and usually involves the portrayal of another's experience through the performer's voice and body. Testimony in the context of Jamaican/African Diasporic life also bears resemblance to and perhaps is influenced by *testifying*, a mode of communication in Black churches wherein the pastor or prayer leader shifts from guiding the meeting and allows the congregation to speak. Members stand up and speak candidly about a life-changing experience—usually their own—with the aim of showing solidarity with other members or inspiring action on the part of those who have not yet *seen the light* in a spiritual sense or are doubtful about another decision they must make. Testimony in Jamaican theatre is intrinsically performative, often involving significant bodily emphasis, shifts in the meter of the voice to convey emotion, and attention to only the most resonant elements of the story. The goal is to make the audience empathize through vocal agreement or through action following the testimony. As Roxana Waterson (2010, 514) writes, "implicitly some work is required of the audience in order to arrive at a satisfactory outcome from such performances; they have their part to play in being actively, not merely passively responsive to what is being communicated."

For the 2009 performance of *A Slice of Reality* in Parliament, while the characters served as the primary audience for one another's testimonies, the intended audience were the members of Parliament and Jamaican society writ large. The skit opened with two women discussing the debates to repeal anti-choice laws in Jamaica. One woman then received a shocking phone call, where someone gossiped to her that a friend's teenage daughter is now pregnant. The news quickly spread to other women, and they eventually gathered on the street to talk about it. The conversation quickly shifted to pregnancy and abortion. Five characters, who were based on the stories HTCG members had collected in their community-based discussions, talked about their experiences:

- An older woman with five children and four grandchildren who planned to go "straight [to] a bush doctor" if she ever got pregnant again because she was unable to take birth control for health reasons
- A homeless woman with a mental illness who said she became pregnant four times after being raped by the same man and was considering going to a "quack doctor" to have an abortion if it happened again
- A woman who related the story of not being able to get an abortion for her daughter, who became pregnant after she was raped by her father
- A middle-class mother who said that she paid for an abortion after her teenage daughter got pregnant, allowing her the chance to attend university
- A woman who had been given a poisonous abortifacient because she couldn't afford a less risky medical abortion and had to be rushed to the hospital

The other characters served as these women's interlocutors, neighbors, and friends and offered many opinions on abortion, the ineffectiveness and side effects of contraceptives, and various difficult scenarios in which women become pregnant.

Two of the stories depicted through dialogues addressed the intersection of gender and class in the conversations about abortion. The first was that of the homeless character, who recounted that the man who had repeatedly impregnated her was a rich man with an expensive car who paid her to keep quiet. This story is even more disturbing when we consider that it was based on a real woman. The other story that focused on class involved the middle-class woman who recalled being able to pay for an abortion for her pregnant teenage daughter, who was now a successful university graduate, wife, and mother to a daughter. She remarked, "I am from uptown, and it is being done plenty up there, but because uptown women can go to private doctors you don't hear about it."[21] Indeed, in much of the conservative anti-abortion rhetoric, the men who impregnate poor women through rape or some form of exploitation are usually implied to be poor men from volatile urban communities, with connections to organized crime and violence. The 2008 submission of the CLDU is demonstrative of this rhetoric: it focuses narrowly on the dangers of "dons" (organized crime leaders) and "garrisons" (urban communities) as instruments of women's oppression.[22] In response to these stigmas, Sistren/HTCG therefore discussed the more deleterious effects of anti-choice laws on poor women, as well as highlighted the ways in which a classist emphasis on their abortions pathologizes them. Further, by juxtaposing stories in which women from disparate social classes were assaulted by well-off men, Sistren/HTCG confronted the tendency for sexual deviance to be associated with poor people. This commentary on class intersected with and supplemented the general commentary on the harmfulness of anti-choice laws and the frequency with which women and girls risk their lives and health to obtain unregulated abortions. One of the most grounded critiques of anti-choice legislation and out-of-touch conversations that focus on moral propriety was a moment in which the women listed a collection of poisonous abortifacients, such as "boiled cobweb with Pepsi, rusty nail, Pepsi and Phensic [tablets], dog blood, john crow [turkey vulture] blood."

Essentially, the skit reflected the general activism of the pro-choice coalition by focusing on the most desperate cases. Pro-choice activists over the years have generally sought to show the inherent callousness of the current legislation against abortion by emphasizing its disregard for women in desperate situations. As such, they tend to focus on the need to change the law to accommodate women who have been raped, women living in poverty, pregnant teenage girls, and those with high-risk pregnancies. They also often use human rights language to present arguments, showing how anti-choice legislation conflicts with UN instruments and policies such as the Convention on the Elimination of All Forms of Discrimination against Women, to which Jamaica is a signatory. In the 2007–9 debates, a frequent argument made was that Jamaica needs to lower maternal deaths in order to meet UN development goals.[23]

In my conversations with HTCG members, some people voiced support for abortion only in extenuating circumstances. This emphasis on extenuating circumstances in the activism as well as in the general public's response to surveys on abortion, provided a rebuttal to the suggestions from mostly Catholic anti-choice lobbyists that adoption is an alternative to abortion. Thus, the focus of HTCG members was on the potential trauma of a pregnancy and its effects, not on the potential inconvenience to parents or their inability to take care of a child. For example, Pauline Blake emphasized the possible psychological effects of bringing to term a pregnancy that resulted from rape: "Every time you look at that child is like you want to call it 'Rape'" (pers comm., 2015). Similarly, the character in *A Slice of Reality* who recounted the incestuous rape of a girl by her own father referred to the pregnancy as a "life-and-death situation!" HTCG members also stressed the need for compassionate care in centers that would offer abortion access. They conceived of such centers as safe spaces that fulfill the physical need for privacy and a judgment-free environment, and that cater to women without the means to go to private gynecologists. As Althea Blackwood noted, "In the inner city now, because we don't have any money we have to go to the quack shop and so that is why we are really trying to come across with the issue to find a safe place, where persons who cannot afford it can go. Because uptown a lot of persons are doing it uptown but nobody knows about it. But in the inner city you have the quack shop and sometimes your life is at risk" (pers. comm., 2015).

Patricia McCrae, in agreement with her, finished Blackwood's sentence with an emphasis on choice regardless of circumstance: "that yu can go in and mek decision pan yu oun. Nubady nuh mek decisions for yu! A your body, a yu a feel it, a your foot ina di shoes a squeeze. A taak bout a only sickness or rape. Ee, wa guh so?" (pers comm., 2015).[24] This emphasis in McCrae's statement on choice regardless of circumstance was not at the forefront of the skit's dialogues.

As part of Sistren/HTCG's goals to present research (and *A Slice of Reality*'s function as a political submission), there were moments in *A Slice of Reality* when it departed from the focus on testimony and experience in order to provide information. For example, a character stated, "I read in the paper the other day that the World Health Organization say [*sic*] there are twenty-two thousand unsafe abortions every year!" The others added to her statement by emphasizing that this number did not include "quack" abortions done by unlicensed or unskilled medical practitioners. One major challenge of research-to-performance techniques is that of crafting a performance while also presenting facts, and enabling the story to reinforce the political message without becoming didactic (the Mothertongue Project faced the same challenge with its production of *Walk: South Africa*; see chapter 2). Sistren and HTCG balanced their research-focused presentation of facts through the use of testimonies, and statistical evidence about the dangers of unregulated abortions through the incorporation of movement, poetry, and singing. These nondialogic aesthetic choices resist the need for social scientific validation, unlike the sections in which the performers essentially provided research. They moved beyond a focus on what to do when a pregnant woman faces extenuating circumstances and instead amplified the message about choice and bodily autonomy. Analyzing the work of space, movement, and orality allows for a profounder understanding of the play's function as an activist performance rooted in gender-justice discourse. I will now discuss two vignettes that made the most critical interventions into the debates and distinguished the input of *A Slice of Reality* most effectively from that of the other pro-choice presentations. These are the choral dub poem performed in the middle of the skit and the song with which it ended.

"Yu Nuh Seet!": Dubbing Out Sexism and Classism

In the middle of the performance the dialogue paused, and the actors performed a poem accompanied by a drumbeat modeled after the signature beat of the Nyabinghi group of Rastafari, the Africa-centered lived philosophy and social movement that originated in Jamaica. Nyabinghi was the name of a legendary East African queen whose spirit was most famously embodied by another warrior-queen, Queen Muhumuza of Uganda, in the twentieth century (Sandner 2018). Reflecting this influence, Nyabinghi is one of the most militant and pro-Black Rastafarian groups, and the drum is defined by a measured, bass-heavy, *Tun Tun . . . Tun Tun . . . Tun Tun Tu Tu Tu Tun Tun*, making it an ideal accompaniment for Black performance poetry geared at advocacy. I refer to the poem as "Yu Nuh Seet" (Can't You See?) after its refrain. Below is my transcription of it.

	Original Jamaican:	English Translation:
LEADER:	Yu nuh seet?	Can't you see?
CHORUS:	Uman have dem raits	Women have their rights
LEADER:	Yu nuh seet?	Can't you see?
CHORUS:	Luk pan di criminal dem	Look at the [real] criminals
LEADER:	Yu nuh seet?	Can't you see?
CHORUS:	More counseling	More counseling
LEADER:	Yu nuh seet?	Can't you see?
CHORUS:	Mek wi choose fi wiself	Let us choose for ourselves
LEADER:	Yu nuh seet?	Can't you see?
CHORUS:	Wi a nuh murdara!	We are not murderers
LEADER:	Yu nuh seet?	Can't you see?
CHORUS:	A cudda uppa, middle, or bottom	It could be upper, middle, or bottom
LEADER:	Yu nuh seet?	Can't you see?
CHORUS:	All kaina uman!	All Kinds of Women
LEADER:	Yu Nuh Seet?	Can't You See?
LEADER:	All Kaina Uman!	All Kinds of Women

The poem's refrain, "Yu nuh seet?" is based on a phrase that Jamaicans commonly use when explaining an argument. My very loose English translation of "Can't you see?" misses the emphatic tone of the original, which is not just an appeal. It is also an exhortation. It says more than just "Pay attention to my needs" and demands self-reflection from the audience.

"Yu Nuh Seet" adheres to most of the conventional features of dub poetry, a genre that developed in Jamaica during the 1970s. The term *dub* derives from the influence of toasting, which entails a disc jockey chanting over the dub (instrumental) side of a record. Toasting mixed with other practices to influence the development of dancehall music in Jamaica and hip-hop in the United States in the late 1970s to early 1980s. Oku Onuora, pioneer dub poet, is credited with inventing the term *dub poetry* to define this genre, in which the performer's intonation often switches to different beats to convey various emotions.[25] Unlike the many popular Jamaican art forms that have an origin in working-class Black Jamaican aesthetics, especially reggae music, dub poetry has maintained a categorically subversive nature as rebel poetry because it has not taken on various modes of use through mass global consumption, reinterpretation, and co-optation.

Women have been central to the development of dub poetry, and many successful dub poets are women. The list includes the dub pioneers Lillian Allen, Jean "Binta" Breeze, and Anita Stewart (a.k.a. Anilia Soyinka), who is mother of dub poet/actor and playwright D'bi Young Anitafrika. As Afua Cooper (1999, 7) notes, from the beginning, women dub poets not only spoke about the same issues that male dub poets covered but also added critical dimensions about women's lives including sexuality, love, spirituality, family life, and gender equality, sometimes with a "feminist stamp." "Yu Nuh Seet" fits within this tradition of dub poetry's use for Black feminist/womanist politics.

Sistren and HTCG's use of movement and singing at the end of the skit functioned similarly to the use of dub poetry, allowing for exploration of the range of physical and other expressive forms in storytelling. It also balanced the straightforward verbal approach of the dub poem with a more implicit one that emphasized the women's delight in their own bodies. While the dialogue involved the presentation of research (cohering with the approach of other pro-choice groups) and the dub poem spoke to the parliamentarians directly, the singing and dancing that ended the skit allowed the performers to speak with one another and with others who would be watching the news broadcast later that day. The closing song is *A Slice of Reality*'s most effective/affective statement about communal bonds forged in the performance and beyond.

"Wi Oun Laif an Raits Inna Wi Han": Ritual Movement, Woman Power

Most of Sistren's full-length plays feature music and singing with a choral song accompanied by upbeat drumming or another genre of bass-driven music. Consistent with this practice, *A Slice of Reality* also concluded with a song, which I refer to as "Wi Oun Laif" (Our Own Lives).

Original Jamaican:
Uman wi have wi oun laif anda cantrol
Wi nuh waa no unwanted pickney pan dis lan
Wi have wi oun laif an raits inna wi han
No matta wa yu try, wi a nuh murdara

English translation:
Women we have our own lives under control
We don't want any unwanted children on this land
We have our own rights and lives in our hands
No matter what you try [to say], we are not murderers

The lines of the song and the dance that accompanies it may at first seem contradictory to what the women expressed in the rest of the play. They spent the previous fourteen minutes arguing that women do not have their own rights and lives in their hands, because of the government's and wider society's refusal to pay attention to them. However, the song functions less as a conclusive statement and more as an exhortation. Its agency-focused lines indicate Sistren/HTCG's resistance to being caught in the victim/victor binary. As is the case with many genres of African Diasporic dance, particularly those used in celebratory and mourning ceremonies, the central focus is to transmit a message of survival and to use movement to bring the action back to a place in which healing can occur. In *A Slice of Reality*, the dance's movement was circular, consisting of various hip gyrations and the performers' use of their bodies to form a circle. This employment of circular movement and circular scripting in a play, especially to embody its resolution, adheres to Omofolabo Ajayi's (2002, 119) concept of the "arc of ritual wholeness." Ajayi states that this arc fuses the past, present, and future. The "resulting wholeness brings about a healing process and resolution to the individual generation, communities or cultural, socio-political and ideological issues."

The final vignette therefore produced a ritual and ontological circle that signifies the connection made in Jamaican/African Diasporic ritual performance practices between fertility, regeneration, and life and death. Sistren/

HTCG chose to center the women's bodies, especially the pelvis, which is the site of sex and reproduction, as opposed to diverting attention from them. They did this in a context in which women's bodies were under interrogation. Dancing at the end of the play represented reclamation of those bodies and minds.

The dance did not transgress the politics of sexual respectability in Jamaica as much as other more popular, contemporary dances do, especially those in dancehall culture involving explicit movements constructed to mimic sexual activity. However, like the affirmative lines of the song it accompanied, the dance resisted categorization into subtle versus explicit, unsexed versus sexual, morose versus joyful. Additionally, the dance, which involved wining (circular movement of the hips and buttocks), was an affirmation of Jamaican and African Diasporic movement, particularly as practiced by Black women. Across the African Diaspora, Black women's dances that focus on the hips and buttocks are important sites of community-making, assertions of sexual agency, and displays of ingenuity and skill (Halliday 2020; Pérez 2016; Springer 2008). Like the speech patterns of dub poetry, these forms of movement are guided by the polyrhythms that are essential to Jamaican/African Diasporic performance (Nettleford 2002, 81). In combination with the other performance techniques and the use of Patwa in *A Slice of Reality*, the dance interrupted the nontheatrical performance of Britishness, middle class–ness, and patriarchy that constitute a major element of governmental procedure in Jamaica.

By utilizing decidedly African Diasporic/Jamaican techniques, *A Slice of Reality* also introduced a nontextual response to the anti-imperialist, anti-choice rhetoric that abortion is a foreign imposition (*Gleaner* 2019). Exemplary of this other side is for instance the Pan-Africanist rejection of abortion voiced by Jamaican child rights advocate Betty Ann Blaine, who, in an interview with the *Daily Post Nigeria*, listed "ideologies and agendas dictating that we must agree with same-sex and prochoice lifestyles and positions" as "common threats Nigeria, the African Continent, the Caribbean and the Christian world face" (Nwachukwu 2021). Of course, pro-choice activists have continually pointed to the colonial origins of the law in order to reject this notion, but it continues as a culturalist argument. By embodying a pro-choice position through Black aesthetics and Jamaican vernacular expression, *A Slice of Reality* rooted gender justice within Jamaican/Black/African Diasporic culture.

The approach to have the characters give deeply personal accounts of their lives, punctuated by poetry, dance, music, and ritual, is similar to that used by several other Black Caribbean women theatre practitioners, such as Trey Anthony (2005) in *Da Kink in My Hair* and Jean Small (1990) in *A Black Woman's Tale*. With regard to its focus on bodily autonomy, *A Slice of Reality* closely resembled Sistren's breakthrough early play *Bellywoman Bangarang* (1978), a semi-autobiographical collectively created production about teenage pregnancy, child abuse, and oppressive societal norms that control girls' self-image. Sistren's executive director, Lana Finikin, recounts that *Bellywoman*'s "message was about tearing down walls—taboo walls" (pers. comm., 2014). It was Jamaica's first major theatrical discussion of sexual topics like menstruation, pregnancy following rape, and childbirth. In her analysis of *Bellywoman Bangarang*, Kanika Batra (2011) draws on legal scholar Tracy Robinson's (2003) theories of citizenship, sex, and gender in the Caribbean to formulate the concept of postcolonial sexual citizenship. Like Robinson, Batra begins from the assumption that women's sexuality, pregnancy, and issues of reproductive rights overlap with questions of nationhood and ideal citizenship. Postcolonial sexual citizenship relies on an emphasis of "the inextricable relationship between sexuality and survival and a concomitant denial of emphasis on the connection between sexuality and morality" (49). Batra puts forward the idea of an assertion of citizenship that centers women's sexual and reproductive concerns. This assertion of citizenship is embodied in daily acts of resistance as well as staged performances. *A Slice of Reality* continued this practice, initiated by *Bellywoman Bangarang* and by Sistren's early plays, through the subject matter of abortion, asserting women's equal citizenship thematically and spatially by performing inside the Houses of Parliament.

A Slice of Reality's Resonances

Sistren and HTCG's major political contribution to the 2007–9 cycle of debates about the Termination of Pregnancy Act was made possible by their subjective treatment of the issue through the novel approach of using drama. As Taitu Heron, Danielle Toppin, and Lana Finikin (2009, 47) state, "Sistren's presentation . . . played an important role in moving the discourse out of the abstract discussions of 'right' versus 'wrong' to address the fact that the law as it currently stands is adversely impacting the lives of large numbers of women in Jamaica." By staging the voices of working-class women, they made clear that an issue that has largely been defined by the elites—including religious leaders, gender-justice advocates, and academics—is also one that is talked about daily among the general public, including in informal community meetings and other spaces in which women gather, such as the one depicted in the skit. In the days after the performance many groups and individuals contacted Sistren and commended the collective's activism: "These emails had a decidedly emotional tone, praised Sistren and expressed renewed commitment and hope" (Heron, Toppin, and Finikin 2009, 59). Additionally, in a letter to the *Gleaner*, a member of the public, Rebekah Lawrence (2009), similarly expressed her appreciation for *A Slice of Reality*. The letter stated, "I urge the parliamentarians to take this opportunity that Sistren has presented them with by their 'slice of reality on the ground' to really study the issues and get beyond dogma and egotism. Women's rights are human rights too, lest they forget."

As was to be expected, the outpouring of emotive praise Sistren and HTCG received from development agencies, activists, and members of the public was not echoed by the parliamentarians, whose tendency it is to maintain a stoic, ostensibly objective demeanor when hearing presentations from activists. This seeming commitment to stoicism was placed under pressure with the performance of a skit, especially one as lively as *A Slice of Reality*, which elicited emotion and kinesthetic responses from foot tapping to laughter. There were also some awkward moments in the performance, when some of the MPs seemed physically uncomfortable, and one MP left for several minutes to talk on his phone. However, the MPs' responses were largely favorable, tempered with the caution that has dominated discussions about abortion in Jamaica for decades.

Minutes from the proceedings feature positive comments such as those from Joint Select Committee members Hyacinth Bennett and Fenton Ferguson, who stated that the play had presented the issues in a realistic manner; and Rudyard Spencer, the chair of the committee, who indicated that "Sistren's presentation would go a far way to helping them to make a decision about abortion at the end of the deliberations" (quoted in Heron, Toppin, and Finikin 2009, 55). Others, such as Dwight Nelson, lauded the inventiveness of Sistren/HTCG: "I do not wish to make a value judgment in respect of the content of the presentation . . . but the format is a refreshing departure. In a manner of speaking, Sistren has made the committee's day" (quoted in Heron, Toppin, and Finikin 2009, 55). Another MP, Lisa Hanna, who has publicly supported the repeal of the anti-choice law, was less inhibited in her praise. She openly commended Sistren in a statement afterward and linked the skit to everyday realities that women face by stating that she was particularly moved by the depiction of the experiences of a woman with a mental illness who was sexually assaulted and considering an abortion: "I've met one lady in my constituency that that had happened to, so it was very emotional for me. She has eight children" (quoted in Campbell 2009).

These comments did not portend wide governmental support for repealing the law. As Danielle Toppin, a member of the pro-choice coalition who was present when the skit was performed, stated, "There was the euphoria; definitely there was euphoria. There was a lot of interest from the parliamentarians that were present in talking afterwards. But you could also see that there were some who took it lightly. . . . I don't think that is the fault of the method but more the topic that was being discussed. . . . The people who are anti are not shifted by a presentation . . . because it is too integrally tied to their views on God; their views on religion" (pers. comm., 2015). A decade later the government is still uncommitted to putting in place a Termination of Pregnancy Act, but a new movement has emerged.

The Current Pro-Choice Movement

In January 2019, ten years after *A Slice of Reality* was performed in Parliament, the government resumed the debates around amending the antichoice law. The time was ripe for a regeneration of pro-choice lobbying in Jamaica, owing to a new wave of women-led activism in Jamaica and the rest of the Caribbean in the early 2010s. From 2014 to 2019 public conversations around sexual violence were heightened, facilitated by social media as well as on-the-ground protests. Thus, there was no escaping conversations about gender and sexuality. The debates about abortion had not ceased in the Jamaican media between 2009 and 2019. From time to time pro- and anti-choice letters and columns were published in newspapers, and influential people, including journalists, occasionally made statements.[26] A public opinion poll was sponsored by the *Gleaner* in 2018, which showed that although the majority disapproved of abortion on request, they made a distinction between their own discomfort around abortion and the government's power in prohibiting it. Most significantly, 67 percent of the men and 82 percent of the women agreed that "the government has no place in determining if or when a woman ends her pregnancy" (Hall 2018). In addition to the plethora of news stories about abortion law reform in traditional media, on social media the subject was ubiquitous. For instance, a Tumblr page titled *Abortion Monologues* was created in 2018 by feminist blogger Jherane Patmore (K. Barrett 2019). She invited comments from Jamaican women who had had abortions, consistent with the increasing tendency on social media for people to speak openly about sex and reproduction.

There was another development that precipitated the new debates. In 2017, Juliet Cuthbert-Flynn, an Olympic medalist and well-known media personality, had become an MP aligned with the majority-governing

Jamaica Labour Party. In 2018, when a woman in her constituency died after complications from an illegal abortion, Cuthbert-Flynn officially demanded by way of parliamentary motion that the government reconsider the APRAG's 2007 recommendation to repeal the country's anti-choice laws and institute a Termination of Pregnancy Act. Additionally, she spoke publicly in the media about having had an abortion when she was younger, after being diagnosed with a brain tumor (L. Barrett 2019). While Cuthbert's physician had recommended the abortion in order to preserve her health and life, consistent with the common-law exception, this admission was significant: it was the first time a member of the government had publicly spoken about a personal sexual experience, much less an abortion.

In response to Cuthbert-Flynn's calls, from January to June 2019 the government heard submissions from pro-choice groups as well as anti-choice activists, and the media was flooded with commentaries on reproductive rights. As usual the anti-choice activism was dominated by Christian groups, the most impactful of which was the Catholic Church, which continues to leverage its moralistic and patriarchal power and political sway in Parliament. Indicative of the church's political influence on Parliament is the fact that the MP who heads the Human Resources and Social Development Committee, which was charged with hearing the submissions on abortion, is a Roman Catholic deacon.

My own public entry into the pro-choice debates was via a May 28, 2019, letter to the editor of the *Gleaner*, Jamaica's most popular newspaper. I wrote the letter, titled "Laws Must Protect Citizens," in response to media reports about the visit of Alveda King, director of Civil Rights for the Unborn, who was the guest of the Catholic organizations Jamaica CAUSE and Missionaries of the Poor. She and her group announced that they were on a "dissuading mission" to convince Cuthbert-Flynn to withdraw her pro-choice stance. She drew on her own experiences with two abortions she regretted, and the purported frequency of abortion among Black women in the United States, to put forward the idea of abortion as an anti-Black practice that went against the much-recycled dream of Martin Luther King Jr., her uncle (Cross 2019). Alveda King's arguments against abortion emerge from a race-conscious sector in the anti-choice movement in the United States, in which abortion is often likened to racial genocide. Carolette Norwood (2021) notes in her critique of the US anti-choice campaign Protecting Black Life that these discourses equate abortion with murder and racist violence, and blame Black women for high rates of Black mortality. They essentially portray Black women's wombs as sites of anti-Black violence.

In my letter I called out Jamaican anti-choice proponents' hypocrisy for using anti-imperialist arguments against the pro-choice movement while unashamedly exploiting connections to powerful US anti-choice activists in their activism. I also underscored the importance of reproductive justice to racial justice, given Black women's high likelihood throughout the Diaspora to be poor and to have inadequate access to proper reproductive health services. Eventually, I cowrote a submission with five other people in support of the Termination of Pregnancy Act and presented it to Parliament on July 25, 2019, on live television. I was thus placed in the same position Sistren/HTCG had occupied ten years prior.

I presented with Maziki Thame, a cowriter of our submission and a member of our group, which we called Women and Men for Women's Reproductive Freedom and Autonomy.[27] Our presentation had been postponed twice because the ten-member committee could not find a quorum to attend the scheduled meeting. Thus, it was with a sense of relief and frustration that we finally presented. My class positioning and presentation format made my presence in Parliament much less remarkable than Sistren and HTCG's when they performed *A Slice of Reality*.[28] However, the formality and elitist nature of the space were daunting. Other pro-choice groups were seated in the same section of Parliament, while to our left was a mostly male group of Christians representing the Joy Town Community Development Foundation, a faith-based anti-choice organization. One of their speakers was Christina Milford, founder of the Pregnancy Resource Centre, who stated that she had gotten pregnant after being raped when she was younger and chose not to have an abortion; she was thus against abortion even for survivors of rape. This was a counter to the argument that abortion should at the very least be legalized when a pregnancy resulted from sexual assault and also seemed to be aimed at rivaling a statement from Opal Palmer Adisa, a professor at the University of the West Indies, Mona, who was one of the pro-choice activists in attendance. Adisa, then chair of the Institute for Gender and Development Studies, recalled having an abortion when she was seventeen years old because she knew she was not "emotionally ready to be a mother" (PBC Jamaica 2019b). Besides Milford, the contingent from Joy Town Community Development Foundation included one other woman and four men. While I generally disagreed with their arguments, I was most dismayed by their complete lack of racial awareness. All their references to so-called experts on abortion, and all their propaganda tools including videos and images, were imported from white American evangelical anti-choice activists. To make matters worse, while every other group was only given fifteen minutes to present, this group (the only anti-choice one that day) was allowed to present for an hour and would have gone on for much longer had we not protested. If anyone doubted the political clout of the Christian church in Jamaica, this spectacle proved them wrong. The pro-choice sector rebutted the arguments from the anti-choice activists, but this was only after many minutes of complaining from us and appeals to the chair from other MPs to allow us to speak again. And it did not end there: the men in the group were given another chance to rebut our rebuttal for around twenty minutes. Thus, after four months of meetings and presentations to discuss Jamaican women's bodily autonomy, a group of Christian conservative men were given the last word.

In November 2019, four months after this final presentation, when the government was supposed to have decided on whether to change the laws, we were told that there would be another holdup. The government announced that it would be inviting another set of submissions from the public. Therefore, more people and groups made submissions and presentations, which ended in March 2020. After receiving the submissions, the committee drafted a report and recommended a "conscience vote" of the House of Representatives (B. Henry 2020). A conscience vote entails having MPs vote based on their own personal opinion and not that of their party. Alongside the legal/constitutional recommendation, the committee concluded with a somewhat out-of-place recommendation that pregnant women and fathers be offered counseling on how to become parents, which seemed like a concession to those who are opposed to abortion.

The conscience vote has not occurred, and the report has essentially been neglected by Parliament. Furthermore, with the government preoccupied with the COVID-19 pandemic, the issue was further overshadowed from 2020 to 2021 and barely even mentioned by politicians in 2022. Of course, the pandemic did not prevent other countries such as Mexico, Thailand, and Argentina from prioritizing reproductive rights and making changes to their laws. Actually, the latest setback is mostly symptomatic of the hold of the church in a country that purports to separate church from state. It is also symptomatic of the lack of priority given to reproductive rights as a condition of democracy—not only by the government but by the most influential citizens.

A Slice of Reality in Retrospect

Looking back at *A Slice of Reality* fourteen years later, I find that the skit resonates as a performed critique of the bodily policing of women and as a theorizing of gender justice rooted in working-class Black women's subjectivities. As a theatre project, it represents a practical redefinition of the link between theatre and politics. The practice of using performance to debate a law has historically been a major facet of activist and pedagogic theatre. However, the unique quality of this skit is its spatial reimagining of the political process by producing a rehearsed performance within a governmental space based on a research-to-performance methodology.[29] Activist performers generally believe that transforming democracy necessitates unbridled public discourse and representations of the lives of marginalized groups, and Sistren abides by the perspective that theatre inspires change by letting an audience think differently about the subject matter. *A Slice of Reality*'s major resonance is the way that it brought to public attention the issues inherent in the debates around abortion, while challenging male-dominated political procedure by bringing women's stories into a governmental space. Its most important role was its use in public education efforts when it was brought to different communities and performed for ordinary Jamaicans. It effectively expressed the arguments central to pro-choice advocacy in a way that does not regularly happen. Perhaps one of the most succinct explanations of how the skit theorized gender justice came from HTCG member Cinderella Green. She stated, "You can't depict my life for me, you can't tell me what threatening to me, because having a child and not being able to feed that child; that life-threatening to me you know" (pers. comm., 2015). This statement speaks to the socioeconomic challenges faced by many women in Jamaica and, like *A Slice of Reality*, shows us that legal-moral and political definitions are often insufficient to deal with the day-to-day lives of society's most marginalized groups. These dictates are usually designed and enforced by people of privilege and subjected to rules of decorum and propriety that do not necessarily reflect the lived reality of the population.

Unfortunately, Sistren and HTCG have been hampered from doing this important consciousness-raising work due to lack of funding, and the skit has not been performed since 2009. Moreover, the voices of working-class Black women were notably underrepresented in the 2019–21 parliamentary conversations. While all the pro-choice groups emphasized that poor people are the most disadvantaged by anti-choice laws, poor Black women who support the Termination of Pregnancy Act did not speak for themselves publicly in the space of Parliament. Neither has there been any sustained project of public education in the proposal for a Termination of Pregnancy Act in Jamaica since 2009. These problems are due to the structure of reproductive rights advocacy in Jamaica. There is no civil organization with the sole purpose of advocating for abortion law reform or, for that matter, reproductive justice in general. The currently active pro-choice Partnership for Women's Health and Well-Being is a loosely organized coalition of individuals and social justice groups, rather than an organization with funding to help realize its objectives.

Notwithstanding the inability of Sistren and HTCG to produce performances of *A Slice of Reality* beyond 2009, and the relative absence of embodied narratives of working-class Black women's stories in the current activism, the skit exists as part of the repertoire of pro-choice activism in Jamaica. As James Thompson (2009, 178) notes, though the material object of performance slips from view, "art's capacity to sustain sensation beyond an initial moment (to paraphrase Deleuze) offers a stretched field of enquiry." In this field of enquiry is a vision of social justice, which activist performers embody, interrogate, and call for. Thus, I will end this chapter in the same vein as the play—with a lack of linear resolution. The scene has been set for continued discussion and activism around the issue of abortion. The response to *A Slice of Reality*'s call is still pending.

CHAPTER 2

"The Wound Is Still There"

Walk: South Africa and the Ontological Violence of Rape

In the final vignette of a 2014 performance of *Walk: South Africa*, performer Nina Callaghan, with her body clothed in plastic bags, moved out of the theatre and into the sunlight. Each of the other performers followed her; then the audience members, without being told to do so, also proceeded. Some stopped on the sidewalk outside the venue, wondering whether they should go farther, while others continued walking until they were fully immersed in the city space of Cape Town. Hopefully they were transformed by the performance they just witnessed, which featured a series of vignettes on the normalization of sexual violence in South Africa: the racial and sexual legacies of colonialism, slavery, and other historical atrocities in modern-day South Africa; the silencing of victims and survivors; anti-LGBTQ sexual assault; and the visceral effects of rape on female bodies.

Walk: South Africa—like its predecessor, *Walk*, created by Indian theatre artist Maya Krishna Rao—is situated in the early 2010s within a nationally based activist movement against sexual assault that arose in response to a horrific rape and murder of a young woman. In India, this young woman was Jyoti Singh Pandey, killed in 2012, and in South Africa it was Anene Booysen, killed in 2013 (Buiten and Naidoo 2016; Lodhia 2015; Shandilya 2015). I learned about *Walk: South Africa* in 2013 after becoming familiar with the work of the Mothertongue Project, prior to beginning my ethnographic research on women's theatre. Sara Matchett, Mothertongue's artistic director, pointed me to the original, incomplete version of the performance, which was produced just a month after Anene's death, and to Maya Krishna Rao's *Walk*, its major theatrical influence. Watching *Walk* (2013) and *Walk: South Africa* (2013 and 2014) for the first time, I was deeply affected and shocked by their commentaries and indeed by the stories of Jyoti Singh Pandey and Anene Booysen. Having seen them numerous times over the last eight years I am still affected by them, but a bit less jolted, because information on sexual violence is more publicly accessible than it was in 2013 and there is now a comparatively more sympathetic global environment in which to discuss it. This is largely owing to women-led activisms that have pushed for more media reporting and the prominence of social media and other campaigns such as #TotalShutdown in South Africa, #LifeInLeggings throughout the Caribbean, #MeToo in the United States, and countless others.

South African activists are among the world's most visible when it comes to gender-based and sexual violence. South African hashtags such as #NotInMyName, #AmINext, and #TotalShutDown, which has been accompanied by an annual march since 2018, are internationally resonant. The activism and global conversation surrounding sexual violence has led to the frequent use of the term *survivor* to underscore the importance of healing as well as to acknowledge that sexual violence is a life-altering experience, one that those who have experienced it must grapple with and hopefully move beyond. I employ the term *survivor* alongside the term *victim*, which is still in use (mostly in justice systems) in recognition of the fact that many people—Anene and Jyoti among them—have not survived this violence. For them, it was a life-ending experience. The word *victim* also denotes the positionality of someone who is still dealing with the immediate aftermath of an attack, before the process of healing begins, or one who prefers that description in order to denote the relationship of domination that perpetrators force on those they harm. The two terms are crucial in analyzing *Walk: South Africa*, a production that profoundly embodies the fact that the trauma produced by this violence can be both life altering and life ending.

The title of this chapter was extracted from a quote by Sara Matchett in my interview with her in 2015. We were discussing the immense responsibility that theatre artists take on in telling stories about sexual violence. On the one hand, focusing only on the violation can downplay the fact that those who experience it are subjects who are actively making sense of the world; on the other hand, focusing too much on them as survivors can inadvertently downplay the trauma of sexual violence as well as create an excuse for it. In *Walk: South Africa*, Mothertongue emphasizes the enduring pain caused by this act of violence, both for those who have survived it and those who have succumbed to it: the wound that is "still there."

As the creators/performers define it, *Walk: South Africa* is a performed critique of rape culture, a concept that refers to the normalization of sexual violence globally.[1] The definition of rape culture offered by Emilie Buchwald, Pamela R. Fletcher, and Martha Roth (1993, vii) is one of the most succinct and influential. According to them, rape culture is the widely held assumption that "sexual violence is a fact of life, inevitable as death or taxes" (see also Herman 1984). This popular perception obscures the fact that sexual violence stems from beliefs, attitudes, and agendas that can be changed. It also creates a neutral atmosphere in which even the description of the event of rape or general comments on it become open to numerous interpretations and terms (Ndashe 2006; Valenti 2014). The irony of rape culture is that while it stresses the inevitability of sexual violence, it requires that those who are most susceptible to it, especially women, devote inordinate amounts of time to adjusting themselves in order to avoid it. And in instances where the violation occurs, the victims/survivors might still be blamed for not doing enough to protect themselves.[2]

Though the production engages with the bodies of the performers in different vignettes, the focus is not on the act of rape itself. It does not have a central plot with a story about a person who has been raped. *Walk: South Africa* was purposefully devised with the aim of sensory engagement, allowing for a conversation that moves beyond individual and social commentaries about sexual violence and toward its material and emotional effects. In name and in content it emphasizes the act of walking as both a quotidian human activity and a principal device in protests against sexual violence. The use of walking as a trope also enables Mothertongue to interrogate gendered and sexed negotiations of the public space from a female perspective. Since 2013, *Walk: South Africa* has been performed in different ways eleven times, with a few new cast members. The 2014 version that I analyze in this chapter, and from which I took most of the quotes from the performance, is the most publicly available because it was recorded and posted to YouTube in its entirety (Mothertongue Project 2014). *Walk: South Africa* remains relevant as South Africa continues to have one of the highest reported rates of sexual violence in the world. This includes numerous cases in which women and girls have been murdered following a sexual assault, and their bodies left in public spaces—as Anene's was. Sexual violence affects women of all races in South Africa. For instance, in October 2018 a young white woman, twenty-one-year-old Hannah Cornelius, was raped and murdered following a robbery and her body left at the side of the road. However, most murder cases in which women's bodies were left in public following a sexual assault have involved young Black women victims. Among these are the cases of twenty-two-year-old Sulnita Manho, fourteen-year-old Camron Britz, seventeen-year-old Jodene Pieters, and nineteen-year-old Uyinene

Mrwetyana, who were murdered in 2016, 2017, 2018, and 2019, respectively.[3] Over the years more names have been added to the list of victims of lethal sexual violence and other forms of gender-based violence, and media coverage and activism have increased. More recently, the 2022 gang rape of eight women while they were filming a music video at a mine dump near Johannesburg received international news coverage. Like other cases, it provoked protests against sexual violence, especially after the charges against the fourteen suspects were dropped (Gouws 2022; Mahdawi 2022). Like other activist initiatives, Mothertongue's multiple iterations of *Walk: South Africa* continue to contribute to consciousness-raising efforts and advocacy.

My analysis of *Walk: South Africa* highlights the theories present within the performance and also places it in conversation with the scholarship of Pumla Gqola (2015) and Louise du Toit (2014), who have written on the need to view sexual violence in South Africa in multidimensional ways, and whose scholarship focuses on the psychological and ontological aspects of rape. In her book *Rape: A South African Nightmare*, Gqola (2015, 80) cites, among other tendencies, what she terms the "female fear factory" or the "manufacture of female fear" as a central feature of South Africa's problems with sexual violence: "The manufacture of female fear works to silence women by reminding us of our rapability, and therefore blackmails us to keep ourselves in check. It also sometimes works to remind some men and trans-people that they are like women, and therefore also rapable. It is a public fear that is repeatedly manufactured through various means and in many private and public settings."[4] Among other tendencies, she writes, the female fear factory depends on "the safety of the aggressor, the vulnerability of the target, and the successful communication by the aggressor that he has power to wound, rape and or/kill the target with no consequences to himself" (80). Gqola's conceptualization describes the interdependent relationship between a potential victim (which all people with female bodies are socialized into thinking they are) and a potential perpetrator, wherein the latter's dominance relies on the former's distress.

In her essay "Shifting the Meanings of Postconflict Sexual Violence in South Africa," du Toit (2014, 120) examines this relationship between a potential perpetrator and potential victim philosophically, asserting that rape must be understood essentially as ontological violence: "The act of rape aims at the destruction of the sexual and personal integrity of the victim, and the rapist intuitively understands the extent to which a person's sexuality lies at the core of her being. . . . Extreme violence that targets a person sexually is an expression of a higher ambition than merely political domination . . . ontological violence aims to re-describe or redraw the very limits of the real, of the truth, of the world itself."

Drawing on Elaine Scarry's (1985) study of the ontological effects of torture, du Toit (2014, 120) further posits that "the new world of the perpetrator is built on the ruins of the victim's world." Essentially, Gqola (2015) and du Toit theorize the centrality of bodily integrity in women's ontology—that is, the basis on which they understand their existence in society, how they interpret gender and sexual perceptions of them, and how they navigate the world through these understandings. Similarly, in a study of students at the University of Cape Town, Simidele Dosekun (2007, 90) identifies a link between the fear of being raped and the daily reality of womanhood or femaleness. Dosekun states, "Even if a woman never actually experiences rape, she may think of it as always inherently possible because of her gender" (see also Gordon and Riger 1991; MacKinnon 1991). If rape is ontological violence, then rape culture normalizes this ontological violence, allowing it to be considered an essential part of human nature and society, and therefore unchangeable. *Walk: South Africa* exposes this normalization by representing rape as abnormal and pain inducing, drawing on the national context of South Africa.

The Context: Sexual Violence in South Africa

The sensationalist label "rape capital of the world" is often assigned in global media to South Africa (Africa Check 2015; *South Coast Herald* 2018), though it is also sometimes applied to other countries in the Global South. According to World Population Review (n.d.), in 2019–20 South Africa had the fourth-highest incidence of rape in the world, with a rate of 72.1 per 100,000. Notably, though this represented a significant decrease from the rate recorded in 2010 (132.4 per 100,000), the "rape capital" label is still applied to the country, and South Africa is still listed among the top five countries with the highest number of reported cases of rape. Using statistics posted online by the South African Police Service (n.d.), I calculated that the rate of reported cases of rape per 100,000 in 2021–22 was 70. This shows a reduction from 2019–20, but an increase from 2020–21, which had a rate of 61 per 100,000. World Population Review has not yet updated its list of comparative statistics per country for the past three years. These numbers, however, do not tell the full story: as the global discourse on sexual assault has revealed, international comparisons of rape statistics often do not account for differences in how countries collect reports on sexual assault, whether rape is disaggregated from other sexual offenses, how widely available resources are for victims to report crimes, and how sexual assault is classified. For instance, in South Africa rape is defined as nonconsensual genital, oral, or anal penetration by any kind of object, in addition to genitalia. It is gender and sex inclusive, and thus forced penetration of a man is also considered rape (Clifford 2021). In contrast, many other countries limit the definition of rape to penile-to-vaginal penetration. There are also apparent prejudices in how these statistics are interpreted by international agencies, wherein some countries receive more nuanced treatment than others. This is the case for Sweden, which has been globally praised for comparatively high levels of gender equity (EIGE 2020; Lane and Jordansson 2020) but which has a high number of reported cases of rape. World Population Review included on its rape statistic webpage as of 2022 a narrative that posits Sweden's relatively high rape numbers as "a positive sign" because the statistics are presumed to be "fueled in large part by Sweden's broader definition of rape and more inclusive reporting rules compared to other European countries." No such analysis is offered for South Africa, Australia, or any of the African, Caribbean, and Latin American countries whose rape statistics were listed alongside Sweden's as being among the highest in the world—despite World Population Review's admission that there are limitations to comparing countries' statistics on rape.

The focus on certain countries as centers of sexual violence has historically obfuscated the global ongoing crisis of such violence—an obfuscation that the recent wave of activisms across the world has exposed. The World Health Organization and the United Nations report that almost "one in three [women worldwide] have been subjected to physical and/or sexual intimate partner violence, non-partner sexual violence, or both at least once in their life" (UN Women 2022). Though there are variations in the kinds of acts perpetrated, offenses ranging from sexual harassment to spousal abuse to rape are prevalent throughout the world. The global stigma attached to sexual violence ensures that the vast majority of these crimes are not reported. In most countries that have provided statistics to the United Nations, less than 10 percent of women who have experienced sexual violence seek help from the police (UN Women 2022).[5] Thus, the title "rape capital of the world" is more problematic than it is useful (not to mention being incorrect, if one relies on current international statistics). A more constructive approach is to examine the problem through the lens of those who live in the country being analyzed. South African people's experiences of rape and sexual violence are no more or no less valid if the country is considered the rape capital. Rape and other gender-based violence including murder are national emergencies that have prompted robust activist campaigns and movements, and bodies of scholarship and art that theorize around the issue. Indeed, some of the most incisive theories on sexual violence that I have encountered were developed by South African scholars and activists, and the country is among just a few in the world in which there are consistent on-the-ground mass demonstrations around sexual violence.

Prior to the first #TotalShutdown of 2018, which involved massive street marches throughout the country, was the One in Nine Campaign. One in Nine, formed in 2006, takes its name from the estimate that only one in nine South Africans who are raped will report their rape because of the secondary trauma experienced by survivors when they make these reports. It began in response to the 2005–6 rape trial of future president Jacob Zuma, three years before his election to the presidency. Zuma was acquitted. My aim, though, is not to proclaim his guilt, but to highlight the fact that patriarchy informed the tone of the trial and much of the public commentary around the case. Some media coverage of the trial, as well as the vocal supporters of the accused man, disregarded the woman involved and centered the rights and motives of the man charged (Gqola 2015; Hassim 2014; Segall 2013). Zuma's accuser was Fezekile Kuzwayo, who is still known by the pseudonym Khwezi, which was used to protect her identity. Zuma's defense—which included his employment of stereotypical Zulu masculinity as a rationale for his sexual proclivities—and the harassment of Khwezi during and after the trial were manifestations of patriarchal violence and foregrounded the normalization of sexual violence in the media.[6] Such ongoing patriarchal and normalized violence was evident in the court's and the media's victim-/survivor-blaming, concentrated mostly on the woman's supposed carelessness; their focus on the man's importance to society (his possible incarceration was cast as detrimental to the common good of Black South Africans, even if he was guilty); their harassment of the alleged victim/survivor, including intimidation; and their accusations that the woman had ulterior financial motives. Khwezi died in 2016, but her name continues to be invoked alongside other women's in activism around rape and other forms of sexual violence.

The on-the-ground activism is complemented by a growing body of scholarship on sexual violence, including its prevalence in the country's history through settler colonialism, racial slavery, and apartheid. As with all societies with recent histories of violent authoritarian rule, scholars face the major challenge of examining a social problem within its historical context while not overemphasizing the influence of that history on contemporary problems. Such an overemphasis can inadvertently provide an excuse for inaction on the part of governments and other authority figures who have the power to address the problem, or allow someone to point to recent events to argue against historiographical analysis. Incidents of rape increased statistically after apartheid, and, as Kimberly Wedeven

Segall (2013) and Desiree Lewis (2009) note, several notorious public spectacles that performed the control or inspection of women's bodies occurred after the democratic transition. Segall (2013, 132) states, "public spectacles demonizing African women as degenerate and corrupting have . . . been central to hegemonic postcolonial definitions of the healthy body politic." For example, the castigation of women in miniskirts at the Noord Street taxi ranks in 2008 and the punitive targeting of lesbians for rape have been mostly postapartheid problems, which developed after laws against gender and sexual discrimination were entrenched in the Constitution. However, these phenomena are integrally connected to the past. Lewis (2009, 131) posits that these relatively recent occurrences are an attempt to reinstate and/or confirm patriarchy in a situation where women's power is legislatively being increased. She notes, "public acts of marking women's bodies not only create meanings for those directly involved in the acts, they also re-enforce the legitimacy of an aggressively patriarchal status quo in the public sphere. In so doing, they seek to confirm and reproduce a brutally hierarchical order, one which is diametrically opposed to the social freedoms associated with legislation and policy-making in post-apartheid South Africa."

Thus, the social structures of patriarchy, racism, and violence that were entrenched in colonial and apartheid South Africa remain part of the fabric of society even amid the democratic gains of the last three decades. What appear to be increases in violence are also modern iterations of historical processes, taking place in an environment that is more open to reporting, discussing, and organizing against sexual and other forms of violence. As the research shows, rape is a major facet of South African history and was integral to the systems of slavery and European colonization that began in the seventeenth century, as well as the later system of apartheid (Y. Abrahams 1996; Armstrong 1994; Cock 1989; Gqola 2015; Irish 1993; Magubane 2001, 2004; Motsemme 2004). In light of this history and more contemporary factors, Hannah Evelyn Britton (2020), writing on gender-based violence writ large, cautions against the framing of sexual violence as endemic to South African culture and, by extension, African cultures. Instead, to understand gender-based violence in the country, we must use a structural approach that encompasses sociohistorical and political contexts. She notes, "Gender-based violence, then, is not isolated from wider institutions of socially sanctioned violence, state violence, or structural inequality and must be approached with an intersectional lens. . . . The South African context of civil conflict, state-fostered racism, social and economic inequality, forced labor, and forced migration created moments and processes through which violence became reinforced as normal, routine, and even unremarkable" (12).

South Africa is not exceptional in this respect. Globally researchers and journalists have found that military occupation, war, and excessive authoritarianism create and depend on sexual violence. This is true across numerous military conflicts throughout human history; the modern wars in Iraq, Syria, and the Democratic Republic of the Congo; the Israeli-Palestinian conflict; military occupation, such as that inflicted on Haiti by MINUSTAH, the UN-backed military (or "peacekeeping") forces; and racial-ethnic systems of terror like slavery, segregation, and the Holocaust (Ayiera 2010; Branche and Virgili 2012; Campbell and Elbourne 2014; Danielsson 2019; El-Bushra and Sahl 2005; Gunne and Brigley 2010; Hartman 1997; Loomba 2005; G. Thomas 2005).[7] And, as critical examinations of systemic racism have shown, "rape has been central to the spread of white supremacy and the way race and racism have organized the world over the last four hundred years" (Gqola 2015, 21). In South Africa, pervasive sexual violence against mostly Black women during colonialism and slavery and under apartheid by men of different races was rarely met with punishment. Not only was rape prevalent as a form of individualized violence, it was also perpetrated by groups and institutions, as for instance with the practices of jackrolling (systematic abduction and rape); the sexual terror meted out by *iintsara* gangsters; *ukuthwala* (abduction for the purpose of forced marriage); and state violence such as the sexual degradation of anti-apartheid activists in prison (see Motsemme 2004).[8] Though this violence affected people of all genders and races, Black women suffered the most. They were least likely to be protected, and if reports were made, their alleged rapists were more likely to be acquitted or never arrested. Apartheid was an assertion of white supremacy, which included a reliance on white male heterosexual supremacy.[9]

The apartheid state not only participated in sexual terror but also encouraged it by ensuring the institutional lack of protection for, and castigation of, the most vulnerable groups. Though white women were also highly unlikely to report rape because of their own subjugation, when they reported it they were more likely to receive justice if the perpetrator was not white. Under apartheid, a convicted rapist could receive capital punishment. However, this was not motivated by a general desire to protect women. Rather, it appears that rape as a capital crime was one means through which the state sought to exact lethal attacks on Black men. Citing the work of Heather Reganass, director of the Institute for Crime Prevention and Rehabilitation of Offenders, Sue Armstrong (1994, 35) notes that prior to the moratorium on the death penalty in the 1990s, only Black men who were convicted of raping white women were hanged. No white man was ever hanged for this crime. And the trickle-down effect of white patriarchy ensured that Black and other men of color also asserted relatively unchecked and unpunished sexual aggression against women of the same race.[10] The transition to democracy created more opportunities for reporting of, and conversations around, a problem that already existed. These historical legacies combine with institutional failures to address the problem; current economic, racial, and gender inequalities; and the maintenance of patriarchal codes that normalize rape.

Du Toit (2014) has weighed the pros and cons of three popular interpretive frames for South Africa's problem with sexual violence. The first frame, "past perpetrator trauma," sees apartheid and the liberation struggles as emasculating phenomena. In this frame, sexual violence is a major way in which [Black] South African men assert their dominance (du Toit cites Moffett 2006, 136; Hamber 2007, 385). The second frame is "current social exclusion," which also focuses on emasculation but emphasizes the legacies of apartheid and new forms of socioeconomic inequality in the country (she cites Altbeker 2007, 100; du Plessis 2007; Cooper and Foster 2008, 10). The third frame, "patriarchal violence," focuses on rape as an enactment of male dominance because of men's perceptions that women's advancement in society threatens their manhood and socioeconomic status (she cites MacKinnon 2005, 129; Moffett 2006, 129). Du Toit (2014) has two central critiques of these frames: (1) they tend to focus solely on Black men, especially with respect to explanations of the effects of apartheid and the notion of male marginalization, even though gender-based violence, and rape in particular, is prevalent among all races; and (2) they offer an insufficient explanation for the sexual nature of the violence that is rape. These frames do not respond to the question of how sexual violence differs from other kinds of violence.

Du Toit (2014) posits that although historical, social, and political explanations provide crucial frames, by focusing on the intent of the rapist they can render invisible the experience of the victim/survivor. Rape, according to du Toit, continues for several reasons, including its limited risk to the perpetrator: most victims/survivors do not report it, and in cases where it is reported, the accuser is usually blamed for the crime and shamed by their community. Furthermore, rape is not taken seriously enough by law enforcement, resulting in low conviction rates. Perpetrators take these factors into consideration and target relatively young and powerless women more than others in order to increase their chances of successfully attacking and/or killing their victims (Du Toit 2014, 119). Taking the focus off the perpetrator's social background and motivation allows the conversation to expand toward the psychic and social environments in which rape, and sexual violence in general, is pervasive. Whereas Gqola, du Toit, and other scholars and activists offer psychosocial and ontological analyses of sexual violence and rape culture, *Walk: South Africa* embodies these analyses with attention to the experiences of victims and survivors. The cases of Anene Booysen in South Africa and Jyoti Singh Pandey in India were the catalysts that led to the creation of the performance.

Making *Walk: South Africa*: The Catalytic Effect of Two Gruesome Cases

On February 3, 2013, seventeen-year-old Anene Booysen was found almost dead at a construction site in her community of Bredasdorp in the Western Cape. Six hours later she passed away in a hospital, where medical practitioners had tried against the odds to save her life.[11] Later that year, in October, her friend twenty-two-year-old Johannes Kana was convicted of her rape and murder and sentenced to two life terms without parole (*Mail and Guardian* 2013). The night before she died, Anene had gone to a tavern in her community and left with Kana, whom she knew well and who had previously accompanied her home at night.

Just six weeks before Anene Booysen's murder, on December 16, 2012, twenty-three-year-old Jyoti Singh Pandey had endured a similar life-ending assault in Delhi, India. She and her friend Avnindra Pandey had taken a bus home after seeing a movie. Six men who were on the bus gang-raped Jyoti for hours as the bus drove through the city and beat Avnindra when he tried to intervene. Jyoti died two weeks later in Singapore, where she had been flown for emergency medical attention. Five men (Ram Singh, Mukesh Singh, Akshay Thakur, Vinay Sharma, and Pawan Gupta) and Mohammed Afroz, then a seventeen-year-old unnamed juvenile, were arrested and subsequently convicted for Jyoti's assault and murder (Dorwart 2021).[12] However, as with Booysen's case, the attackers' convictions brought neither closure nor reassurance that the justice system on its own can correct what continues to be a prevailing problem. The brutality of the attacks on the young women shocked all who heard about them. Not only had they been raped, their bodies had been mutilated and disemboweled. And both had been left out in public to die—Jyoti on the street and Anene at the construction site. Additionally, in both cases the convicted men expressed no remorse.

In South Africa as in India, there were nationwide protests, conversations, and commentaries on what had happened, and Anene and Jyoti became symbols of the horror of sexual violence in their respective countries. Jyoti is known as India's Daughter, and the Sanskrit moniker by which she was known in the Indian media—Nirbhaya (Fearless)—has become an inspirational symbol. Anene is similarly referred to as South Africa's Daughter, and she was named South Africa's Person of the Year in 2013. She shared this title with white South African Reeva Steenkamp, who was murdered that same year by her boyfriend, white South African Paralympian Oscar Pistorius. In addition, the Anene Booysen Skills Development Centre was opened in Bredasdorp as a memorial to her in July 2016.

These cases provoked conversations on the normalization of rape, including the prevalence of victim blaming. Anene was criticized by some for her purported lack of caution and discretion; that is, for being a seventeen-year-old girl who had gone out to have a good time and supposedly created the situation for her rape and murder to occur. As Gqola (2015) points out, even in the absence of direct victim blaming, speculations about her diverted scrutiny away from her attackers. Questions were raised about her foster parents' level of care for her, including whether they had properly protected her.[13] In the case of Jyoti, some people, including her murderers and their lawyers, questioned her decency for being out late at night and argued that she caused her own murder by fighting back during the assault. The language used in the victim blaming of Jyoti was notably more abhorrent than the insensitive comments made about Anene, and the hurtful and misogynistic statements from the defense lawyers and convicted men circulated internationally.[14] However, in both cases there was significant public discourse on gender norms, women's vulnerabilities, and the reason for the persistence of rape in the respective country.

Notwithstanding the general similarities in the two murders, the Booysen case drew far less attention than Singh Pandey's, which attracted extensive international attention for years. A large protest movement sprang up the day after the attack in Delhi and spread to other cities throughout India and to bordering countries. As a result, India's political leaders were forced into action. Prime Minister Manmohan Singh, and the head of the governing Indian National Congress, Sonia Gandhi, met the plane carrying Jyoti's body from Singapore. Additionally, the protests led to legal changes, though substantive transformation around sexual violence did not occur in the aftermath (Shen 2013). In the film and theatre industries, Jyoti's story has also been told. In 2015, the British Broadcasting Corporation produced *India's Daughter—The Nirbhaya*, a documentary directed by Leslee Udwin.[15] Also, South African playwright and director Yaël Farber created a critically acclaimed play called *Nirbhaya* in 2013, which had a successful run in

Britain (Brantley 2015). In stark contrast, Anene's murder provoked only limited protests and vigils in some parts of the country, and the world did not take much notice (Swart 2013). Politicians, including President Jacob Zuma and opposition leader Lindiwe Mazibuko, made statements denouncing the crime, but no real governmental action took place, and neither President Zuma nor any highly influential national leaders attended the funeral, though several politicians did. There were also a few international reports and a statement from Navi Pillay, the UN high commissioner on human rights (UN News 2013). Overall, in contrast to the mass protests that destabilized India after Jyoti's murder, the protests in South Africa for Anene were small scale. They were mostly organized by members of the Bredasdorp community, gender-rights activists, and a few high-profile people like Scottish singer Annie Lennox, whose involvement was widely publicized. Gender activists, including Mothertongue members, could not help but think about Jyoti's case and the strikingly different response in India.[16]

Mothertongue's artistic director, Sara Matchett, stated that she and some of her colleagues in India wondered whether the location of Jyoti's attack—Delhi, a large, urban space—had influenced how prominent the case had become in relation to others in rural India. In addition, they speculated about whether Jyoti's status as a university student, despite her poor background, might have figured into the contrasting responses between her assault and others (Matchett, pers. comm., 2015). Some authors have noted that Jyoti, who was a physiotherapy student from a humble background, became a symbol utilized by political factions to further their own objectives (Lodhia 2015; Simon-Kumar 2014). According to Krupa Shandilya (2015, 465), before her identity became public, some activists and influential media outlets constructed her as an "everywoman" within an upper-caste Hindu conceptualization in order to garner sympathy for her. This was consistent with how the middle-class Hindu woman had become "the de facto subject of Indian feminism," at the expense of Dalit women.

It is hard not to notice the differences in the national and global responses to Anene's and Jyoti's murders. However, we must also acknowledge that the Delhi protests began as a set of peaceful marches at the houses of the chief minister and president, and evolved into a major countrywide uprising after the protestors were attacked by the police (Shandilya 2015, 467). The massive public response to the incident in India arguably motivated the international response. Thus, national context as well as the timing of the attacks, place of the attacks, and identities of the victims must be considered when we analyze the responses to these two similar cases. It is possible that racial and geographic hierarchies that rank South Asian women above African ones played a role in how the international media responded as well; however, this would have been easier to discern if Anene and Jyoti were from the same country. Given the range of contextual differences in which these murders took place, it is more productive to analyze Anene's case within the context of race, class, and gender in South Africa than to rely on transnational speculation about the disparate response to her and Jyoti's murders.

Notwithstanding the classist tones that commentaries on Anene's demographic status may have taken, it is still necessary to unpack the ways in which her race, age, class, and gender made her more vulnerable than white women, and middle-class and rich Black South African women, to sexual assault and murder within a public space. As a teenager she also was more at risk of sexual violation than older women (Salo 2009). These vulnerabilities can get reinforced within the justice process. For instance, the police investigation into Booysen's murder included only limited follow-up on her statement that she had been attacked by five to six men. Despite the somewhat underwhelming response from the South African government, the death of Booysen was a pivotal moment in South African activism against sexual violence, reinvigorating public discourse about the problem following a lull in activism and media conversations about it (Buiten and Naidoo 2016). Anene's experience was one in a series of gruesome attacks.[17] Thus, feminists, activists against sexual assault, and others in South Africa felt that while her case may have shocked the nation—albeit not enough to cause a nationwide uprising—discussions needed to be centered on the daily reality of sexual violence and, in particular, on its normalization.

Two weeks after Anene's murder, Sara Matchett was contacted by Maya Krishna Rao, an Indian theatre artist whom she had met once before. Rao asked Matchett to watch a YouTube video of a performance called *Walk* (Rao 2013), which she had created in response to Jyoti's death, and invited Matchett to collaborate on a transnational project. The following week, Matchett met with Koleka Putuma, Genna Gardini, and Rosa Postlethwaite, three of her students at the University of Cape Town (UCT), where she teaches in the Department of Drama. Later, they contacted Siphumeze Khundayi, a UCT graduate, Mothertongue board member, and theatre artist. They employed a collaborative method wherein they devised individual ideas around the theme. In the following weeks and months, they conducted research and improvised, drawing on various performance forms and traditional and new techniques.

Walk: South Africa was first presented to the public in a YouTube video of a dress-tech rehearsal at UCT's drama auditorium in 2013 (see Mothertongue Project 2013). It has evolved as the performers incorporated audience feedback with their own self-reflections, and adapted it to suit each venue. The structure is that of a performance installation. This is a live theatrical performance, influenced by visual art installations, in which a series of vignettes combine the artist's body, props, acting, and poetry to convey specific messages. The performance I analyze in this chapter was done in 2014 as part of the Cape Town Fringe Festival.[18] The venue was the popular nightclub the Dragon Room, a space that is normally marked for music and entertainment and that seems to be a disjuncture from the topic of the play. However, as with other forms of site-specific performance, including Sistren and Hannah Town Cultural Group's (HTCG) *A Slice of Reality* (2009; see chapter 1), *Walk: South Africa* transgresses conventional bounds of theatre. The choice of a nightclub signifies a questioning of whether spaces are to be classified for entertainment purposes only, or also for serious consciousness-raising work. Additionally, nightclubs hold sexual meanings. Globally, these places are considered erotic because of their function as meeting spots for potential sex partners, the usually revealing types of fashion worn there, and the combination of music, liquor, and dimly lit ambience. Therefore, a play about sexual violence at this venue confronts sexual respectability politics as well as victim blaming geared at women and girls like Anene Booysen, who were sexually assaulted or murdered after they went to parties, bars, and nightclubs.

Walk: South Africa: The Performance

Walk: South Africa addresses various questions: What are the historical contexts of sexual violence in South Africa? How do we prioritize the voice of the victim/survivor? How do we memorialize victims/survivors and repair the damage caused to them and their communities? And how do we conceptualize differences of race, gender, class, age, and sexual orientation? With regard to the last question, the 2013–14 cast of *Walk: South Africa* embodied this intersection of age, race, class, and sexuality in the conversations around rape. Three of the performers were Black and three white. One performer, Nina Callaghan, might be referred to by many people as mixed race and would have been classified under apartheid as *coloured*. However, she identifies as Black based on her view of Black as not just a phenotypical descriptor but a political identity that "embraces everyone who is not white." For her, it also encompasses the cultural identity of Camissa: an "Indigenous Khoena word that attempts to embrace the historical, geographic, and place heritage of mixed-race people in South Africa" (pers. comm., 2020). The cast's racial composition did not proportionally reflect South

African demographics, considering that Black people are in the majority in the country, are the most socioeconomically subjugated group, and are the main victims of lethal sexual violence. However, their racial differences generated the possibility for cross-racial understandings of rape that are integral to the examination of violence and its effects in the country. In 2014, the ages of the performers ranged from early twenties to middle-aged. Their sexualities varied, but most identified as queer, and all six continue to make space for sexual and gender difference in their bodies of work beyond *Walk: South Africa*. Their varied sexualities and awareness of sexual difference are significant because they expose the flaws in heteronormative and gender-normative constructions of sexual violence.

I have identified three key performative themes that define the six vignettes in *Walk: South Africa* and their various ontological engagements. The first was the production's representation of female bodies, enabling a conversation around how they are differently marked according to race and sexuality. The second was its engagement with voice and sound as counterperformative mechanisms to the silencing of victims/survivors, and the third was its reliance on an affective connection with the audience. Together,

Figure 3. The creators/performers of *Walk: South Africa* in 2014. *Left to right:* Genna Gardini, Siphumeze Khundayi, Rosa Postlethwaite, Sara Matchett, and Koleka Putuma. Missing: Nina Callaghan. Photo by Catherine Trollope, courtesy of the Mothertongue Project.

they commented on the sexual dimensions of European colonization and racism in South Africa; highlighted the silencing of victims and survivors and the need for avenues through which their voices can be centered; and, finally, offered a call to action against sexual violence through a symbolic emphasis on movement, or what I have termed *mobile prompting*. The act of walking at the end of the performance constituted its final vignette and moved the audience from passive spectators to active participants. It was standing room only; the audience had to walk through the space, with only a few stage lights and the guide's flashlight to illuminate the room. Because *Walk: South Africa* was both installation and performance, stillness and movement functioned equally in it. The vignettes were positioned throughout the space and became mobile after being prompted by a guide with a flashlight. Each one contributed a unique insight into the normalization of sexual violence in South Africa.

Marked Bodies: Rosa Postlethwaite and Siphumeze Khundayi

Walk: South Africa began with Rosa Postlethwaite's location of sexual violence within the history and geography of South Africa. The vignette was inspired by the legend of Princess Vlei, a Capetonian story that might be based on a real event or a collection of events transformed into an allegory. According to this story, in the seventeenth century European colonizers raped a Khoekhoe woman. Afterward, she escaped, climbed to the top of a mountain, and cried, and out of her tears emerged a *vlei*, a large body of water.[19] That body of water is now the Princess Vlei nature reserve. In another version of the story, the woman did not create the *vlei*. Rather, she was bathing in it when she was abducted and raped by Portuguese sailors. According to that alternative version, the *vlei* is so named because it was the site of her violation. Despite their differences, both versions are allegories of original colonial violation in South Africa, and in certain respects Princess Vlei is a personification of South Africa. Postlethwaite visited the site multiple times in preparation for the performance, so this example of short-form storytelling was partly autoethnographic. Her props were a table, sand collected at the site, and a large fish tank with cloudy water that she had drawn from the *vlei*. She began her performance by scooping sand onto the table, then climbed atop it and awkwardly held the tank, while speaking: "If you ask the question of people, 'Is it possible to cry under water?' somebody tells you that you asked a really stupid question. But I've noticed that there is a difference between being submerged in a tasteless, odorless liquid and feeling like something's escaped. I wanted to feel the tears but I accidentally fell into the water."

Throughout the rest of her monologue, she remained atop the table. With a projected video of the *vlei* in the background, she then concluded: "It was her tears that formed the *vlei* that I fell into. I didn't know her, but I can see she knew how to have a good cry. . . . I knew I wouldn't find her out there in the landscape. It was my bones resting in their graves that she had stirred. She had stirred me." In this last line she posited a connection between herself and Princess Vlei by underscoring how the story resonates within her in a way that comes close to being spiritual. This emphasis on the near-spiritual resonance of Princess Vlei indicates the complexities of the legend as well as its use as a point of departure for a performance about sexual violence. On the one hand, this legend problematically relies more on the mythos of tears forming a body of water than it does on the tremendous violence experienced by the princess. The rape is the stimulus for a miracle, which appears to salve the traumatic effects of a story about sexual violence. On the other hand, Princess Vlei is an actual geographic spot evoking wonder and caution, and it symbolizes the ways in which South African society is marked by colonial sexual violence. That violence is hidden in plain sight in that famous body of water. However, the ambiguity that characterizes the story in text was largely absent in performance. Postlethwaite's physical discomfort, standing on a table that appeared as if it would break under her weight and that of the fish tank, with her knees and shoulders bent and her head turned diagonally to the audience, was slightly disturbing. It was consistent with the general mood of *Walk: South Africa*, which challenged the audience to perceive sexual violence as a categorically painful phenomenon.

As a white British woman, Postlethwaite is descended from one of the major European groups that colonized South Africa, and belongs to the set of women who possess racial privileges in the country. She is simultaneously privileged racially and nationally and also penalized according to her sex and gender—an illustration of the matrix of domination as articulated by Patricia Hill Collins (2008). Therefore, an interrogation of her racial and national identity adds some racial tension to the vignette and was part of the work of reflection that the audience had to engage in. Her original vignette from 2013 was a nude durational performance that involved her rolling around on broken glass. At the time she had only lived in South Africa for a year, while attending UCT as a graduate student. She was therefore aware of her limitations in representing South Africa and the ways in which she could be perceived as a white foreigner speaking for Black South Africans. Thus, instead of focusing on a verbal narrative she decided to engage the audience on a physical, nonverbal level that depicted the "pedestrian" nature of sexual violence through the nude body (Postlethwaite, pers. comm., 2016). The 2014 Princess Vlei vignette continued that meditation, but referenced the experience of a historical Black South African woman through engaging with a beloved landmark.

Siphumeze Khundayi's vignette, which occurred toward the end of the performance, can be juxtaposed with Postlethwaite's since they both performed the different ways that race and sexuality figure centrally in the conversation through explicit representations of their bodies. Khundayi wore a white dress, white bandages, and white body paint/clay, evoking the ritual clothing of the Xhosa, Khundayi's national/ethnic group. The performer knelt, agitatedly reciting a supplication to the ancestors in isiXhosa, calling on them for strength and simultaneously thanking them for their guidance. The supplication ended with the word *camagu*, which is akin to the Christian *amen*. This moment was "a prayer to the queer humans who have lost their lives. The parts of rape victims that die" (Khundayi, pers. comm., 2022). From the kneeling position, Khundayi then contorted her body into different positions before recoiling and trying to fight off an invisible perpetrator. What followed next was a performance of the silencing that occurs in the moment of rape and long after. Khundayi removed a long piece of white cloth from her underwear and then quickly used it to gag and blindfold herself, before partially removing the white dress to reveal bound breasts. The piece ended with Khundayi trying to speak and attempting an attenuated version of the Xhosa movement *umxhentso*, a traditional move consisting of foot stomping and a raised, open-palmed hand indicating surrender.[20] This vignette centered the experiences of Black South African lesbians and other queer female-bodied people who have been targeted for sexual assault based on their sexuality and gender. In general, it reflected the silencing of survivors and victims. The vignette's most effective/affective resonances were in the bodily torment and precarious physical representation that characterized it, including the binding of the breasts to make the body appear less feminine (as some lesbians and trans men do). Khundayi performed a spectacle of violence while centering the body and the whole self. The influence of Xhosa ritual, specifically through ancestral pleas, linked South Africa's legacies of racial terror to current problems of sexual violence, and also honored the ancestors and centered their guidance in current activisms. Khundayi is a Black South African woman, and the sexual and political violence of colonialism and apartheid, combined with heteropatriarchy, resonate within her body. The performer is the ontological and racial descendant of the legendary Princess Vlei, with a body marked as Black, queer, and Xhosa (see also Matchett and Cloete 2015).

To embrace and claim these physical and cultural identifiers is an act of defiance against demonizing, objectification, and domination. The violence perpetrated in 2014 against twenty-four-year-old Disebo Gift Makau—whose name was projected at the end of *Walk: South Africa*—went beyond sending a message to Black lesbians.[21] It was, as du Toit (2014) notes, a message that affirmed the dominance of the perpetrator while denying the humanity of the victim, and it typified the female fear factory (Gqola 2015). Disebo was considered a victim of *curative* or *corrective* rape, in which the perpetrator allegedly aims to change the victim's sexual orientation. I refer to these kinds of assault as *antilesbian* or *antiqueer punitive* rape, given that the perpetrators clearly aim to punish the victims for what they see as a sexual transgression personally offensive to them. The terms *curative* and *corrective* rape have been critiqued by Madhumita Lahiri (2011) as problematic culturalist tropes that imply that these antiqueer assaults are unique to South Africa. Their use, however, is in response to other culturalist arguments that posit that LGBTQ identity is un-African and thus deserving of castigation and correction.

Essentially then, by making ancestral linkages in a performance that centered queerness, Khundayi's vignette resisted well-known antiqueer ideas about LGBTQ identity being a degenerative force in South African society and an un-African orientation. Khundayi and *Walk: South Africa* rendered queerness visible and allowed simultaneous understandings of sexuality and gender within the conversation, engaging in what Xavier Livermon (2012, 298) refers to as "queer(y)ing freedom" in South Africa. The piece fit within a genre of visual and performance art by contemporary African women in which they center their bodies in decolonial, feminist, or other liberatory conversations, defying an overwhelming tendency in African societies to not engage in sexually explicit performances or such artistic commentaries. Ayo A. Coly (2019) emphasizes that colonial histories have affected discourses about African women and African people in general, resulting in an inclination to avoid presenting the unclothed or sexualized body in artistic work. The legend of Princess Vlei invoked in Rosa Postlethwaite's performance acts as a redemptive piece of oral history to recall the sexual exploitation of South African women by Europeans, even when the archival basis of the story is not easily available. In contrast, the history of another Black South African woman, Sara (Saartjie) Baartman, is preserved in the archives of Africa and Europe, popular culture, literature, and multiple works of scholarship (Chase-Riboud 2004; Magubane 2001; Mitchell 2018; Parks 1997). Baartman's experience is perhaps the most globally known instance of an individual African woman's sexual exploitation by Europeans. Named the Hottentot Venus when she was first exhibited in England,[22] Baartman was one of at least two Khoekhoe women who were displayed in European freak shows in the eighteenth and nineteenth centuries. Posthumously, she continued to be subjected to racist violence when she was publicly dissected by French naturalist Georges Cuvier. Afterward her genitalia, brain, and other body parts were placed on display in the Muséum National d'Histoire Naturelle and Musée de l'Homme in France for 150 years, before being repatriated and buried in her homeland in South Africa.

The experiences of Baartman and others like her display the sexist and racist tendencies within the long history of colonial domination and conquest in Africa. Coly (2019, 3) notes that "the colonial history of un/clothing black African women and inscribing grotesquerie and sexual aberration on the black African female body has inflected postcolonial African discourses surrounding womanhood." Hence, with a few recent exceptions, "the tradition in postcolonial African visual discourses has been to cover up,

Figure 4. Siphumeze Khundayi in *Walk: South Africa*, 2014. Photo by Catherine Trollope, courtesy of the Mothertongue Project.

desexualize and decorporealize African womanhood" (136). Black South African visual artists and performers such as Nelisiwe Xaba and Tracey Rose have moved beyond this tradition by framing their bodies as works of art through which to put forward commentaries on race, sex, and colonialism. Similarly, Khundayi centered her body in the performance in order to question racial-national antiqueer discourses and affirm Black lesbians as integral citizens within the body politic of the South African nation and, in particular, as inheritors of ancestral legacies like every other Black person. While Khundayi's and Postlethwaite's performances examined the effects of rape culture in different bodies—the Black female queer body and the geographic spaces of South Africa—others utilized speech and sound to depict the silencing and unsilencing of the voices of those who want to rail against the normalization of rape.

Voicing Trauma: Koleka Putuma, Genna Gardini, and Sara Matchett

Walk: South Africa confronted the silencing of rape survivors in three vignettes featuring poems and a nonverbal sonic performance. The second and third vignettes in the 2014 performance were by poets/playwrights Genna Gardini and Koleka Putuma, delivered in distinct fashions and with different meters. The performer Nicole Fortuin understudied for Putuma in the performance featured in the 2014 video on YouTube. She entered wrapped in plastic from her head to her torso, beginning with a guttural moan that lasted for about a quarter of the duration of the vignette. Her use of the plastic over her face evoked a violent image of strangulation, which, in part, tracked with Siphumeze Khundayi's vignette. With the aid of a megaphone, and pushing against the distortion of her voice by the plastic, she then shouted:

> Speak!
> Ears splitting and vulgar
> summoning their walks to harken
> Bitter taste
> Speak!
> Vomit the gag, amputate the festering wound inflicted on you,
> Speak!
> Stifle silence . . .

Putuma's poetry is usually confrontational and often deals with racism and sexism.[23] For example, another one of her poems, "oh dear god. please! not another rape poem," sarcastically references some people's resistance to hearing discussions about rape, especially by women artists. The poem in *Walk: South Africa* reflected the rallying cries of the movements throughout the world to end gender-based violence: "Speak!" "Stop the Violence!" "End Violence against Women!" and so on. However, it did not employ these rallying cries in a facile way. Rather, it directly questioned the use of these slogans as tropes that may or may not result in change and subverted them by elaborating on their meaning. The poem was delivered as part exhortation, part chastisement, and part venting:

> Gushing from the pit of tunnels
> In the dark
> In the park
> On the bus
> Scrape your way into the morning if you must
> For they have come to bury us
> Paraphrase us
> Erase us
> Demean us
> Diminish us
> Walk on us
> Walk in us . . . !

This was the only vignette that appeared to address the audience directly and was also a more instructive performance than the others, in that the actor explicitly emphasized the need for action. It was also the only vignette in *Walk: South Africa* to draw on Maya Krishna Rao's (2013) narration in the original *Walk*, in its spoken-word technique and its content: "In the dark, in the park, on the bus . . . " Putuma's goal was to produce a direct conversation with the original *Walk* (Putuma, pers. comm., 2017). The resulting riff affirmed the transnational feminist content and aesthetics of the two performances.

The vignette ended abruptly, and the performer exited the room, leaving the audience standing in the dark. This break was cut by Genna Gardini's cowbell, the introduction to her vignette, which used poetry to call to mind graphic images of child sexual abuse and pedophilia. The poem, which is part of her published repertoire (Gardini 2015, 29), is titled "Mister." I have partly reproduced it below.

> You are as thready as a wear in the leather,
> puffing from the crook of your collapsed chin,
> asking to let you run one of my powder stockings,
> cobbled, down your shin

> until, with one fowled swoop of your sciatic,
> Methuselastic,
> hip-replacement-in-the-attic arm,
> you sit me slap on your knee. "How old are we?" say "Pretty,
> pretty in your yellow dress!"
> (And, of course, you can guess the rest.)
> . . . .
> I find your tweed hands itching and
> plying my two dumpling knees apart
> as if to trace by heart a start on a sore
> that isn't even a scab, yet.

The poem's descriptions of a perpetrator call to mind an elderly man, a grandfather-like figure that reminds me of Martin Tindle Knoetze, a sixty-year-old white South African who in 2015 was convicted of raping three Black girls over several years with the collusion of the mother of one of the girls.[24] Gardini's femme melancholic appearance, in a black dress and black stockings, enhanced the poem's grimness and emphasis on the vulnerability that results from constant silencing. As a climax, Sara Matchett's later sonic performance embodied and encapsulated through sound the relationship between silencing and a phenomenon that Malika Ndlovu (2014, 3) describes as an "unmuting." This vignette occurred after Siphumeze Khundayi's and was the last one that took place indoors.

Matchett's presence as a white, middle-aged woman served two purposes. It functioned as one of Mothertongue's responses to the widely held notion that sexual violence does not affect white women and is essentially only a problem found in Black communities. Also, her presence emphasized that although rape is mainly perpetrated against young women and girls, older women are also affected and have a personal stake in speaking out against it. This vignette was accompanied by music from Maya Krishna Rao's original *Walk*, mixed with womb sound effects.[25] Matchett utilized breath manipulation to produce varied sounds, beginning with a slow moan that built to a melody, then to a crescendo, and then to a guttural wail that indexed all the pain displayed in previous vignettes. Her chest quivered. Her eyes bulged. Her skin turned bright red as if seared by fire. This vignette responded to Putuma's exhortation to "Speak!" Yet Matchett's sonic performance was not decipherable speech, but rather an expression of indefinable emotion. This piece was influenced by Rasa breath patterns that she learned at Adishakti Laboratory for Theatre Arts and Research in India; female Koodiyattam breath performance; and Alba Emoting, which was developed by neuroscientist Susana Bloch, theatre director Pedro Orthous, and neurophysiologist

Guy Santibáñez (see Bloch 2017; Sajnani and Gopalakrishna 2017). When applied to acting, Rasa breath patterns evoke the sensations that the actor perceives within the audience, while Alba Emoting involves effector patterns, a technique of charting emotion onto an actor's performance through posture, breath, and facial expression. The scream at the end was influenced by Matchett's study of one of the roars in Koodiyattam Rasa breath patterns. Matchett's breath performance, like Putuma's and Gardini's poetry, was a counterperformative of silencing and shaming. Joined with the other vignettes, including Postlethwaite's and Khundayi's, these pieces were an attempt to recuperate the female body and voice. All five vignettes dramatized the ruining of the world that occurs with sexual violence (Du Toit 2014), as well as an attempt to vocalize this damage through the representation of material and mental effects, verbal articulation, and the employment of not-quite-discernible but still palpable sound. However, they left questions unanswered: Where do we go from here? Is there any room to move toward justice? The final vignette intervened to respond to these questions.

Mobile Prompting: Nina Callaghan

Originally, the performance ended with Matchett's vignette, followed by the projection of names of South African victims/survivors of rape and murder on the wall. Most of the names were of women whose assaults had been featured in the media, while others were of women who had volunteered to have their names included.[26] The projected names offered the opportunity for the audience to look beyond statistics as well as beyond the actors' performances to the numerous lives affected by sexual violation. However, staring at the names, especially following the intensity of the previous vignettes, was harrowing. Some audience members—and Nina Callaghan, who joined the project in 2014—thought that the ending did not offer space for the audience's reflection or a break from the traumatic nature of the performance. And, in contrast to many other productions by Mothertongue that focus on traumatic subjects, there was no ritual to ease the emotional difficulty that the audience felt from experiencing the embodiment of a painful subject matter. Callaghan had the idea to introduce her character, adorned with plastic bags, to reflect the small glimmers of light in the dark room. *Walk: South Africa* thus began and ended with her.

While the audience waited in the lobby of the second floor of the Dragon Room, Callaghan entered unassumingly, dressed in black pants and a black blouse, sat astride a countertop, and began orally inflating clear plastic bags slowly, with an expressionless face turned away from the audience. After

Genna Gardini took the audience inside to view the other vignettes, Callaghan was not seen again until she entered the space at the end and led the other performers and the audience outside. Subsequently, everyone dispersed into the city. This final vignette acknowledged that there was a question regarding how the audience may move from spectatorship to acting on the problem, but it provided no verbal response, no explanation, and no resolution. How Callaghan's vignette came to be part of *Walk: South Africa* is deserving of analysis because the matter of whether the production was previously too pessimistic and traumatic is at the center of the debates around speaking about sexual violence and representing it onstage. To engage more with the issues at hand in *Walk: South Africa*, I will now put it in conversation with another South African play that tells the story of a young girl's experience with sexual abuse.

In October 2015, before my interviews with most of the members of Mothertongue who worked on *Walk: South Africa*, I traveled to Johannesburg for two weeks. My primary aims were to attend the Olive Tree Women's Theatre Festival and interview Olive Tree founder Ntshieng Mokgoro and other theatre artists participating in the festival. (Mokgoro's individual work as a playwright and the work of Olive Tree Theatre are the subjects of chapter 4.) At the festival I saw Gcebile Dlamini's *Nomzamo*, a play about a young Black teenage girl who is repeatedly raped by an older male relative. Unlike many plays I had seen that addressed rape, *Nomzamo* spent most of its thirty minutes describing the girl's pain and only diverted from this in the last five minutes, after the rapist died from natural causes. Some members of the audience thought that the play focused too much on Nomzamo's pain. Others were relieved that she finally took on the stance of a survivor at the end. She became a "victor" as opposed to a "victim," said one man during the postshow discussion. Her small step toward the audience and fleeting smile at the end represented the character's empowerment.

The focus on survival is an important part of the process of healing from sexual violence and a necessary aspect of addressing rape trauma syndrome. Therefore, I understand why these audience members yearned for Nomzamo to heal and thrive. From a dramaturgical perspective, there were constructive suggestions for revising the play's lengthy monologues. I am also acutely aware that retraumatizing can occur among audience members who have experienced sexual violence in a play that focuses on pain. This too should be an issue that theatre artists take seriously. In my contribution to the talkback, I asked Dlamini about her dramatic choices.[27] She revealed that she decided to emphasize the trauma of rape, which she felt is often denied in public discourse. She also told us that she was sexually assaulted as a young girl by a family member. The fact that the playwright/director was a survivor of rape meant that the play was semi-autobiographical—a fact that an audience should factor into their reception of the play. It is possible that the play's emotive nature functioned as catharsis for her and the young girls with whom she has worked, given that she was motivated to write it after she met a girl who related her experiences of sexual assault (Dlamini, pers. comm., 2022).[28] I thought of all these factors during the talkback, that night when I got back to the hotel, and for months and years afterward. My fixation on *Nomzamo* indicates that Dlamini achieved her aim, however disturbing the play was to some audience members. In sum, I found the focus on pain important to an understanding of the ontological effects of sexual violence. It was necessary to see Nomzamo go from being a bubbly young girl to an utterly traumatized one, seeking through soliloquys to make sense of what was happening to her.[29] The tendency in plays and movies about sexual violence at the time was to emphasize survival, and this at times obscured the seriousness of the subject matter. In later years the global rise of activisms that centered the voices of victims and survivors would act as a corrective to historical silencing and as a refusal to publicly engage with the trauma of sexual violence.

A central commonality among feminists and other gender-rights advocates throughout the world is an emphasis on the need to deconstruct the belief that pain is women's lot in life, whether that is the biological pain of childbirth, pregnancy, and menstruation, the emotional pain of heartbreak and betrayal, or the psychological and physical pain of gender-based violence. This expectation has produced various tropes that are used to inspire and empower, as well as to minimize women's experiences of trauma: the single mother who sacrifices all for her children; the devoted wife who stays with an unfaithful husband; and the strong Black woman who thrives against racism, classism, and patriarchy and is also there to help the more fragile white woman through her difficulties (see Beauboeuf-Lafontant 2009; Daley 2021; Mama 1995). These tropes are often considered virtues within themselves, rather than characteristics that women have had to take on as a means of survival. Therefore, activists have had to negotiate the line between representing the full breadth of the trauma of sexual violence and figuring out a path toward healing, while dealing with sex and gender expectations around how women, girls, and queer people should express themselves.

I spoke with the performers about *Walk: South Africa*'s embodiment of trauma: though significantly different in technique and content from *Nomzamo*, the production also focused on the violence of rape and attracted the same kinds of comments about its intensity. We discussed the fact that many women who were raped were also killed, as was the case with Anene Booysen and countless others throughout the world. We also talked about the trauma that survivors of sexual violence have to work through. Thus, is there a danger in downplaying trauma to focus on survival? And is the requirement to move beyond pain at times a type of inadvertent victim blaming? In order to interrogate the centrality of pain in discussions about rape without necessarily responding to these questions, the creators/performers of *Walk: South Africa* decided to weave trauma into their techniques. They also decided from the beginning that they would aim to move the audience through the performance's aesthetic rather than to develop a didactic relationship with the viewers. Most importantly, they wished to emphasize the social and psychological damage done by sexual violence and its perpetuation. As Nina Callaghan stated, it was "an attempt to be completely unapologetic about the horror we are in" (pers. comm., 2015). Koleka Putuma similarly stated, "When we are addressing this issue there is no out. There is no exhale. There is no release. It is important to be confronted with a piece about rape where the ending reflects the reality we are existing in" (pers. comm., 2015).

Not all audience members were receptive to this aim. As Sara Matchett recounted, in early performances in 2013 and 2014, some felt that it was too depressing. I can concur with them to an extent, based on watching the first performance in 2013, which focused entirely on the trauma of sexual violence. After this initial critique, they changed the production to add aspects that seemed more hopeful. This did not work. As many theatre artists who modify their pieces to please critics have found, "it felt manufactured" (Matchett, pers. comm., 2015).[30] Nina Callaghan's durational plastic bag performance was the only new element that successfully introduced a less traumatic component to the production. Her introduction of hope was not mawkish; in part, this is because her performance can open itself to many interpretations. For instance, the first time I watched the 2014 Dragon Room performance I was disturbed by her entry at the end because it distorted the names of victims and survivors that were projected on the screen. Callaghan told me that some audience members felt that the bags evoked an image and sensation of being suffocated, which was different from what she intended. However, once she started moving out of the theatre and into the sunlight, the reflection of the sun's rays signified some confidence in activism as well as a collective call to action.

Rather than prescribing a binary focus on depression versus happiness/hope/survival, the vignette turned in the direction of movement that the audience had to then work through. This approach is similar to that taken by Sistren and HTCG in their skit *A Slice of Reality* (2009; see chapter 1). The skit's middle and ending featured exhortative and proclamatory poetry, singing, and dancing. However, Sistren and HTCG were much more instructive in their techniques, given that they were presenting the skit with the specific objective of convincing politicians to change a law. In contrast, in *Walk: South Africa* the performers did not tell the audience what to do. Audience members had to decide for themselves. As Genna Gardini put it, the ending of the performance with the movement outside emphasized the ability to "move lightly through the shit and horror and take on another meaning, a meaning you choose for yourself" (pers. comm., 2015).

Conclusion: *Walk: South Africa*'s Resonances and Affects

The act of walking served both physical and heuristic purposes in *Walk: South Africa*. It was a performative device exhorting the audience and the community to action through literal and political movement, as well as a mnemonic method of locating the experiences of the two women whose deaths influenced the development of the performance. Both Anene Booysen and Jyoti Singh Pandey were in transit to their homes on those fateful nights, and Anene was literally walking home. One of the major preoccupations of contemporary gender justice movements is the way women's bodies are policed as they move through their societies on a daily basis. For example, global advocacy against sexual harassment—such as the US-based SlutWalk campaign, started by model and activist Amber Rose—focuses partly on the act of women walking in public while wearing whatever they choose (Sayej 2018). *Walk: South Africa* fell within this framework of embodied activism. It enacted an affective engagement that centered an active spectatorship, depending equally on the audience's engagement in the moment of the performance and their reflection after its end. In her response to one of the performances of *Walk: South Africa* at the Dragon Room, Malika Ndlovu (2014, 3) wrote: "None of us are left unmoved. We must take what we have been given and apply it in the 'real world,' in our lives. . . . My mind is both full and empty." In her interview with me, Ndlovu similarly spoke about *Walk: South Africa*'s significance in bringing an emotive voice to discussing rape in South Africa. I write about Ndlovu's reaction to the performance not as an attempt to validate its effectiveness, but as an example of one audience member's encounter with it in a way that escapes static definition. Her short-term response to the performance was to stop at a sidewalk café in Cape Town on the way home and compose a poem that functions as possibly her most articulate expression of what she experienced. Other audience members were frustrated by the play's lack of resolution. After the 2014 performance at the University of Witwatersrand in Johannesburg, one person said, "You just leave us there" (Matchett and Gardini, pers. comm., 2015). This comment, which was meant as a negative critique, ironically suggests that Mothertongue achieved its purpose to leave the responsibility of resolving the problem of rape and rape culture in the hands of the audience.

It is impossible to predict the specific political actions that individuals will participate in after seeing a performance. However, one indication of the impact of *Walk: South Africa* is that at the performance analyzed in this chapter, the audience members continued to walk with the performers until they got tired. This display of kinesthetic empathy (Reynolds and Reason 2012), in which the audience shows its affect by following the gestures and movements of the performers, proves successful the Mothertongue Project's aim to "move [the audience's] feet" (Matchett, pers. comm., 2015). Using Eve Kosofsky Sedgwick's (2003) formulation, Kimberly Wedeven Segall (2013, 139) speaks about the sort of sociopolitical change that Maya Krishna Rao's original *Walk* and Mothertongue's *Walk: South Africa* both called for: "Emotional residues and audience moods are not extra, arbitrary, unimportant, or distractions from the rational forms of legislation; no, emotional responses, especially when they are repeated in diverse forms and inscribed on numerous bodies, become a political force."

Essentially, *Walk: South Africa* uses the aesthetic of a moving installation as a repertoire of the critical features of the normalization of sexual violence in South Africa: its historical resonances, the way women of different ages and races become vulnerable within it, Black women's and queer people's particular experiences, the junctures and disjunctures between white privilege and gender marginalization, and the way people's movements throughout the country are interrogated. The performance is also a memorial and testimony linking the past with the present and future. This was most clearly evident in 2014 in Rosa Postlethwaite's and Siphumeze Khundayi's vignettes, but it is a thread running through *Walk: South Africa*, as it does in many postapartheid theatre productions and theatre by Africana people throughout the world.

Walk: South Africa is also a living, evolving performance. It has changed over the years as some of the original creators have stopped performing in it or changed their vignettes, and others have joined. The newer cast members who performed in the two iterations in 2019 were Jacki Jöb, Vathiswa Nodlayiya, Stembiso Sibanda, and Lukhanyiso Skosana. The performers have not repeated the walk at the end as they did in the 2014 Cape Town Fringe Festival and the Sex Actually festival held at the University of Witwatersrand. *Walk: South Africa*'s different manifestations have added new perspectives. However, the paradigm shaped by the 2014 performances remains with the new content. *Walk: South Africa*'s major resonances are in its resistance of a resolution or any form of didactic appeal to the audience. It is therefore both ambiguous in its refusal to give the audience a conclusive narrative and unequivocal in its statement that sexual violence and its normalization are complicated problems that cannot be abolished by a single story or collection of stories on a stage. Ultimately, the resolution is the responsibility of the community, the nation, and the globe.

CHAPTER 3

"Mi a go try release yu"

Mourning, Memory, and Violence in *A Vigil for Roxie*

"I would like if they stop to kill our children." These words were inscribed on a card in the awkward handwriting of a child, accompanied by a stick figure of a boy. And under that image was another sentence that said, "Omer has died," seemingly referring to a child who had passed away.[1] This card was left by an anonymous visitor from the after-school program at Liberty Hall: The Legacy of Marcus Garvey, a Pan-Africanist institution in Kingston, Jamaica, which hosted an exhibition and performance titled *Song for the Beloved: Memory and Renewal at the Margins of Justice* in May 2015. Visitors to the exhibition had been invited to reflect on social justice and place their words on cards that adorned a large memorial table covered in soil, candles, and stones that bore the names of people who had died violently in Jamaica.

The play *A Vigil for Roxie*, the theatrical highlight of the exhibition, had been staged in the same space a few days before the child who left the card visited, and coincidentally, the words on the card connect with one of the most emotional scenes in *Vigil*. In this scene, which occurs within the first ten minutes of the play, Iris, a single parent of a young boy named Roxie, reads a composition that he wrote for one of his classes. In it he states, "In my community, people say that if you come from down here, you not going to live long. They say sooner or later a bullet will find you" (Lawes et al., 2015, 4).[2] However, Roxie is inspired by the resilience of his mother and is committed to working hard in school so that he will not become another perpetrator or victim: "Mama say to survive you have to pick sense outa nonsense. Not because I come from down here. As long as I take the education and work hard I can be anything I want" (4). Several scenes/years later, Roxie's mother discovers a gun in the same schoolbag, and this signifies his

Figure 5. Section of the interactive exhibition *Song for the Beloved: Memory and Renewal at the Margins of Justice* at Liberty Hall: The Legacy of Marcus Garvey, 2015. Photo by the author.

transition to a gang leader and ultimately seals his fate to die at the hands of the state. Roxie the fictional child, much like the real child who visited *Song for the Beloved*, expressed his frustration with the violence that enveloped his community and envisioned another kind of life for himself. Roxie the man, however, had few qualms about engaging in violence as a means of providing for his mother and community and asserting power over his enemies. As a result, the women in his life were left to deal with the consequences of his decisions and with the overarching structures of violence, poverty, racism, and economic inequalities that plagued his life and death. His mother still memorializes him through an annual vigil in which she relives the events leading up to his death. The play's story takes place mostly during the vigil she is conducting on the fifth anniversary of his murder, when, though still traumatized, she has the benefit of enough time to fully assess everything that happened. At the end of the play, she utters a final monologue, in which she declares, "Mi a go try release yu" (I will try to release you) (Lawes et al., 2015, 29). I titled the chapter after this climactic statement, which indicates that Iris has started the process toward healing and has been able to assess the social milieu in which her son lived and died. The story resonates because it provides a deeply subjective perspective on one of Jamaica's most pervasive problems—its rate of homicides.

In 2020, Jamaica's murder rate was among the five highest in the world, despite fluctuations over the previous two decades (WorldAtlas 2020). In 2022, amid the socioeconomic upheavals caused by the COVID-19 pandemic, the rate increased from the previous two years to place Jamaica second on the list of countries with the highest homicide rates (Statista 2022). Much of this violence is concentrated in densely populated urban areas and is tied to gangs and the illegal drug trade. Violence committed by, and directed against, young men has taken countless lives, as have extrajudicial killings by police officers and soldiers mostly in economically disadvantaged urban communities. The goal of the play *A Vigil for Roxie* and its creators is to attend to the ways members of these communities engage in social justice advocacy and memorialization, in order to allow a deeper understanding of their experience of violence, beyond the often pathologizing narratives about them.

This chapter analyzes the 2015 performance of *Vigil* in the *Song for the Beloved* exhibition. I worked on *Vigil* and *Song for the Beloved* as coordinator from January to June that year. Thus, *Vigil* is the only performance I analyze in this book in which I was directly involved and had some input. The play and the exhibition are products of the Letters from the Dead project, which documents and represents through performance the ways in which people in urban communities affected by violence memorialize loved ones through street art, vigils, and other commemorative practices. The project's focus on the way communities cope with violent deaths and on the effects of local and global socioeconomic issues de-individualizes violence and treats it as interconnected with structural factors. Chief among these factors are neoliberal processes, which have intensified inequalities in Jamaica and throughout the Americas and operate in conjunction with the legacies of slavery and colonialism; the militarization of the police; the growth in transnational crime networks; the primacy of guns as tools within these networks; the normalized disposability of Black bodies, including by other Black people; and notions of manhood that lead many young men to become involved in organized crime and violence. *A Vigil for Roxie* builds an alternative archive through theatre, which participates in the larger conversation about the connections between violence (whether by civilians or state agents) and deeply embedded socioeconomic structures.

Several scholars have written on violence in Jamaica from different perspectives (Crawford-Brown 2010; Gray 1990, 2004; Irish-Bramble 2012; Tafari-Ama 2006; D. Thomas 2011, 2019). *Vigil* participates in this conversation but allows it to flow through the experiences of working-class Black Jamaicans, drawing on their memorial rituals as a source of knowledge. By depicting the processes through which people affected by violence remember as well as forget—i.e. suppress—their experiences of it, the play centers the complex emotional lives of Black people amid centuries of slavery and colonialism, as well as current inequalities that disparage their humanity. Through theatre, they are made into agents who not only react to their circumstances but also resist and transcend them.

I analyze five of the play's main characters and argue that through them, *Vigil* illustrates how gender intersects with race and class in the production, circulation, and experience of violence in Jamaica. Most of these characters are women. This dramatic choice is representative of the reality that women are central in public mourning rituals and play crucial roles as heads of households affected by the deaths and incarceration of loved ones. They are also vulnerable to sexual and other kinds of violence. There is a growing body of scholarship globally on Black women and other women of color in situations of intense conflict, including wars and state-sanctioned violence (see Barajas 2018; Downs 2016; Perera and Razack 2014; Richie 2012; Segal 2016; Shalhoub-Kevorkian 2014; C. Smith 2008; Theobald 2012). For example, Christen Smith (2015, 2016, 2018) has written about the "slow death" of Black women who have had to bear the effects of police and military violence in the United States and Brazil. Likewise, in Jamaica, while more men than women are killed by agents of the state (the police and soldiers) and by civilians engaged in crime networks, women often suffer long-term problems related to the stress of losing children, boyfriends, husbands, brothers, and fathers. This is in addition to being victims of reprisal murders in disputes among men, and killings and assaults at the hands of state forces. To unpack the various ways in which people of different genders participate in and are affected by violence, *Vigil* features both men and women, focusing on mostly women who are related to the eponymous Roxie. After the story ends there is a postlude featuring readings of letters that participants in the Letters from the Dead project in 2009 wrote to their deceased loved ones, as well as letters that they imagined could have been written by the dead. This emphasis on the connection between the living and the dead, the past and the present, is influenced by African and African Diasporic religious and cosmological understandings of ancestral connections. At the time of the 2015 performance of *Vigil*, Letters from the Dead had been in place for eight years, with an already impressive repertoire of performances.

The Letters from the Dead Project

Letters from the Dead was conceived in 2006 by artist-scholar Honor Ford-Smith and is based at York University in Toronto, Canada, where she teaches. It is most accurately defined as the performance component of the "Memory, Urban Violence and Performance in Jamaican Communities" research project, which Ford-Smith initiated and oversees as the chief researcher. This project explores "how people in different social and spatial locations remember and forget the losses inflicted by urban violence. It examines the side of inner-city violence that escapes official reports."(Ford-Smith, n.d.). Ford-Smith (2014, 263) writes that despite Jamaica's high murder rate, and the simplistic narratives that circulate internationally about violence in Jamaica, memorial acts such as vigils "demonstrate that far from being pathologically and inherently violent, Jamaicans actively resist violence in ways that are rarely reported."

The project draws on these performance practices in its productions. Its aesthetic is also in part a continuation of the performance methods that Ford-Smith and her colleagues affiliated with the Jamaica School of Drama in the 1970s–80s developed in their mission to build a Jamaican theatre aesthetic. Thus, Letters from the Dead exists within the same genealogy and with many of the same collaborators as Sistren Theatre Collective. Sistren is a partner on the project; and the members of the Hannah Town Cultural Group (HTCG), which created *A Slice of Reality* (2009) with Sistren (see chapter 1), have been instrumental as performers and participants.

The first performance was a street march in Toronto in 2007, which made visible the losses that Aboriginal/First Nations, African-descended, Asian-descended, Caribbean, and working-class white communities suffer as a result of violence. The march culminated at the Eaton Centre, a major shopping mall, at the spot where a young white woman was killed in 2005. Communities of color in Canada felt that the problem of violent deaths had only been made visible in the media because of this murder and that although they had long suffered the physical and emotional consequences of violence, their losses had been ignored. This street performance was influenced by memorial practices and public demonstrations connected to various antiwar, anti-state-violence, and peace movements throughout the world, including Women in Black against the Palestinian occupation, Madres de la Plaza de Mayo in Argentina, and rituals created by First Nations people in Canada (Ford-Smith 2011). Following on the success of the site-specific street performance in Toronto, the next one was held in Jamaica in June 2009 in response to an increase in Jamaica's murder rate at the time. There, the performance was an image event in which people dressed in black marched with photos of deceased loved ones through the streets of downtown Kingston. There were elements of the Toronto performance in that image event, including the wearing of black by participants and a cardboard coffin decorated with images of deceased people; however, the major influences were Jamaican religious and memorial practices such as those found in the Afro-Christian religion of Revival. Since the original Canadian and Jamaican performances, the project has developed many exhibitions and performances in Canada, Jamaica, the United States, Britain, Colombia, and Chile. In each site, it connects local problems with global struggles.

For instance, at the 2016 exhibition and performance of *Song for the Beloved* in Santiago, Chile, in which I was one of the performers, the country's ongoing project to memorialize the disappeared and murdered people who were victims of the Pinochet regime's (1973–90) systematic violations of human rights provided a local context for a wider conversation.[3] Visitors to the performance installation, who were asked to talk about their visions for social justice, were vocal about Latin American and region-specific problems, including the killings connected to the transnational drug trade in the Americas. Police violence in the United States emerged as a recurring problem that visitors spoke about as well, and the performance was dedicated to Black Lives Matter, cofounded in 2014 by Patrisse Cullors, Alicia Garza, and Ayọ (formerly Opal) Tometi. Since this performance was one month after the mass shooting at Pulse, a gay nightclub in Orlando, Florida, several visitors to the exhibition also commented on anti-LGBTQ violence.

I was involved in this 2016 Chilean performance because I had joined the project in 2015 to coordinate *Song for the Beloved* and *A Vigil for Roxie*. The 2015 exhibition and performance occurred during the same week as the fifth anniversary of the violent events known as the West Kingston or Tivoli Incursion, and while the Jamaican government's West Kingston Commission of Enquiry was holding nationally broadcast hearings. The inquiry featured testimonies about the week in May 2010 when the police and army entered Tivoli Gardens in order to execute an arrest warrant and disarm the community but instead committed massive human rights violations.

Urban Communities, Politics, and Violence: The West Kingston Incursion

A Vigil for Roxie includes commentary on the political nature of violence in Jamaica, especially the relationship between politicians and men involved in organized crime, and the use of excessive force by the police and soldiers to curtail crime in urban communities. While the play does not focus on a specific community, the fifth anniversary of the Tivoli Incursion provided a real-life memorial moment in which to understand the relationship between organized crime and state violence.[4] Tivoli Gardens is one of twelve communities described as "garrison constituencies" because of their close alignment with one of the two major political parties and their position as a base for transnational crime, mostly through gangs headed by leaders known as dons (Stone 1983). The development of garrison communities and the importance of dons reached their pinnacle in the late 1970s, during clashes between the People's National Party (PNP) and the Jamaica Labour Party (JLP), which advocated democratic socialism and liberal capitalism, respectively. The formal political competition influenced and was buoyed by intense violence in the inner-city communities associated with the two parties. As Obika Gray (1990, 2004) has documented, the political element in urban violence in the 1950s–70s was a consequence of politicians punishing people who were not loyal to their parties while soliciting and rewarding those who were. Politicians exploited and co-opted moral and social tendencies associated with the urban poor as well as their racial and class consciousness. Among these tendencies is what Gray (2004, 129) terms "badness-honour," which he defines as "a repertoire that employs language, facial gesture, bodily poses and an assertive mien to compel rivals or allies to grant power, concede respect, accord deference or satisfy material want." According to Gray, badness-honour occurs globally, finding expression in Jamaica through "badmanism" or "badness," as displayed through the activities of the "rude boys" of the 1970s. While badness-honour is largely performative it can lead to real violence, and in the 1970s, postcolonial political rivalry between the PNP and JLP intensified violence throughout Jamaica, especially in urban communities.

At the international level the US government interfered economically and militarily to ensure that Jamaica did not become an ally of the Soviet Union like its neighbor Cuba, and to contain the spread of socialism and communism in the Caribbean, which was a major preoccupation during the Cold War. Over eight hundred people were killed in the year leading up to the 1980 elections, including Roy McGann, the minister of national security. Several mass atrocities, such as the Orange Street Fire of 1979 and the Eventide Home Fire of 1980 (in which 150 elderly women died), were strongly alleged to be political, possibly involving the US Central Intelligence Agency (Carr 2002; C. Robinson 2011).

After the 1980 elections, the JLP—and, consequently, liberal capitalism and a bourgeoning neoliberalism—emerged supreme. Some of the violent tendencies that had characterized Jamaican politics during the 1960s–70s have remained since then, but without the obvious ideological divisions of democratic socialism versus liberal capitalism. As governments have decreased access to public resources through structural adjustment policies they have created conditions in which citizens increasingly find illegal means of survival through organized crime. Writing on Latin America and the Caribbean with a focus on Jamaica, Michelle A. Munroe and Damion K. Blake (2017, 582) argue that "the implementation of public sector neoliberal reforms and policies from the 1980s, as well as increasing access to the drug trade by nefarious community leaders known as dons, resulted in a transformation of violence in Jamaica." Nowadays, with the deaths or imprisonment of Jamaica's most powerful dons, organized violence is marked more by gang and other group activities led by individual men who are relatively unknown beyond their communities, the police, and crime networks. These men may not have the same transnational political and economic power as dons, but they exercise enough authority within their communities to be feared. Alongside the tendency for young men who are involved in crime to operate as protectors of their communities, political paternalism and clientelism continue in Jamaican society. These tendencies are characterized by politicians' provision of resources to marginalized communities in a tacit exchange for votes, especially during election time.

A stronghold of the JLP, Tivoli Gardens operated for many years in a semi-sovereign position in relation to the rest of Jamaica, with its own systems of leadership and crime control. This position was sanctioned through political paternalism and maintained through violence targeting persons thought to be infringing on the community's autonomy, including the police and utility bill collectors.[5] This situation led the then chief of the Jamaica Defence Force (later commissioner of police), Rear Admiral Hardley Lewin, to refer to Tivoli as "the mother of all garrisons." Similarly, Owen Ellington, the commissioner of police in 2010, described it as a "state within the state" (Jamaica Ministry of Justice 2016, 26).

The Tivoli Incursion was the violent high point in a yearlong conflict emerging from the government's delay in deciding whether it would extradite businessman and don Christopher "Dudus" Coke to the United States on charges of conspiracy and murder.[6] After a year of uncertainty, on May 17, 2010, the prime minister announced via a national TV broadcast that Coke would be extradited and that a warrant had been issued for his arrest. The decision precipitated a series of conflicts between the Jamaican police and residents of Tivoli Gardens, gunmen, and others who supported Coke. In the most damaging of these events, men allegedly working for or on behalf of Coke attacked several police stations, bombing one and destroying another by fire. At least two police officers were shot and injured and several others fired on when they attempted to clear roadblocks allegedly set up by people affiliated with Coke. Unarmed community members also showed their support for Coke. One day hundreds of people, mostly women wearing white, marched to downtown Kingston to protest his extradition, some declaring on placards that they were willing to die for him. Neither the violent attack on police stations and officers nor the peaceful mass demonstration changed the mind of those in government. If anything, these events increased their resolve to disarm Tivoli and the rest of West Kingston and to arrest Coke. In the days leading up to the incursion, residents were told to leave. Some people did leave, doing so via buses that the government had provided, but many Jamaicans argued that these buses were inadequate and that the government's plan did not consider the physical and psychological difficulties that people would face leaving their homes.

On May 24, over eleven hundred police officers and soldiers from the Jamaica Defence Force entered a barricaded Tivoli Gardens with the official mission to arrest Coke (who was reputed to be hiding there) and to disarm the community. Armed men who engaged them in battle were overpowered. But the incursion did not stop there. Testimonies from residents, police officers, and soldiers, as well as a video recording made by a surveillance plane operated by the US Department of Homeland Security, disclosed that the police and soldiers stormed through Tivoli Gardens, assaulting civilians who had not engaged them in battle. Homes were ransacked, informal interrogation procedures employed, and summary killings carried out. Additionally, by the end of the week around five hundred men and boys from Tivoli and neighboring communities were being detained; they would be held for many days in the National Arena, a site usually used for sporting and official events. The official record states that at least seventy-three persons were killed during the incursion and the search for Coke, including three members of the security forces and seventy civilians (Jamaica Ministry of Justice 2016, 15, 476).[7] Countless others were injured, lost loved ones, and suffered long-term trauma. Adding to the shock of it all, the bodies of many who died during the incursion stayed on the street for several days and were only removed after the police and army completed their initial operation. Two of the people killed were nineteen-year-old Lundy Murphy and seventeen-year-old Jamain Murphy. I knew these brothers because they had been students in the after-school program at Liberty Hall when I worked there—just like that anonymous child who left the memorial card.[8] Neither Lundy nor Jamain was associated with Coke or any crime networks, and neither was armed when he was killed.

Coke was eventually arrested in June 2010 and extradited, but the soldiers and police maintained a presence in West Kingston, which became predominantly a female space following the death and detention of so many men and boys. The national human rights group Jamaicans for Justice, community peace activists, and international human rights organizations strongly condemned the incursion. Amid this disgrace, Bruce Golding resigned as Prime Minister at the end of 2010, and two publicly broadcast commissions followed. The first was the Commission of Enquiry into the Extradition Request for Christopher Coke, referred to more popularly as the Manatt Commission of Enquiry. It was held in 2010–11 to investigate the government's overall mishandling of the extradition request and the unethical hiring of a US law firm (Manatt, Phelps and Phillips) to advise the majority-governing JLP on the extradition. This first inquiry led to a plethora of talking points, satirical cartoons, catchphrases, and even songs and was largely treated as entertainment by Jamaicans.[9] Much less entertaining and more consequential was the West Kingston Commission of Enquiry, held from December 2014 to February 2016 to address the human rights violations in the police and army's operation. Jamaicans tuned in live to see victims and their families recount what happened during the incursion. Testimonies from civilians, soldiers, police, politicians, attorneys, activists, and others were carried live on Jamaican televisions, mobile phones, and computers for a year. News reports summarized and analyzed the sittings of each day, while pundits, academics, lawyers, and human rights experts weighed in on the usefulness and shortcomings of the commission. A secondary drama within the primary drama was that the inquiry laid bare Jamaica's problems with socioeconomic class in the legal system. For example, I was annoyed with how the attorneys representing the government seemed to talk down to the alleged victims, and I noticed the civilians' polite manner despite what was often a patronizing process. As an example of the elitism in the legal profession, one defense lawyer for the civilians was routinely mocked on social media for not enunciating his English words perfectly (Paul 2015).

In the final analysis, the West Kingston Commission of Enquiry found that the police and military had committed human rights violations and recommended, among other measures, financial recompense. In December 2017 the government earmarked 200 million Jamaican dollars (approx. 1.5 million US dollars) as compensation to those who could demonstrate that they had unjustifiably suffered personal injury or lost family members. As of May 2018, 190.4 million dollars had been paid to 418 persons (*Jamaica Observer* 2018). As of 2022, however, no individual has been held criminally responsible for what happened. And yet, even in the absence of justice, the inquiry did have the lasting effect of enabling Jamaicans and international audiences to hear testimony about this extraordinarily violent event. The inquiry achieved something that had been elusive for decades: it allowed the nation and the world a glimpse into the violence that plagues many communities in Jamaica.

I have recounted the West Kingston incursion in great detail because this was a pivotal moment in Jamaica's history of violence by state agents as well as by transnational crime networks. This event entailed more than police brutality against poor Black people. It was a military event. Although some Jamaican men fought in the British Army in the First and Second World Wars, when the country was a British colony, Jamaica has never gone to war against another country. Yet, the human rights violations committed by Jamaica's soldiers and police resemble those committed by armies in the course of international and national warfare. The incursion and related events were the consequence of entangled uses of violence as a tool of social control: politicians' turn to violence for political gain, particularly in the founding of garrison constituencies; historical class-based and racial inequalities held in place by the state's limited services to poor communities; the social power exercised by men involved in organized crime over their communities; and the transnational criminal networks and efforts by police and military to combat or control them.

While the fifth anniversary of the West Kingston Incursion contextualized the 2015 performance of *A Vigil for Roxie* within a contemporary memorial moment of inordinate state and civilian violence, the major and ongoing engagement of the Letters from the Dead project is with the cumulative effect of decades of violence on families and communities. It uses performance to explore processes of healing, visions of justice, and struggles for survival. Justice for victims and survivors of violence cannot be conceived in purely quantifiable ways, such as through monetary compensation. Justice also means engaging the subjectivities of marginalized people and the communities in which they live.

Situating the Performance

From the outset, *A Vigil for Roxie* and the wider exhibition, *Song for the Beloved*, were to be staged in downtown Kingston and made free to the public, rather than being held at a commercial theatre in uptown Kingston, the middle-class and wealthy area of the city. Eugene Williams, cocreator and director of *Vigil*, stated that some people felt that the play would get more exposure in the theatre community if it were staged at a commercial theatre. For example, he spoke of a well-known theatre administrator who, commenting on a 2014 performance in downtown Kingston, stated that the community members who participated in the discussion afterward were "a distraction" (Williams, pers. comm., 2014).

Despite the logistical and financial advantages that would have accompanied having *Vigil* at an uptown theatre, both of its Jamaican performances (2014 and 2015) have been held in downtown Kingston, with free admission and audience interaction. We explored several venues for the 2015 performance, including the Hannah Town Community Centre in West Kingston, one of the areas in which people were most affected by the 2010 incursion. However, Hannah Town was at the time experiencing sporadic flare-ups in violence, which made it difficult to host a large event there. Next was the courtyard of an artist's studio in the downtown Kingston business district, but this again did not work because of the costs of physically converting the space into one that could contain an exhibition as well as host a performance for hundreds of people. Both of these spaces would have aligned with Letters from the Dead's emphasis on shifting the geographies of performance to areas of a city that are primarily accessed by working-class people and to spaces not thought of as theatre venues. After several months of exploring venues we decided on Liberty Hall. The 2014 performance of *Vigil* had been held there, so staging the 2015 performance there simply meant reconnecting with this venue. My own relationship to Liberty Hall was twelve years long by the time I coordinated the performance. I worked as researcher there from 2003 to 2011 before moving to the United States, and then became a member of the Friends of Liberty Hall Foundation. Liberty Hall is the former Kingston and international headquarters of Marcus Garvey's Universal Negro Improvement Association and African Communities League (UNIA-ACL), and it maintains a focus on Pan-Africanism, Afrocentrism, and Black uplift through education. It houses the Garvey Great Hall, where the exhibition and play were held; the Marcus Mosiah Garvey Multimedia Museum; a library; and community outreach programs for children and adults. Given its broad demographic focus and multiple functions, Liberty Hall is visited by people from all walks of life and from different communities across Jamaica and internationally. Though the building is now owned and mostly funded by the government, it is not considered to be aligned with a political party or community, and its location in the center of downtown Kingston makes it readily accessible. Thus, it was an ideal place for the event.

Song for the Beloved was advertised as an exhibition and performance, with *Vigil* serving as the main event that launched it. In hindsight, it could more accurately be defined as a performance installation like

Mothertongue's *Walk: South Africa* (see chapter 2). As with other iterations of the Letters from the Dead cycle, the central installation in *Song for the Beloved* was a long memorial table designed in the format of Jamaican Revival tables, with candles, soda bottles, and live plants. Images of memorial murals were projected on a screen parallel with the table, while at the other end were posters of people who had died violently and placards from the Letters from the Dead image event held in 2009. The exhibition was interactive, encouraging audience members and visitors to add the names of people they wanted to remember to the stones and cards on the memorial table. Another table held memorial buttons of people who had died violently. For the opening, which featured *Vigil*, audience members were seated on either side of the table. The semicircular seating structure with the memorial table in the center, and the placement of the play within the already highly interactive exhibition, facilitated the aesthetic and physical closeness between audience and performer. Adding to the focus on African-centered, Black-affirming memorial and artistic practices, the play was preceded by drumming and a performance from Abbebe Payne, a Rastafarian poet based in downtown Kingston.

Vigil was performed as a staged reading followed by a discussion. The format of the staged reading is influenced by a range of approaches to theatre that emphasize its pedagogic value by encouraging audience interaction and reflection. Such approaches include mimetic storytelling, call-and-response, and Boalian forum theatre. By reading from the script while performing, actors invite the audience into the process of creation, showing that the play, like the topic it speaks about, is a work in progress. At the center of the performance of a staged reading is the bare-bones story, not the ability of the director to create a naturalistic or realistic interpretation of the events it depicts.

The audience expressed differing opinions about the aesthetic value of the staged reading; some who had seen the 2014 performance, in which the actor performed her lines from memory and with more costuming, were a bit disappointed. However, the play generated much thought and feedback from the audience in the fifteen-minute discussion during the intermission, the ninety-minute conversation that followed it, and a community workshop held the next day.

Vigil is a research-to-performance production collectively devised and written over the course of two years (2009–11) and then revised in 2015. The playwrights—Amba Chevannes, Honor Ford-Smith, Carol Lawes, and Eugene Williams—based it on research conducted on memorial practices in urban communities in Jamaica. Women from two volatile communities influenced the storyline as well as the rituals constructed in the play. The first is Monica Williams, whose son Jason Smith was shot and killed by the police in 2002.[10] While legal justice remains elusive, Williams continues to hold an annual vigil for Jason at her home in Spanish Town, a major urban area close to Kingston. Second, Hannah Town Cultural Group members, particularly those who are Revival practitioners, have been vital to the construction of the play. The play's central prop is a table draped with white and red cloth, and the main actor sings Revival songs throughout.[11] The fabric of the story is woven through the narratives and interactions of five central characters who belong to the same family. Each character generates insight into gender and racial norms around grieving in the context of historical and present violence: Iris, Roxie's mother; Shanika, Roxie's girlfriend; Dimples and Stacey, Roxie's cousins; and Roxie. They are supported by four other characters, most of whom are unnamed.

By emphasizing a set of characters who are linked but who each have their own motivations, flaws, and virtues, and who exist within a space that is intensely affected by violence, the play reflects the womanist emphasis on commonweal, which, according to Layli Maparyan (2008, 10), "requires an understanding of the whole within each individual; each individual recognizing both the necessity of coordinating with the whole and the role of one's own freedom and self-expression within the co-constitution of the whole." The whole (that is, society) is embodied in a middle-aged Black woman: the actor who plays Iris also depicts every other character, including Roxie. Her body in performance serves as an archive of memories, documenting and reliving the traumatic event of Roxie's death and the violence that led to it.

The Performance

The play opens while Iris is preparing her annual vigil for Roxie, who died five years earlier. In a series of flashbacks that perform the spatial, temporal, and role shifts generated through the Revival ritual, the audience learns about Roxie's metamorphosis from an innocent child to a noted gang leader and then to victim of an extrajudicial killing by soldiers. Throughout his short life we see the havoc that his violence wreaks on his family, in which he is the only man. His family members, especially his mother, have to endure the damage that he causes them, including the grief they suffer after he is killed. In addition to having to deal with Roxie's demise, his girlfriend, Shanika, is gang-raped by the same soldiers who killed him. Stacey and Dimples, Roxie's cousins, are in survival mode in differing ways. Secondary characters connect the familial tragedy to inequalities in the country's justice system, classism, colonialism's racial, economic, and gender legacies, and imperialism in Jamaica as manifested in the tourism industry.

In all, the play has nine characters depicted by one actor. This is an impressive feat of acting even by Jamaican standards, where theatre aimed at raising awareness about a social problem is often minimalist and involves role shifts by actors. Watching the staged reading performed in the installation was a remarkable visual experience. The actor, Carol Lawes, became a living installation herself in embodying these roles and in demonstrating the mutable experiences of gender, racial, class, and other inequalities within a single Black body. Most significantly, Iris's performance of her memories of the years leading up to Roxie's murder produces an alternative archive that may not make it into a mainstream narrative about the life of a notorious gang leader.

The use of ritual to perform time shifts occurs in many other Jamaican theatre plays and productions as well, most notably Dennis C. Scott's *An Echo in the Bone* (1974), Sistren's *QPH* (1980), and Trevor Rhone's *Old Story Time* (1981).[12] These plays similarly comment on race, class, gender, and the connections between the past and the present, with some actors playing multiple characters. In *Vigil* it is deeply resonant that the mother, Iris, is who brings all the characters to life. Black Jamaican mothers historically and currently serve as the container for all kinds of social codes. As I stated in chapter 1, much of the rhetoric around respectability in the African Diaspora has relied on the figure of the unmarried Black mother. *Vigil* uses this Black mother's body as a vessel from which to embody a multiplicity of positionalities and identities:

1. A poor mother mourning the loss of a wayward son (Iris)
2. The vendor in the tourist zone using Jamaican stereotypes to sell souvenirs
3. The corrupt but sympathetic police officer who retires because of his disillusionment with his colleagues' recent murder of a young man
4. The classist, middle-class woman oblivious to her privilege
5. A schoolteacher whose husband was murdered, who also serves as a voice of conscience and forces Iris to stop idealizing Roxie (Miss Robb)
6. A young woman who survives sexual assault at the hands of her boyfriend's murderers (Shanika)
7. A Jamaican immigrant in the United States trying to support herself and also take care of her demanding family back home (Stacey)

8. A young woman who uses indifference as her coping mechanism (Dimples)
9. A young man who is both victim and assailant in the violence that continues to consume Jamaican communities (Roxie)

In addition to playing these nine characters, Lawes also voiced the two soldiers who sexually assault Shanika, during a monologue toward the end of the play.

While Roxie is the only one who commits lethal violence, several characters are morally flawed. For instance, the police officer who disagrees with an extrajudicial killing by his colleagues admits to taking bribes, and Iris and Shanika not only know about Roxie's criminal activities but also comply with them. In Iris's case this is out of a sense of loyalty to him and desire to protect her only child. The objective of the creators was to resist a dichotomy between victims and perpetrators and to emphasize the characters' common experiences of violence in their pasts and presents. Commenting on this dramatic choice, playwright and cocreator Amba Chevannes stated,

> We are all products of that kind of... legacy of that experience of hundreds of years of violence and being violated. And so, when we divide ourselves into the victims and perpetrators I think we miss that bigger point. And the one who is actually victimizing is also damaged and is also damaging themselves when they are committing that act. So, we address one but not the other, and so this is how I guess the cancer continues to grow; how it manages to grow without us being conscious of it. (pers. comm., 2015)

Anchoring this cast of characters, who are each negotiating their role in creating violence as well as coping with their own violation, is Roxie's family. The family can be defined as matrilocal and matrifocal in that women dominate numerically and have most of the caregiving and economic responsibilities. In many working-class communities in Jamaica, most households are headed by women, and women serve crucial roles as business owners, organizers, and activists. And yet they operate amid men's legal and illegal economic, military, and political leadership. Janet Momsen (2002) refers to this existence of matrifocality and matrilocality alongside patriarchy in Caribbean communities as "the double paradox."[13]

Women are often complicit in, or participate in, the violence that plagues many Jamaican communities, but their roles tend to be determined by their relationships to the men involved in these networks and heavily mediated by their gender. Thus, Iris's positionality is inextricably tied to Roxie's role as gang leader. Their relationship begins and ends the play and is the emotional thread that ties together all the events in it. As Honor Ford-Smith has pointed out, the inspiration behind having the mother-son relationship

Figure 6. Carol Lawes in *A Vigil for Roxie*, 2015. Photo by the author.

serve as the center of the story was the Peruvian play *Rosa Cuchillo* (2002) by Ana Correa, which is based on the 2000 novel of the same name by Oscar Colchado (Ford-Smith, pers. comm., 2015).[14] In that play, a mother searches the netherworld for her disappeared son. *Vigil* places Iris not in the netherworld but instead in her home space, the site of her memorial ritual. Roxie is resurrected through his mother's memories, and her grief is the transformative device that makes the story happen.

Iris: The Grieving Black Mother as Agent

Iris and (to a lesser extent) Roxie's girlfriend, Shanika, are the only two characters who have dialogues with him and the only ones whose reactions to his death and its immediate aftermath are depicted. As a poor Black mother, Iris is engaged in a struggle to rise above her own suppression, and she sees Roxie as a path to progress, which is a role he is first unable and then unwilling to fulfill. In her final monologue, she repeats all the career paths that he could have taken, stating in one of her final lines, "Mi did see yu as a doctor. Dem see yu as wicked" (I saw you as a doctor. They saw you as wicked) (Lawes et al., 2015, 25).

"Mi a go try release yu"

Iris's investment in Roxie is partly a general investment that most parents make because they want their children to do well, and partly a hope that she may be able to live vicariously through him. She also yearns for him to assume the position of respectable patriarch, to become the protector and provider for his family in a social order in which middle-class and wealthy men within the ostensibly law-abiding economy are accorded ultimate respect. Her maternal love for her son enables her to sympathize with him when he fails to live up to the elements of respectability that must go hand in hand with assuming this role as patriarch. We would perhaps not be wrong to surmise that had Roxie lived longer, her faith that he could change and become the man she envisions him to be would have remained firmly in place, even if he had continued to be involved in crime and violence. There are similar conflicts in the mother-son relationship between Lena Younger and Walter Lee Younger in Lorraine Hansberry's 1959 play *A Raisin in the Sun*. Iris and Lena experience a deep disappointment in their sons' failings, yet in their eyes redemption is always a possibility. Most notably, in the penultimate scene of *A Raisin in the Sun*, Walter Lee rebuffs an offer from the white man from the Clybourne Park Improvement Association after the latter tries to convince the Younger family not to move to that white residential area. Following the altercation, with profound pride Lena says to Walter's wife, Ruth, "He finally come into his manhood today, didn't he? Kind of like a rainbow after the rain" (Hansberry 1996, 146). Unfortunately, before Roxie could fulfill his mother's expectations as Walter Lee manages to do, he dies. The certainty that this expectation will never be fulfilled because of Roxie's death is one source of the deep sorrow Iris experiences.

Jamaican men raised solely by their mothers often express reverence and a constant affirmation for these mothers' role in their lives, indicating the special bond that mother and son share. Raymond T. Smith (1956) refers to this tendency among Afro-Caribbean people as matrifiliation. Reggae and dancehall music feature numerous songs about "Mama," some by women but most by men, who dominate the popular music industry. These songs praising mothers are interspersed with the frequent offerings from male artists of highly sexualized, sometimes misogynistic songs about young women. Despite the glorification of single mothers' resilience in Jamaican culture, however, we cannot ignore the gender frictions that exist in these relationships.

Vigil does not comment on Roxie's father, and we can assume that he does not play a role in his son's life. As a result, parental blame falls on Iris, whose ritualistic idealizing of Roxie is in large part an attempt to absolve herself of any responsibility she thinks she might have for his tragedy. Early in the story, we see her perform a common practice found among Black parents throughout the African Diaspora: excessive punishment of children in a misguided effort to protect them from an early death at the hands of another Black youth or the police. These punishments are enduring symptoms of the cycle of violence produced during transatlantic slavery and colonialism. Her physical punishment of Roxie begins after she discovers that he has started to carry a gun. These beatings, of course, do not have the desired outcome and arguably harden Roxie even more. As a poor Black child he has already been framed by social expectations and law enforcement as capable of enduring physical maltreatment and deserving of such (see Patton 2017). Additionally, the trauma that Roxie experiences from living in a violent community, as evidenced by his school composition, is arguably heightened by this experience of violence within the home (see Crawford-Brown 2010). His aggression toward his mother later on, after she refuses to wash his bloody shirt, may be his attempt to assert his position as a man who can no longer be scolded and punished.

As Iris goes from being a disciplinarian to a compliant mother, then almost her son's victim, and finally a mourner, she suffers at the junctures of maternal love, violence, and grief. Roxie's demise may or may not be related to her parental choices, but in the final analysis his own motivations and the social milieu in which he is caught and eventually dies transcend Iris's role as his mother. Deeply rooted racial and gender ideologies and historical and contemporary power structures ultimately place him in a precarious social position: he is a Black man from a poor background, operating in a system of power that was neither designed by him nor expected to serve him; and he becomes invested in the very same power structure that oppresses then kills him.

Roxie: Violence and the Precarity of Poor Black Manhood

In August 2010, three months after the Tivoli Incursion and two months after the arrest of Christopher "Dudus" Coke, the police killed one of Jamaica's most wanted men, someone who was allegedly responsible for up to one hundred murders. Cedric "Doggie" Murray was a member of the notorious Stone Crusher gang and a known contract killer. Like many other gangs in Jamaica, Stone Crusher had transnational affiliations with the United States, the source of its guns. Murray himself had lived in the United States for a while, and his involvement in crime began there. He was eventually sent to prison and then deported to Jamaica, where he soon became integrated into criminal networks. Once the authorities stepped up their hunt for him, he found refuge in Tivoli Gardens. He was among the men who fought with the police and military during the May 2010 incursion and, at least for a time, escaped capture.

Even more newsworthy than the death of Cedric Murray was the discovery of his diary by the police, which they found on his body alongside his gun. Subsequently, excerpts from the diary were published in various Jamaican newspapers and on social media sites:

> My life right now is a jigsaw puzzle with a missing piece, my woman. I am in great distress and agony. When does my pain end? . . . she make [sic] me happy and I make her unhappy. . . . My gun is my best friend[;] we are always together, always. . . . I have seen all my friends killed by the police in cold blood or shoot out. I make no excuse for my past. I am a real gangster hard-core. (*Gleaner* 2010a)

"Doggie's Diary," as it was dubbed, portrayed not a two-dimensional image of a cold-blooded killer and social menace, but instead a young man who thought deeply about his life, his society, his role in it, his responsibilities as a man to his woman and children, and his mortality. Numerous letters and public opinion articles commented on what the diary revealed about Murray's personality. People who had known him weighed in as well. For instance, in an interview with the media his high school teacher described him as a polite, "quiet and unassuming" boy who loved to read cowboy comics (*Gleaner* 2010b).[15] Whether he could have been rehabilitated became a topic of public debate as well (Reid 2010).

One of the perspectives offered was by Ian Boyne (2010) in the *Gleaner*, in an article titled "That Doggie Diary." Boyne saw the diary as an opportunity to have a conversation about how social factors, especially economic status, affect whether a person turns to crime and violence: "It is true that poverty does not deterministically 'cause' crime and produce criminals and terrorists. But it is also a fact that economic deprivation and social alienation are associated with certain types of outcomes." His comments track with the approach used by the Letters from the Dead project to examine the structural scope of violence. As such, Cedric Murray's diary was one of the dramaturgical influences behind the construction of Roxie as a character. Like Murray, Roxie was initiated into violence at an early age and died at the hands of state agents while he was still young.

The play traces Roxie's experiences from childhood to adulthood in three central scenes. In the first, his mother, Iris, reads a brilliantly written school composition in which he articulates his concerns about violence in his community and his aspirations for his future. In the second, she finds a gun in his schoolbag, which epitomizes his loss of innocence as well as his forced transition into manhood. In the third scene, after he has become a known gang leader, he erupts in anger at his mother after she refuses to wash a blood-stained shirt. These scenes establish how the community and the country at large have shaped his life choices. Roxie's frequent mood shifts indicate a struggle to reconcile the various roles he plays in his community with his positioning as a Black Jamaican man from an impoverished family who remains on the fringes of society, despite the power he exercises over his enemies and the fear with which they regard him. His final monologue is particularly evocative. After he almost hits Iris, his mood changes to one of conciliation and sadness:

> Mama yuh know sey me love yuh man. Sometime me jus talk hard to yuh for me under pressure, seen? How yuh tink mi feel when dem kill all Andre? Him was just a likkle youth. An him was so sensible. Him deserve better dan dat. Why tings like dat haffi happen? Life is just a book of puzzlement . . .

He then quickly shifts to a vengeful persona:

> North Side man a go feel it fi this. Dem fi know seh dem can't cross dis yah border. Nuff a dem a go tun duppy tonight or a no me name Conqueror.

After turning his rage toward the audience, he combines a self-righteous judgment of Jamaican elites for their hypocrisy with an assertion of his status as a leader in his community:

> Wha, weh you a look pon me fah? Yu tink yuh better dan mi? Look inna di mirror and examine yuself! Run along Mr. and Miss Innocent because you are jus a vampire. You tink you coulda live if we never a fight we one anodder? Open your eyes. Me a di master now. None shall escape. Yu done know. (Lawes et al., 2015, 32)[16]

Like other men in Jamaica with limited education, Roxie does not have access to the sociocultural and economic networks and wealth that allow elite men of various races to exercise political control over the country. Within his community, however, he can gain access to economic capital through the informal economy, to protomilitary power through illegal guns, and to the respect of the community through his role as its provider and protector. His community becomes a protonational entity, his gang serves as his governmental system, and his guns are his munitions to show dominance in a hostile environment.

Gang members, men involved in crime, and those who serve as protectors of their communities often refer to themselves as "soldiers" and to conflict as "wars"; they also sometimes use military and governmental titles for informal community leaders and protectors. Among these are the titles "general" and "the president" (as Christopher Coke was called).[17] Roxie, whose title is "conqueror," is the leader of the Conqueror Crew when he is killed. These titles and symbols are not merely meant to evoke deference and perform fearlessness; they are distinctly attached to gender norms and expectations. Barry Chevannes (2001) states that among the ways Afro-Caribbean boys and men prove their manhood are: serving as protector and provider for their families; eschewing open displays of emotion, especially sadness; focusing on immediate accumulation of wealth in order to support women, their families, and their communities; and displaying dominance over women, especially in sexual relationships. These codes circulate and shift in different contexts. Once boys begin earning money, no matter at what age, they begin to be seen as men. This yearning for financial independence, combined with lower expectations for boys than girls in academic performance, as well as opportunities to earn a lot of money in jobs that require limited education, can in turn affect their performance and attendance in school (Figueroa 2004; Lindsay 2018; Miller 1991).[18] Amid generational poverty, gender expectations and norms become intertwined with economic survival and the desire for wealth that confers social status in a capitalist society.

Roxie was almost on track to becoming the lawyer or doctor his mother wanted him to be. But preparing for a professional career requires many years of study and, for those living in poverty, tremendous economic sacrifices. Roxie got a scholarship to a top high school, but his grades soon began to slip, coinciding with, or caused by, his interest in crime. The play does not detail how Roxie was initiated into crime or explore whether he had other reasons to drop out of high school. However, it is safe to assume that this happened because of his family's economic needs, combined with his own early maturity, individual motivation to become a leader in his community, and rejection of the social expectations that he should have a formal middle-class career—expectations that benefit those already born into the middle-income and rich classes. There are other men from a similar socioeconomic background who might have chosen a conventional career path despite its difficulties, but Roxie did not.

It is difficult to speak about the suppression of Black men while also maintaining that they are capable of bad decisions, just as it is difficult to speak about Black women's experiences with racism and sexism without treating them as perpetual victims. Common rhetoric in the African Diaspora portrays Black men as endangered, at risk, and marginalized. These conversations usually call attention to high rates of Black male deaths and incarceration and their victimization by the police and racist white people. Some scholars have directly challenged feminist critiques of patriarchy and male privileging among Black people by focusing on how Black men suffer racial and gender discrimination historically and currently (Curry 2017; Johnson 2018; Miller 1991, 2004).[19]

Avoiding the dichotomy of privileged versus oppressed that often pervades conversations about Black men's actions, *Vigil* offers a path through which to view working-class Black men involved in crime as both active subjects and objects of others' actions; as marginalized by the wider society, but dominant in their communities. Where manhood is intricately linked to the ability to provide for, protect, and defend one's family and community, guns and other lethal weapons can perform both material and symbolic roles to safeguard sociopolitical power. Control of guns serves a crucial purpose in the absence of other means to access this power, such as formal political office, middle- or upper-class position, control over the state's police forces, and higher education. Marlon Moore, who worked for many years as a violence interrupter with the Peace Management Initiative, surmises that the gun is for all intents and purposes a phallic symbol, a marker of manhood and power (pers. comm., 2019). This significance is affirmed in the loving way in which Cedric "Doggie" Murray referred to his gun in his diary, and in Jamaican popular culture, especially gun music in dancehall.[20] Imani M. Tafari-Ama (2006, 44) writes, "Having grown accustomed to surviving by the fear caused by his 'tool' many inner-city men feel powerless without it." This indicates that the power wielded by men involved in crime and violence is unstable. Although several powerful gang leaders enjoy impunity in Jamaica, they are still unequal to the men who control formal politics. This imbalance was strikingly visible in the West Kingston Incursion, just as it is in the state's success in killing many notorious men involved in crime and violence. Formal political and military power often dominates in a stable nation-state in which there is either general deference among citizens for the government's authority or widespread governmental coercion of the population. Moreover, lethal rivalries among gangs, crews, and dons and their marginalized communities make their power insecure in contrast with state forces.

The story of Roxie's family also illustrates the dependency of poor Jamaicans on their formal political representatives. In one scene, Iris speaks positively about her relationship with the community's member of Parliament

(MP), who enabled her to get the house she currently lives in. She is an unofficial political worker who cooperates with the MP to obtain resources for the community. For example, with the MP's help, she was able to get computers for the community's internet café and help build a homework center (Lawes et al., 2015, 12). Like his mother, Roxie himself participates in this unofficial political relationship. The evening before he dies, he meets with the MP. When the soldiers come to kill him, he tries to leverage this political connection, only to find out from them that they are acting on the same MP's orders. Thus, the patriarchal military, economic, and political power of the state prevails. Through this extrajudicial killing, conducted with impunity, the MP and his henchmen send the message that they can win the war with Roxie in the domain of formal power as well as in that of criminal activity. In addition to exerting their military power over Roxie, the soldiers rape his girlfriend, Shanika. While Iris's grief emerges from her parental affection for Roxie and her disappointment and guilt because of her perceived failings as a mother, Shanika's experiences allow insight into the intricacies of loss from the perspective of women who have forged sexual and romantic relationships with men involved in crime and violence.

Shanika: Love in the Shadow of Violence

One of the play's major achievements is that it lends a voice to women attached to men involved in crime, women who suffer because of larger circumstances and structures in which loving relationships are heavily constrained by violence. Throughout the African Diaspora, Black women's labors as defenders of families and communities, as activists in Black radical movements (including armed struggle), and as wives and girlfriends loyal to their partners are so important that we associate these tendencies with Black womanhood in general. In the context of Black men involved in illicit activities like organized crime, popular cultural tropes have developed around Black women's love and support.

Because of the global influence of hip-hop in relation to other Black popular music forms, perhaps the most commonly circulated trope of the loyal girlfriend or wife is the "ride-or-die chick" as depicted in songs like Apache's "Gangsta Bitch" (1993) and "'03 Bonnie and Clyde" (2003) by Jay-Z featuring Beyoncé.[21] The ride-or-die chick is usually a young, sexy Black woman who assists her man in illicit activities and commits to keeping him safe even at the cost to her own freedom or life. She was particularly popular as a trope in hip-hop during the late 1990s and 2000s, when that genre of music became part of the global mainstream and more marketable to white consumers. Margaret Hunter and Kathleen Soto (2009) argue that amid the "pornographic gaze" in mainstream hip-hop during the 2000s, which depicted Black women as hypersexual beings or as gold diggers only interested in men's money,[22] the ride-or-die chick was one of the few images of Black women as noble and caring. Similarly, in movies depicting Black men involved in crime, such as the US film *Belly* (1998) and the Jamaican film *Shottas* (2002), the loyal girlfriends may be secondary to the plot, but they are essential to understanding how the main characters receive sexual pleasure, love, and support in the Black community.

In Jamaican popular culture, perhaps the best articulation of the dynamics of Shanika and Roxie's relationship can be found in dancehall artiste Tanya Stephens's song "Gangsta Gal" (2004), featuring dancehall artiste Spragga Benz, from her hugely acclaimed album *Gangsta Blues*. "Gangsta Gal" describes a woman assisting her man in criminal activities and going to great lengths to protect him. In the lyrics Stephens lists all the things she is willing to do for her man, including hiding his gun from the police, loading his gun, keeping his money safe, and lying on the witness stand. Spragga Benz in turn pledges his commitment to her despite having multiple other women. Notwithstanding Spragga Benz's input, the woman's perspective is the point of departure for "Gangsta Gal," which allows some nuance with respect to the gender power dynamics depicted in the song. In a later song, "These Streets Don't Love You like I Do" (2006), Stephens depicts the downside of this kind of relationship. "These Streets" focuses mostly on the loneliness faced by women involved with men engaged in crime and the added stresses that result when these men go to prison. The song therefore emphasizes that this loyalty often entails a tremendous personal cost. Like "These Streets," *A Vigil for Roxie* complicates the two-dimensional trope of the ride-or-die chick as well as the tough exterior of the gangsta gal by making Shanika one of the most compelling characters with whom the audience sympathizes.

For Shanika, Roxie's death and her violation constitute the ultimate traumas that emerge from her relationship with him. She is somewhat aware of her dangerous positioning before these events occur. In one scene she boldly declares the sacrifices she has made to keep him safe, even though she has not gained substantial economic benefits from her relationship with him. In an argument, she erupts so assertively that Roxie is forced to placate her, even after she insults him:

> A so you waah do mi, Roxie? Yuh figet sey a mi have yuh back out deh? How much time mi pre the corner fi yuh and tell yuh who a plot gainst you and a try sell you out. . . . Yuh better go deal! Leggo affa mi bwoy.[23]

Even after she calls him a boy, Roxie shows virtually no aggression toward her and is at his softest and most vulnerable around her:

> ROXIE: Cho Shanika man, jus cool nuh. A me, Roxie, you a deal wid so?
> SHANIKA: Me sey fe let me go man!
> ROXIE: Shanika! Cho baby! (Lawes et al., 2015, 10)[24]

Roxie's attachment to Shanika is evident in the fact that she is the only character who physically touches him, in a tender scene when she braids his hair. For this scene Lawes depicted Shanika's actions by looking down and interlacing her fingers in a braiding movement, and depicted Roxie's positioning by looking up with her head leaning to one side. It is overall a sensual though conflict-filled scene. In contrast, there are no scenes with Roxie and the other characters (with the exception of Iris), and his monologue toward the end indicates that he distrusts most people.

Shanika herself gains some social currency from her relationship with Roxie, who is a powerful man in their community. Yet the pleasure she enjoys in this relationship has limits, and her loyalty has severe consequences. When the soldiers come to get him, Shanika is forced to witness the violent murder of the man she loves. Afterward, they rape her as punishment for her involvement with him and as a means of asserting their military power. Shanika's monologue, which narrates her torture at the hands of soldiers, was inspired by Salima's monologue in Lynn Nottage's 2010 play *Ruined*, which is set during the civil war in the Democratic Republic of the Congo (1998–2003). *Ruined* depicts the stories of women whose sexual and reproductive lives are almost irreversibly damaged by the war, mostly through the sexual violence that was an integral part of it. By signifying on this well-known monologue, the coauthors of *Vigil* depict the rape of Shanika as an instance in which sex is weaponized as a tool of torture and control.

Shanika's monologue is undoubtedly the most difficult to handle from the perspective of the audience and performer. Not only does it narrate Roxie's death in detail, it does so through a character who has also been violated. Furthermore, as in all cases in which sexual violence must be described or represented, the dramatic goal was to give an account of the rape without descending into gratuitous violence. The performance technique the play's creators eventually settled on allowed the character to momentarily embody the position of first-person witness while not depicting the scene in the actor's delivery. Though Lawes switched between Shanika's and the soldiers' voices during the scene, the soldiers did not appear as characters, and the action of the assault was not depicted in any way. As Ford-Smith explained, in the actor's delivery it is important "not to sensationalize the violence ... to have her do it almost deadpan," almost looking through rather than at the audience (pers. comm., 2015). My experience of this scene as an audience member is that the decision to have Lawes not emote until the very end was more intuitive than counterintuitive, if one is guided by how victims and survivors tend to give account of their violation. It made the scene the most powerful of the play. Though the audience tended to visibly and verbally react during most of the 2015 performance, complete silence and a somber air fell over the room when Shanika narrated Roxie's death and her assault:

> One tek out a Glock and fire one shot. Just one. And Roxie stop talk. One a dem sey "Shut up yuh mout. No you name bad gal. No you deh wid bad man. Bad girls don't cry. No mek up no noise." Him push mi down and di one wid di Glock turn it pon me. Di other one draw down him pants. "Mek mi see what yuh man a go say now." And dem a do what dem waan to do. All di while the sun did a shine bright, bright through the hole dem inna the zinc. After dem go way everything get quiet. So quiet. Like no shot never fire and everybody still a sleep. Like nobody no hear nutten. (Lawes et al., 2015, 24)[25]

It might be tempting to view Shanika through the lens of dramatic tragedy. Certainly, she is in the story because of her connection to a flawed and ill-fated man, like the Bride in Wole Soyinka's play *Death and the King's Horseman* (1975) or Ophelia in William Shakespeare's *Hamlet* (1601). In both mainstream theatre and popular culture, so many representations of women attached to troubled men are situated in a male perspective. It is true that Shanika's suffering emerges from her relationship with Roxie. Yet she exercises significant agency in her relationship with him even if not with the soldiers, and she is a major character in the play.

In the first version of the play, devised and written in 2010, Shanika was not fleshed out. Her function was to narrate Roxie's death in graphic detail. However, the character developed depth when the process of devising the play through improvisation became more sophisticated. Lawes remarked, "The more we kept doing it ... the more each character became solidified. We came to address more of the issues that Shanika would have been interested in; because we started off with our focus on Roxie" (pers. comm., 2015). Shanika came to embody significant aspects of the ethnographic research conducted for the "Memory, Urban Violence and Performance in Jamaican Communities" project. For example, the details of Roxie's murder were based on the death of a young man from a community in West Kingston who was killed in the same way and whose mother had recounted the event of his death to Honor Ford-Smith.[26] With regard to Shanika's violation, although the playwrights did not draw on an individual Jamaican woman's story, her experience is based on information recounted by women who participated in the research project. One finding from the interviews was that there were frequent instances of sexual harassment and in some cases sexual assault by the police (Ford-Smith, pers. comm., 2015), even though this aspect of gang and state violence is marginalized in mainstream discussions. For instance, it is publicly known that sexual relations took place between soldiers/policemen and the women in West Kingston following the 2010 incursion. Even though this fact has not been fully analyzed in research as an example of the sexual aspect of militarism in Jamaica, the media has featured reports on it. For instance, Nationwide 90FM reported that six soldiers were disciplined for "inappropriate behaviour." One of them was sentenced to military prison for "soliciting sex" from a woman, and his supervisor demoted (Minto 2015). Another media outlet, the *Jamaica Star* (2010), a popular tabloid, published a sensationalized story claiming that women and girls in West Kingston were competing for the sexual attention of the soldiers. Even when the women involved ostensibly consented to these relationships, the power imbalance is palpable since the soldiers and police were part of an occupying force responsible for the deaths and detention of the men from the community.[27]

A few scholars have attended to the links between sexual violence and civilian and state violence in the Caribbean. Claudette Crawford-Brown's (2010) *Children in the Line of Fire* documents her psychological research with children in violent communities in Jamaica and Trinidad and Tobago. The book includes reproductions of drawings by the children who participated in the study. One of the most disturbing drawings is by a ten-year-old girl: a man with a gun comes to a mother and demands sexual access to her daughter. Also, as Imani M. Tafari-Ama (2006, 47) states, "While not homogeneous, women are particularly disadvantaged in the inner-city scenario where women's bodies are themselves literal battlefields in the reproduction of structural, discursive and gender power dynamics. Women are often raped as a statement of conquest over some men by other men."

Shanika's rape is arguably the play's greatest irresolution. While ritual enables Iris's testimony on Roxie's death and helps her achieve some measure of healing, the specter of the sexual violence that Shanika experiences weighs heavily within the story, even though it is limited to the one scene in which she narrates it. This is in a sense reflective of the reality in which sexual assault is generally suppressed in narratives around organized crime and state violence in Jamaica. Shanika continues to live, but the play has no representation of her after her monologue; she disappears with the same swiftness as she appears. When Iris calls out to her and to Roxie's cousin Dimples at the end, Miss Robb enters and states, "They're gone Iris. They want to forget" (Lawes et al., 2015, 26). Miss Robb's interpretation of Shanika's departure is not reinforced by Shanika's own words, though the quickness in which she departs indicates a struggle to move on with her life. In contrast, Roxie's cousins, Dimples and Stacey, make direct statements about not wanting to participate in the vigil. Of course, forgetting would be easier for people like Dimples and Stacey, who have not experienced direct violation, even though they grapple with grief and loss. But this act of forgetting or refusing to memorialize is still painful. Through these two characters, the play examines how the suppression of memories might occur within a milieu of violence and in anti-Black socioeconomic global systems that already try to frame most violence against Black people as forgettable or nonexistent.

Stacey and Dimples: Forgetting and Economic Survival

As everyone gets trapped in the tentacles of neoliberal economics, survival means negotiating the state of affairs that David Harvey (2007, 33) refers to as "the financialization of everything." How do mourning and memorialization fit into a system that relies mainly on what is marketable, quantifiable, and infinitely exchangeable, and that is committed to the farce that the most important aspects of economics are current investment opportunities and their financial rewards? We only have to look at successive Jamaican governments' increasing privatization of the country's natural resources (especially beaches) and their plans to lease land protected by environmental and other laws to understand how deeply the state has disregarded the lives and well-being of its predominantly Black citizens.[28]

Vigil spends a great deal of time on economic commentary, particularly through two satirical secondary characters: the oblivious and privileged middle-class woman, and the vendor in the tourist zone who sells all kinds of products and services and is willing to barter marijuana for guns. However, its exploration of people's lives within a global neoliberal system is most poignantly embodied in the characters of Stacey and Dimples, Roxie's cousins, who were raised by their aunt Iris. Stacey was sent to the United States as a child by Iris, presumably to have a better life and perhaps to make enough money to take care of her family in Jamaica, while Dimples is probably unemployed and living off Stacey and her aunt.

Stacey represents the working- and lower-middle-class people of the Jamaican Diaspora, who struggle in the United States even while those at home regard them as well off. She harbors a quiet resentment toward her aunt for sending her away and forcing her to deal with xenophobia, child abuse, and isolation in the United States. However, this resentment is somewhat tempered by her own realization that migration is a last resort to which many Jamaicans have turned. One of the more ironic features of neoliberal rhetoric in Jamaica (and in other Caribbean and Latin American countries) is that politicians promised their policies would lead to widespread prosperity for the country, but these policies have increased inequalities to such an extent that many must leave Jamaica to achieve even a modicum of economic well-being. Jamaicans in the diaspora contribute to the country by sending remittances, which constitute the country's main source of foreign exchange, and more recently by increasingly purchasing Jamaican real estate. When the audience first meets Stacey, she is in the United States interviewing for a wide range of jobs that are not commensurate with her level of education and experience. She had been a supervisor at a travel agency, but now she is applying to become a caregiver for an elderly person, and having a "degree in Psychology from City College" seems irrelevant to the jobs for which she is applying. Stacey juggles the constant demands from Iris and Dimples for money and her responsibility to her son, whose father is in prison in the United States. She does not want to dwell on the tragedy of Roxie's death, and says as much to Iris: "me nah come a no more memorial. Right now[,] mi no waa remember all wah tek place" (Lawes et al., 2015, 17–18).[29] She is preoccupied with managing her financial commitments, motherhood, and bail money for her child's father.

While Stacey is caught within the system as a worker who has personal ties in both the United States and Jamaica, Dimples reaps the rewards of Stacey's labor as her beneficiary. Dimples represents quotidian survival, with very few prospects for upward mobility—the scenario in which so many impoverished Jamaicans live. Most importantly, Dimples seems to have surrendered herself to that scenario and has found a way to thrive within it. Unapologetically materialistic and unashamedly demanding of Stacey's financial support, Dimples does not grieve because doing so would limit her ability to focus on consuming as much as possible. It is through the character of Dimples that the notion of Black men as expendable emerges most clearly, when she declares that there is no sense in Iris building a memorial since so many men have already died. She is only interested in men who are alive: "De whole a de man dem dead already. Live man deh a dance and a live man me want" (Lawes et al., 2015, 18).[30]

She goes on to suggest that Iris should learn more about the possibility that DNA evidence would enable the men who shot Roxie to be identified. Even DNA testing as a tool of justice is financialized by Dimples, insofar as she sees it as a commodity that can be imported. One of the more hilarious statements in the play indicates Dimples's conflation of DNA with DNA testing, as well as her view that the vigil will not be necessary if Roxie's killers are punished: "God bless di man who invent DNA. A dat we need—dem need fi bring DNA come a Jamaica. Maybe that time Miss Iris can stop build memorial" (Lawes et al., 2015, 18).[31] For Dimples, the fact that Roxie's killers haven't been caught and punished means that there is no space for healing; the memorial serves no purpose. Thus, only the material, legalistic space of the justice system counts, not the spiritual, contemplative one that Iris relies on. In the community workshop held the day after the performance, the attendees in my discussion group generally expressed derision for Dimples and focused on her selfishness. She seemed reprehensible to them because she loves money and looks out only for herself, despite the social expectation that Black women must be self-sacrificing. Thus, she exists in sharp contrast with the other women in her family and Shanika—all of whom are preoccupied with taking care of their families and supporting the men in their lives. In the workshop session that I led, after one woman commented on Dimples's selfishness I asked the group whether her behavior could be interpreted another way, as a coping mechanism and a method of self-preservation. After a long pause, they agreed.

Dimples ignores her aunt's calls to help with the vigil and goes to a dance instead. Dancehall music is usually part of Jamaican memorial events, such as funerals, Nine Nights, and vigils, though it is not as dominant as religious songs and music. Iris's vigil actually begins with a dancehall selector getting ready to play music. However, Dimples sets up a sharp dichotomy between the two spaces. She rejects the vigil and its associations with loss, memory, and grief and chooses the dancehall and its repertoires of enjoyment, displays of money, eroticism, and occasional violence. These differences are clearly demarcated through Dimples's body as she dons a green wig, applies skin-bleaching cream, and practices the puppy tail, a popular dance that emphasizes the dancer's buttocks by mimicking a puppy wagging its tail. This self-presentation contrasts with Iris's donning of a long Revival dress and singing of Revival songs with their religious content.

Stacey's position as the mother of a Black boy, the spouse of a Black man in prison in the United States, and the main provider for her family back in Jamaica limits the extent to which she can participate in an alternative performance of enjoyment, as Dimples does. Working in a rampantly capitalist economy and doing care labor in her family means she lacks the emotional resources or leisure time necessary to enjoy entertainment or, for that matter, to participate in memorial practices. Dimples and, to a lesser extent, Stacey represent forgetting. They embody the suppression of memories as they seek to survive within a global system in which neoliberal capitalism disregards the humanity of Black and poor people while profiting from their labor. To forget is not simply to try to erase a person, an event, or a historical period from individual memory. It is impossible for anyone to erase all traces of their own experiences. Stacey's proclamation that she does not want to remember what took place is a conscious decision not to participate in the performance of that memory. If memory is performed through embodied acts such as building memorials and holding vigils, so too is forgetting, and both entail selective engagement with the past (see Connerton 1989; Hutchison 2013; Roach 1996; D. Taylor 2003).

In addition to each having conscious reasons for their refusal to participate in the vigil, Stacey and Dimples are somewhat disconnected from the loss of Roxie—Dimples through her seeming lack of a close relationship with him, and Stacey through her residence in the United States. Moreover, while Dimples and Stacey have lost a loved one and continue to feel the effects of this loss, they did not experience the violence through which Roxie was taken. At the same time, they are not immune from the violent milieu that consumed and destroyed Roxie's life, given their own personal positioning within families and communities that are plagued by violence and as Black women in the Americas. When Roxie proclaims "None shall escape" in his final monologue as a message to his enemies (Lawes et al., 2015, 23), he ironically sums up his and his family's, community's, and region's relationship to violence. It is perhaps the most haunting statement of the entire play.

A Vigil for Roxie as a Political Event

After the first performance of *Vigil*, which took place in 2010 at the Hemispheric Institute of Performance and Politics in Bogotá, Colombia, the audience was moved to tears. Mostly white American theatre practitioners and theorists, they came onto the stage at the end in a groundswell of emotion—to the deep dislike of director and coauthor Eugene Williams, as he recounted to me (pers. comm., 2014). In his thinking, the audience's outpouring of emotion did not translate into serious reflection. Williams explained that he and the other creators had resisted suggestions that the play be produced as commercial theatre because it had to incorporate audience feedback and critical thought rather than be viewed as solely an art product: "I don't want it to be seen as a theatrical or aesthetic event. It's a political event." That dimension went beyond the play's emotional affects: "If you are moved and then you can tell me critically what moved you in this clash of forces, and you can see the political argument, that's different." Commensurate with the aim to focus on critical reflection, after that first performance in Colombia, *Vigil* became more minimalist in its character depictions, costuming, and set design. When the play was next staged, at Rutgers University in New Jersey in 2012, the audience responded differently. Williams recounted that a woman who had also attended the first performance came up to him: "She remembered it being a very moving experience, but this one was not as moving. . . . This one made me think more" (pers. comm., 2014).

Community-engaged theatre aims to utilize the art form to contribute to social change through pedagogy, which requires an understanding of aesthetics beyond the pleasures of art. However, this does not discount the expression of emotions and the development of empathy. In fact, *Vigil*'s aesthetic relies primarily on the emotive space that is opened up through memorial rituals innovated by Black women in order to construct its political critique of violence. Honor Ford-Smith underscored this aspect of the performance when commenting on the audience's emotional reaction at the 2010 performance. She viewed it as a "moment of self-consciousness about what has happened." In her thinking, following their crying, the audience members would have then experienced "a moment of deep discomfort" about their own ability to solve the problem (pers. comm., 2015). Since the play's structure changed after the 2010 performance, it is difficult to speculate about how subsequent audiences would have reacted at the end. Moreover, most audiences for whom it was performed after 2010 were in Jamaica or communities in the Jamaican Diaspora, and their relationship to the story was different from the largely academic and non-Jamaican audience in Colombia. When *Vigil* was staged in Jamaica in 2014 and 2015 for members of communities affected by gang and state violence, audiences used the play as a point of departure, speaking in the discussions that followed about the social problems most of them have experienced firsthand. At the 2015 performance, I noticed that none of the audience members commented directly on the play during the discussion. As a theatre lover and practitioner, I found this unsettling. *Vigil* had not just highlighted the deep embeddedness of violence in Jamaica and the Americas and the importance of memorializing to excavate the roots of this violence, it had also displayed some of the best innovations in Jamaican theatre. The script, props, costuming, and Lawes's virtuosity as a performer made for a master class in the combining of African Diasporic ritual performance and mimetic storytelling with various other theatre methods, especially minimalism; role and space shifting; and the removal/neglect of the fourth wall. It had taken a long process to get from the original script to where the play arrived in 2015, so I wondered whether the audience was not interested in the production process. Before the performance, Ford-Smith and Anique Jordan, curators of the exhibition *Song for the Beloved*, had spoken to the audience about the research and artistic process. The chair of the event, Afolashadé, also explained that this was going to be a different type of theatre, not the kind that would suit anyone "who comes for a performance and to sit down and be entertained."[32] However, I had expected some commentary on the play as a work of art.

An audience's ability to view *Vigil* as a work of political theory and as a representation of the Letters from the Dead project's research is linked to the play's status as an artistic work. Perhaps, for the audience who saw the 2014 and 2015 performances, much about the play was so identifiable and familiar that they saw it explicitly as pedagogy, or a "political event" as Williams states. Many people approached me and Ford-Smith with suggestions to raise money to take the play to different communities in Jamaica. The question of finding an actor who could perform it elsewhere also emerged. This person would have to undertake the demanding task of performing the play in different communities in short periods of time. Or, there would have to be a switch from the monodramatic structure to one with multiple actors.

Since 2015 (and as of 2022), *Vigil* has not been staged again, though there are plans to do so. However, the exhibition *Song for the Beloved* has been installed five times since 2015 in different locations. As a theatre production *Vigil* requires substantial resources, including the labors of the actor, director, and stage manager, rehearsal time, rewrites, travel, meals, and salaries for everyone involved. These expenses are considerable despite the fact that the people who have worked on the play and other aspects of Letters from the Dead have been paid less than they would receive for a commercial theatre project. This is because the performance relies heavily on grants, since there are no admission fees. (In Jamaica *Vigil* has been community focused and geographically based in the spaces that inspired it, while in other countries it has depended on hosting from educational institutions, especially universities and conferences.) These practical, less exciting elements of theatre work affect every production, but take on more vital significance in projects such as *Vigil* and the other elements of Letters from the Dead. In our neoliberal times, projects that are not seen as profitable—cultural productions and social welfare provisions—receive less and less public funding and governmental support (see Nielsen and Ybarra 2012). Moreover, while the play and the wider Letters from the Dead project involve cross-class collaboration, they are primarily about working-class and poor Black people, who lack the social and economic capital to invest in them. Additionally, the creators maintain that its Jamaican performances must always be held in urban spaces accessible to working-class people and made available without admission fees. This means that it will continue to rely on grant funding. Unlike the popular theatre industry, which gets significant sponsorship from private companies, plays like *Vigil* are not driven primarily by entertainment, which in Jamaica often involves racial, gender, and class caricaturing.[33] Productions like *Vigil* force us to take a look at the interior lives of Black people and the contexts of racial, class, and economic oppression that reproduce violence.

In her introduction to the 2015 performance of *A Vigil for Roxie*, Afolashadé stated that the conversations around violence in Jamaica are "about Black lives." Her unapologetic formulation of the problem centers race within a Black-majority country in which racism is often concealed under classism. She went on to say, "Blackness is not about the color of your skin, but it's a livity" (a lived reality, a philosophy). *Vigil* makes its audience think through the deaths and survival of Black people in a way that excavates painful histories and connects them to present inequalities. At the end of the play, after Iris ceases her idealizing of Roxie, she utters the words "Mi a go try release yu" (I'll try to release you) to her dead son, expressing her desire to not see others suffer his fate and stating her need to carry on with her life. After this final statement, the play ends, and audience members and collaborators on the project come to the stage and read letters from, and to, the dead. The majority of these are about love, family, and community. Participants in the research project on which the play is based wrote these letters, including ones that imagined what their deceased loved ones would say if they could communicate with the living. The play and this ritual afterward emphasize how loss and memory figure in our notions about violence, and connect the past to the present in a cyclical rather than linear way. They create spaces of mourning and memorialization in communities that are marginalized, utilizing the memorial practices originated by the people in these places. Through each character, *A Vigil for Roxie* shows how common experiences of violence take on distinct manifestations based on gender, age, and geographic positioning within and beyond Jamaica. Thus, the play's creators point to a path toward justice in which all viewpoints are needed,

Figure 7. A section of the audience at the staged reading of *A Vigil for Roxie*, 2015. Photo by the author.

even those of the dead; and these viewpoints allow an understanding of the ways in which social hierarchies and structures determine which communities suffer the most from systemic violence. Therefore, memorializing and grief are not just emotional processes, but economic and political ones as well.

CHAPTER 4

Alternative Spaces

Black Self-Making, Space-Making, and the Work of Olive Tree Theatre

It was the first day of the fourth Olive Tree Women's Theatre Festival in October 2015, and I was attending a theatre-writing workshop led by Mwenya Kabwe, a lecturer in theatre and performance studies at the University of Cape Town. She asked us to tell her what kinds of stories we were tired of seeing onstage, and the all-female group responded almost uniformly: plays about apartheid, plays about rape, and plays about poor Black women's oppression. Then, after a lengthy discussion, we realized that maybe the problem was not that those topics are ubiquitous in theatre in South Africa. More accurately, the group felt that the portrayals were often limited to the same narratives about Black people's experiences of racism and patriarchy.

Afterward, we discussed how theatre practitioners can create stories that are not in the mainstream, and Kabwe asked us to come up with an outline for an "unstageable play." I was delighted and intrigued by this assignment, because I was in the process of writing the second act for my play *Afiba and Her Daughters*, which later premiered at Rites and Reason Theatre/Department of Africana Studies at Brown University in 2016. I was thinking about how so many elements of the story I was creating could not work onstage. The play took place over the course of 150 years and chronicled the life of an enslaved Black woman and three generations of her descendants in Jamaica. To show the connections between the past and the present, I had time trips that were not chronological. Also, most of my scenes were short, and I had actors singing in a play that was not a musical. Part of my concern was that my experience of theatre-writing up until then had involved a constant acknowledgment that a playwright must be guided by the practicality of the stage, including the limits of live performance within a small space and the importance of organic flow, while ensuring that the production was translatable to the audience. The latter requirement is subject to racial, gender, class, and ethnic biases, particularly when Black theatre-makers present their plays for majority-white audiences or when artists from the Global South have their work presented to audiences in the Global North. Thus, by engaging with the possibilities for an unstageable play we were not simply considering artistic freedom or technical proficiency in abstract ways. We also had to consciously resist racial, economic, and other constraints on artistic expression in theatre as a commercial activity. In the interest of protecting the attendees' intellectual property because they outlined plays they had not yet written, I will not give examples of the ideas they came up with. However, I will report that what we envisioned was a collection of concepts for plays that were peculiar and compelling, as well as impossible to stage according to current theatre conventions and technology. Later on, I would witness the kinds of ingenuity that are on display when artists are allowed to explore the full range of possibilities that exist in performance—all within one-act plays directed by women. The Olive Tree Women's Theatre Festival, founded by Black woman theatre artist Ntshieng Mokgoro, created the space for these ideas to flourish and for a light to be shone on Black women directors' experimentation, information sharing, and knowledge creation.

While they have been integral to theatre-making and to consciousness-raising about social inequalities in South Africa, Black women directors and playwrights have not historically been given their just regard. The majority of South African theatre artists whose writings have become canonical are men: Zakes Mda, John Kani, Athol Fugard (the most internationally successful South African playwright of the apartheid era), Barney Simon (cofounder of the Market Theatre), and Gibson "Bra Gib" Mthuthuzeli Kente, who is known as the "Father of Township Theatre" and "Father of Black Theatre in South Africa." Only a few women gained mainstream success as playwrights during apartheid, among them Gcina Mhlophe, who eventually became better known as a children's book author, but whose 1985 play *Have You Seen Zandile?* is still one of the most well-known plays written during the apartheid era; and Fatima Dike, whose 1976 play *The Sacrifice of Kreli* was the first play published by a Black South African woman playwright.[1] However, they are exceptions in an industry dominated by men. And while there have been opportunities for women to gain acclaim as playwrights, directing and theatre management are even more exclusive domains.

Among the reasons for this gender disparity is Black women's historically limited access to the urban and suburban spaces in which commercial theatre flourished. These spaces were mostly populated by men, who worked as migrant laborers or in cities in the early twentieth century and early years of apartheid, albeit subject to the controls imposed by racial pass laws. In contrast, women and children largely resided in the poor and under-resourced rural land reserves. Additionally, mainstream theatre and international recognition relied on the playwrights' ability to speak and write in English, and Black women were less likely to master that language because of their marginalization in the education and economic systems. A third reason is that, just as for women across the globe, the business of theatre, with its long hours and constant traveling, does not accommodate the domestic responsibilities that most women face disproportionately to men (see Perkins 1998, 2009).

In the postapartheid era, white women playwrights and directors such as Lara Foot (artistic director and CEO of the Baxter Theatre in Cape Town) and Yaël Farber have attained the most international acclaim among South African women and published their plays widely. Black women, on the other hand, are only recently attaining leadership positions as directors and producers in the country's mainstream theatre. The list includes Warona Seane, former artistic manager of the Soweto Theatre and the first Black woman to run a state theatre; and writer and director Napo Masheane. Still, they have to work amid the legacies of a historical disadvantage in artistic opportunities. The Olive Tree Women's Theatre Festival and Olive Tree Theatre, founded by Black woman theatre artist Ntshieng Mokgoro, sought to redress these disadvantages by providing mentorship and exposure for Black women theatre artists.

In previous chapters, I focused on the theories present in three performances in Jamaica and South Africa, staged from 2009 to 2015, within a tradition of women-led movements for reproductive and sexual rights and community-based antiviolence work. In contrast with Sistren, Mothertongue, and Letters from the Dead, Olive Tree was a physical commercial theatre space that operated primarily as a business, with an accompanying activist commitment to racial and gender justice through mentoring young playwrights and directors. Mokgoro has spoken about the need for alternative spaces to cultivate women's theatre work: "There is still lack of trust in women that they can actually produce work. Olive Tree Theatre for me is an alternative space. This is where women can come any time and just do their work and experiment, even if you fail" (pers. comm., 2015).

I center Mokgoro's conceptualization of alternative spaces to examine the work of Olive Tree Theatre and the Women's Theatre Festival. I argue that Olive Tree contributed to an ongoing process of transgressing oppressive racial, gendered, and economic structures in urban South Africa. The theatre conceived of its environs (first Alexandra and now Marlboro) beyond the narrative of urban decay and volatility usually attached to South Africa's townships and urban peripheries. By serving as an alternative space for theatre in a poor, majority-Black community as well as organizing a festival for women directors in a field dominated by men, Olive Tree fashioned a womanist geography in Alexandra (Alex) and Marlboro. The Women's Theatre Festival emerged from Black South African artistic practices and liberatory ideas that are rooted in Black South African women's self-concepts, activism, space-shaping, and art. By extension, Mokgoro's work as a playwright and the work of the women directors she mentors contribute to carving out spaces within the repertoire of postapartheid South African theatre for a multiplicity of stories. Mokgoro's own artistic approaches wrestle with ongoing projects of personal and communal healing amid the legacies of apartheid. Thus, she and Olive Tree emphasize the importance of theatre to processes of social development and Black freedom in South Africa.

Like the Women's Theatre Festival for which Olive Tree is most well known, the story of the theatre's founding is one of Black space-making and self-making through entrepreneurship and art. Several authors have conceived of self-making as an integral concept in the study of African and African Diasporic communities and identities (Allen 2011; Ulysse 2007). In "The Austin School Manifesto: An Approach to the Black or African Diaspora," Edmund T. Gordon (2007) acknowledges the dominating historical context in which Blackness and African Diasporic identity have been formed. However, the manifesto moves beyond a focus on how Black and African people are unified through the common experience of racist oppression toward a recognition of how Black and African Diasporic people have shaped their identities over various geographies and time periods: "our idea of Diaspora focuses on Black agency and the processes of self-making; the Black/African Diaspora as a transnational cultural, intellectual, and, above all, political project that seeks to name, represent, and participate in Black people's historic efforts to construct our collective identities and constitute them through cultural-political practices dedicated to expressing our full humanity and seeking for liberation" (94).

With a more specific focus on Black women in Jamaica, Gina Athena Ulysse (2007) applies the concept of self-making to her study of informal commercial importers (ICIs) in her book *Downtown Ladies*. Her analysis focuses on the women's forging of a collective identity as successful, savvy, and fashionable Black/dark-skinned business owners amid the classism, sexism, racial/skin-color discrimination, and other suppressive conditions they face in Jamaican society. Ulysse states, "By self-making, I mean the various ways ICIs shape their gendered and racial/color identities through choices that affect how they view themselves and how others perceive them" (10). In ¡*Venceremos?* Jafari S. Allen (2011) similarly attends to the gendered dimensions of Black self-making, here focusing on its interplay with sexuality and the erotic domain in Cuba. He utilizes the concept of "transcendent erotics and politics," which range from "momentary transcendence experienced in flashes of self-awareness, love relationships or *communitas*, to the transgression of the hegemonic rules of a particular public, to the potential transformation of standard practices of the public" (3).

My definition of Black self-making parallels the perspectives offered by these scholars, with attention to the imperatives of Olive Tree Theatre and its existence amid the social, economic, and artistic legacies of apartheid in South Africa. The concept of self-making as applied in this chapter refers to processes of creating strong communities, emancipatory ideas, and individual and communal economic wealth through everyday practices. Black self-making involves constant negotiation and resistance. It is carried out implicitly through economic and cultural ingenuity in the face of extreme denial of opportunity, and explicitly in confrontations with the gatekeepers of racial, gender, and economic systems of oppression. Often, it involves leveraging limited access to resources usually provided for the elites into opportunities for marginalized people. Space-making is fundamentally tied to Black self-making in the sense that Black people have globally had to exercise limited agency amid economic and spatial containment. The story of Alexandra, Ntshieng Mokgoro's birthplace and the original location of Olive Tree Theatre and the Women's Theatre Festival, exemplifies the nexus between Black self-making and space-making within South African urban and peri-urban contexts. Conversely, the theatre's closure in 2020 also exemplifies the precarity faced by theatre institutions and community-centered initiatives founded by working-class Black people in their communities. This indicates the difficulties of space-making and self-making amid the historical and contemporary contexts of economic inequalities and racism.

Alexandra as a Site of Black Space-Making and Self-Making

Poor majority-Black urban spaces throughout the world generally have overwhelmingly negative narratives attached to them. Alexandra is no different in this respect. In 2015, whenever I told the South Africans I met that part of my research was located in Alex—and then in 2018, when it was located in Marlboro—I was cautioned about venturing into such places. Their advice was valid, and it showed their hospitality toward a foreigner who had not spent much time in South Africa. They wanted to ensure that I was properly counseled about exercising caution in my travels. Indeed, Alexandra has a high crime rate, which is connected to its high levels of poverty, overcrowding, and limited infrastructure, in contrast to the neighboring affluent suburb of Sandton and other middle-class and wealthy areas in Johannesburg. Also, in the first two decades of the twenty-first century, it developed a reputation as the main site of xenophobic violence against immigrants from other African countries. In fact, I knew of Alex's reputation as a poor and violent community before I knew of its role in the anti-apartheid struggle and the fact that its historically tense relationship to South African state structures is not simply based on its poverty and volatility but also reflects its function as a major site of Black resistance. Thus, South African governments have treated the township as a nuisance because of its socioeconomic problems as well as its status as home to some of the most militant anti-apartheid activism in the country's history.

Alexandra holds the distinction of being one of very few surviving Black freehold townships in South Africa. These townships were so named because they contained significant amounts of land and numbers of dwellings that were not owned by white people. In apartheid-era South Africa, which was defined by white control of land stolen from Black South Africans, the existence of a large set of Black property owners in urban or peri-urban spaces was an anomaly. Among the most iconic freehold townships were Sophiatown (or the Western Areas of Johannesburg) and Cape Town's District Six; less iconic ones included Korsten (on the outskirts of Port Elizabeth) and Besterspruit (Bonner and Nieftagodien 2008, 3). Most freehold townships were eventually taken over completely and their residents removed or in other ways destabilized by the apartheid government. However, Alexandra maintained a significant amount of nonwhite property ownership throughout the apartheid era.

It became a native township in 1912, when the original owner, a white farmer named H. B. Papenfus, began selling plots of land to Black people. He named the land after his wife, Alexandra, and initially intended it to be a white area; however, its distance from Johannesburg made this unfeasible. Its eventual status as a Black freehold township was possible because it was established one year before the passing of the Natives Land Act of 1913, which limited Black ownership of land to 7 percent and stated that Black people could only occupy or buy land as employees of a white person (South African Government 2013).[2] Most people who ended up owning property in Alexandra were former sharecroppers or labor tenants who had been forced off their land or oppressed by limits placed on the amount of livestock they were allowed to own in Orange Free State and the Transvaal (now Free State and Gauteng). These property owners developed among themselves a distinct identity, emerging from their pride in their relative economic independence and aspiration to the metropolitan lifestyle that came with living close to a major city. Eventually, through legislation such as the Group Areas Act (1950) and the Influx Control Law (1923), the apartheid state prohibited Black ownership of land throughout South Africa and enforced geographic and socioeconomic segregation. White people populated the well-maintained and developed cities and wealthy suburban areas, while Black people were forced into rural communities and poor townships on the peripheries of cities. Pass laws policed the movements of Black people into white spaces; and members of the different racial groups (categorized under the 1950 Population Registration Act as African, Indian [South Asian-descended], coloured [usually mixed race], and European) were only permitted to utilize social services and educational facilities assigned to them. Within this categorization system, Africans and Black people were the most oppressed as they were the main target of apartheid laws. White people exploited Black South Africans' labor while also preventing them from accessing land, wealth, and, at the most basic level, adequate social services. While white South Africans enjoyed standards of living and life expectancy that were on par with those experienced by white people in North America and Europe, Black South Africans experienced living standards and life expectancy that were lower than those that existed in most countries in Africa and the rest of the Global South (L. Thompson 2014).

The migrant labor system, which began before the institutionalization of apartheid, exploited Black people's labor for capitalist gain. To make way for white-controlled mining operations and farms, whole communities were moved to underdeveloped spaces called homelands, land reserves, or Bantustans. As Hannah Evelyn Britton (2005, 10) notes, citing Fiona McLachlan (1987), "these small underdeveloped reservations constituted only 13 percent of the land of South Africa, yet they were intended to hold and sustain over 70 percent of the population." The homelands/land reserves were mainly populated by women and children because of men's employment in the migrant labor system. However, by the latter part of the twentieth century, the expansion of industries and increased wealth among white families led to a demand for mostly Black women's labor in urban and suburban areas. As Britton (2005) writes, women's entry into the migrant labor system further impelled their political activism against apartheid.

Many Black South Africans left land reserves to access better economic opportunities close to major cities and lived in townships like Alexandra and Soweto. Eventually, Alex became a major immigration destination for poor South Africans and people from other African countries. There, racial affiliations were stronger than class affiliations, leading to well-educated and middle-income residents living side by side with the unemployed and poor (Bozzoli 2004, 25). By the 1950s, increasing migration and overcrowding alongside conflicts between new residents and others (particularly property owners) led to various problems, including an increase in crime and violence. The location of Alexandra on the periphery of Johannesburg, the physical closeness in which the population lived (in overcrowded yards rather than individual housing blocks like in Soweto), and the existence of a large class of landowners and politically radical young people eventually led to Alexandra playing a vital role in the anti-apartheid movement. Landholders became increasingly loyal to the African National Congress (ANC) political party, while subtenants, who were not as politically loyal to one party, responded to political leaders who were seen to act in their interests. Meanwhile, the significant population of coloured South African subtenants were mainly affiliated with the Communist Party. Alongside their involvement in these formal political institutions, Alexandra's residents constantly mobilized at the grassroots level, including through activisms that focused on better and more equitable social services such as running water, garbage collection, sewage systems, and public transportation. There were, for example, a series of bus and store boycotts throughout the decades, leading up to major revolts in the latter years of apartheid.

The large number of young residents, who were mostly students, also functioned as a cadre of intellectuals and activists in their own right, forming the Alexandra Youth Congress and building a strong membership in the Congress of South African Students. These younger activists would eventually be key to three major historical events: the 1976 Soweto student protests, the 1986 Six-Day War, and a six-month-long uprising in 1986–87. In 1976, Alexandra was positioned as a major supportive base of the Soweto student uprisings, which began in June and were among the most important protests in apartheid history. These uprisings were met by the deadliest use of force from the apartheid government against children in a single event, and were followed by another protest in Alexandra on the next day. The Six-Day War of 1986, for its part, was a series of riots led by young people and heavily repressed by the police. These events were precipitated by police tear-gassing of mourners at the funeral of Michael Diradeng, a youth leader who had been killed by a security guard. Soon after was the third major event: a six-month-long uprising in which there were standoffs between the police and mostly youth, and burning and destruction of homes, buildings, and sites associated with the police and alleged collaborators with the apartheid system (Bozzoli 2004; Bridger 2018; Britton 2005). These events displayed young people's radicalism, including their willingness to utilize revolutionary violence in confrontation with state officials, gang members, and others who were deemed to be working against Alexandra's survival, racial justice, and the anti-apartheid struggle. Girls and young women participated in this militancy, including practicing their own form of justice against accused perpetrators of sexual violence, which was rampant in the apartheid era and intersected with racial violence (see Bridger 2018; Britton 2005). In sum, Alexandra has served a critical role as a locale of radical politics, including youth militancy. Simultaneously, the township was the target of intense policing from the apartheid government as illustrated in the slum clearances of the 1930s, the removal of significant numbers of the population to Soweto in the 1960s, and various commissions of inquiry from the 1920s to the 1960s.

With the end of apartheid, Alexandra's constant confrontations with the state and repression by the police have subsided. However, the township's socioeconomic problems continue. On April 2, 2019, residents organized a protest called #AlexTotalShutDown to express frustration about irregular garbage and waste collection, inadequate crime-control mechanisms, drug use, and an increase in illegal construction (mostly the erecting of informal homes) in the township, this last a consequence of overcrowding (Dlamini 2019). More recently, in July 2021, following the conviction of former South African president Jacob Zuma for corruption and the worsening of economic inequalities due to COVID-19, Alexandra became a site of violent protest (Ntshidi 2021).

While not as large or as famous as Alexandra, neighboring Marlboro has similarly undergone demographic and socioeconomic problems over the past decades. Freehold land ownership was abolished there after the instituting of apartheid in 1948, and it was branded a "black spot," leading to the forced removal of most of its residents. The remaining population had to be tenants of the government and to live in small, inadequately resourced dwellings. The community is now divided into two sections. The first, Marlboro Gardens, is mainly populated by Indian South Africans and is a residential area. The second, Marlboro Industrial, where Olive Tree Theatre was located, is mostly Black, populated by both South African people and recently migrated people from other African countries. Many residents of Alexandra used to make their living in Marlboro by working in factories, but over the last twenty years most of these factories have closed and relocated, leading to a high rate of unemployment in Alexandra and Marlboro. Consequently, a lot of poor and unemployed Black South Africans and African immigrants have made informal housing out of old factory buildings and vacant lots (*Mail and Guardian* 2014). In reaction, the municipal government has carried out a series of evictions, and there have been ongoing legal conflicts between the community and the Johannesburg city council. Thus, like Alexandra, the much larger neighboring township, Marlboro is often characterized as a neglected, volatile area and one in which the people express ongoing dissatisfaction with the government (Majola 2007; Parker 2012). It is within these geographic, historical, and political contexts that Ntshieng Mokgoro was born and established Olive Tree Theatre.

The Founding of Olive Tree Theatre

Mokgoro is the inheritor of the legacies of Black South African women in political organizing in Alexandra: "sub-tenant, beer brewing, churchgoing African women" and others like Lillian Tshabalala, Deborah Mabiletsa, Annie Twala, Alinah Serote, Marjorie Manganye, Patience Pashe, and Sarah Mthembu (Bonner and Nieftagodien 2008, 7, 16). These women were consciously aware of the connections between economic empowerment, education, racial and gender justice, and democracy. Like Mokgoro's, their work was not always explicitly confrontational with the government, but they recognized the importance of quotidian ways of reforming and empowering their community.

She is also the inheritor of a century-long tradition of blending social justice imperatives with the founding of permanent commercial theatre spaces. Within this tradition, Black women are newcomers, as it has been mostly white and mostly male. Mokgoro's work can be compared to that of Gibson "Bra Gib" Mthuthuzeli Kente. He is called the father of township theatre because he took the industry into townships at a time when professional theatre production was mostly associated with established institutions in majority-white spaces. Kente infused his stories with representations of township life and definitively Black Diasporic genres like gospel and jazz music. Along with being credited for creating the genre of the township musical, he trained hundreds of theatre practitioners and produced twenty-three plays, including two that were banned by the South African government. He was also jailed for six months from 1976 to 1977 for the anti-apartheid messages in his work.[3] Kente was perhaps the most popularly acclaimed and economically successful South African playwright of the apartheid era, even though his productions did not benefit from state subsidies (Duval Smith 2004; Kruger 1999; Schauffer 2011). Unlike him, however, Mokgoro established a theatre space, which, under the apartheid era in which Kente and other Black South Africans worked, would have been subjected to the strict spatial and economic controls of the apartheid state.

While not formally trained in theatre, Mokgoro developed such a strong reputation for herself that she was able to garner national recognition and create a space and a platform for other Black theatre artists. In 2009, she won the Standard Bank Young Artist Award, South Africa's most prestigious prize for emerging artists, and was the first Black woman to win this award in theatre (it had been in place for twenty-eight years at the time). She had spent most of her adult life thus far writing and staging plays in her hometown of Alexandra. Mokgoro began her theatre work by participating in community plays and then using drama as a public education initiative while she worked as a library assistant. She eventually decided to quit her job and dedicate herself to writing and producing. The Standard Bank award validated her decision to enter the precarious occupation of theatre artist despite her lack of formal training. She invested her prize money into a production company called Olive Tree Theatre Productions, which was named after her play *The Olive Tree* (2009). Then, with the goal of showcasing the work of women theatre directors, she organized the first Olive Tree Women's Theatre Festival, at the Joburg Theatre in 2012. However, she felt that "the project got swallowed up by this huge theatre space," in that she had to rely too much on the administration of the institution to approve the logistics of the festival even though she was the organizer (pers. comm., 2018). Moreover, she dreamed of building a theatre in her township. Thus, she and her business partner, Kerryn Irvin, sought a space in Alexandra where they could host the second women's theatre festival, in 2013, and they named the space after the production company. Olive Tree Theatre was ultimately born on the top floor of Yarona Mall, a shopping center in Alexandra. When I first visited, in 2015, Mokgoro and Irvin did not have to pay rent, though they were in charge of the electricity, water, and other bills. This arrangement enabled Olive Tree to develop a strong roster of performances and to survive economically. Five years later, after the owners of Yarona Mall decided to sell the building and the lease ended, the theatre relocated to a bigger, self-owned space in Marlboro, where it eventually closed down.

Olive Tree Theatre featured a wide variety of events, from various plays to film screenings to exhibitions; and the theatre was visited by people from inside and outside of the township. In this sense, Olive Tree is comparable to

Figure 8. Street scene of Alexandra from the ground floor of Yarona Mall, 2015. Photo by the author.

both the Soweto Theatre and the Market Theatre (this latter being the most famous theatre in South Africa and a major hub for emerging theatre artists).[4] From an African Diasporic perspective, Olive Tree's work also bears some affinity to that of the National Black Theatre of Harlem in the United States, which was founded by a Black woman, Barbara Ann Teer, in 1968.

From the outset Mokgoro was determined to have the theatre in Alexandra. The plan was that audiences and practitioners would come to the township (and later to Marlboro) for an experience of theatre that is usually only available in the elite areas of major cities at spaces like Joburg Theatre and the Market in Johannesburg, and the Baxter Theatre in Cape Town. One challenge, however, is that most of Olive Tree's audiences are not from Alexandra or Marlboro. In Mokgoro's opinion, the reason for this is not the expense of going to the theatre, but rather the view of it as an exclusive form of entertainment:

> People would rather spend 3,000 bucks on liquor than spending 80 Rand on theatre because they don't understand. . . . We still have people who think theatre is for the elite. Theatre is for people who have money. . . . I am trying to create a tradition of people paying money and I'm trying to get

professional work.... So, I am trying to teach them instead of paying 20 Rand you have to pay 80 because this is professional work.... You want to be at a point of, "Do I want to go to Market Theatre?" "No, I want to go to Olive Tree Theatre." Theatre in townships are competing with taverns and shebeens.... You really need to be patient with people and keep educating people. (pers. comm., 2015)[5]

Mokgoro's observation that theatre is not generally viewed as a popular art form in her township is consistent with the decreasing influence of theatre as a major pastime and a site of political organizing in the postapartheid period. Alex Duval Smith (2004) notes that in the early years of the democratic transition from apartheid, with the growth in media, access to predominantly white spaces of entertainment, and other forms of recreation, there was a decline in theatre patronage among ordinary South Africans. This decreased significance of theatre as a popular pastime seems to have been more pronounced in townships than in major metropolitan areas like Cape Town and Johannesburg, where large theatre institutions benefited from government funding, support from wealthy national and international patrons, and increased international exposure following the end of apartheid. Further, since many of these theatres now include the work of Black artists, they are also considered crucial spaces in which to highlight the work of Black and other emerging artists, which essentially makes it difficult for the emergence of other spaces that also do that important work of mentorship. Amid its economic constraints, Olive Tree Theatre asked South Africans to consider a poor township as a space in which a professional theatre can exist. Mokgoro's commitment to patiently (re)educating people about theatre's importance is consistent with Olive Tree's imperative to mentor and develop the work of younger artists. It also aligns with the pedagogy that characterizes her repertoire. She uses the concept of healing to describe this work.

Healing and the Exploration of Black South African Lives in Mokgoro's Plays

Commenting on the difference between working at a large, long-established theatre and founding her own institution, Mokgoro stated,

My stories tell itself [sic]. They just choose me. I love dealing with the spiritual realm in most of my productions.... Because I am not a healer, I feel like using theatre is how I heal people ... and therefore you cannot tell me how to heal people at that time.... Creativity means creating something from scratch. You are like God. . . . In order to break the ceiling, you need to start creating your own thing. And I guess I am glad in that way, because I am not following anybody's rule. (pers. comm., 2015)

In this statement, she connects the creative process with spirituality, the work of healing as a practice of recuperating stories that are marginalized, and the mission to help communities cope and move on from trauma. Spirituality as a conduit toward healing is also a major theme in the work of the Mothertongue Project, Sistren Theatre Collective, and Letters from the Dead. Their work, and African Diasporic theatre in general, usually involves the recuperation of agency, cultures, and philosophies that have been demeaned by Eurocentric thought and supremacy. Theatre performance is therefore part of the process of repairing the ontological damage caused by traumatic events and regimes built on racial violence, such as slavery, colonialism, and apartheid. But the techniques they employ are more than a reaction to European cultural hegemony. Black theatre artists draw on what they know, including the cultural forms they partake in. For instance, regarding African-based healing rituals such as those found in South African shamanic practices and Yoruba Ifa cosmology, Mothertongue Project cofounder Rehane Abrahams (2006, 16) states, "In Africa, these practices are not New Age, they are continuous 'Age-less' techniques for the restoring of psyche amongst other things."[6]

Commensurate with the focus on healing, Mokgoro's plays feature strong themes of loss and trauma. Her repertoire includes *The Anger* (written when she was a teenager), *The Olive Tree* (2009), *Paradise Fall* (2013), *Distant Faces* (2014), *Phases of Mirah* (2014), and *Memories and Empty Spaces* (2017). *The Olive Tree*, for which the theatre was named, features acts of matricide and, in Mokgoro's words, is essentially about "three generations of women hating themselves" (pers. comm., 2015). At the time of my research, the script for *The Olive Tree* was not available, and so I rely here on her summary of the play, which did not include the names of characters or other details. Regardless, the story deserves analysis alongside her other plays since it is Olive Tree Theatre's eponymous play.

The story begins with a fourteen-year-old girl arguing with her mother about what to do about her pregnancy. The mother, who has previously gotten an abortion for the girl, suggests that she abort the pregnancy again. The girl refuses because of how horrific her first experience with an abortion was. Eventually the argument gets heated, and the girl stabs her mother to death. She buries the body in the yard and plants an olive tree over it in order to conceal the grave. The girl grows up to also have an antagonistic relationship with her own daughter, later getting pregnant by her daughter's boyfriend, aborting the fetus, and burying it in the same spot as her mother's body.

In a later play, *Paradise Fall* (2013), Mokgoro also centers a young woman's encounters with violence. The play tells arguably the most graphic story of sexual assault in her body of work. As a young girl, the protagonist, Samantha, is abducted by a man who enslaves and sexually assaults her for many years. The first abductor is then killed by two other men who also enslave and rape her. Toward the end of the play, she eventually escapes by killing one of the men and walks toward a place called Paradise Fall. The loss of her father (who was murdered by the first kidnapper) haunts the character throughout the play, and her decision to go to Paradise Fall, a place her father used to tell her about, is a means of distancing herself from the traumas she suffered as well as reconnecting with the memory of the only parent she knew. Another play, *Distant Faces* (2014), is an adaptation of a Mozambican novel, Mia Couto's *Sleepwalking Land* (1992).[7] The play dramatizes the conflicts in a South African family following the apartheid-era exile of men who fought in the uMkhonto we Sizwe, the military arm of the ANC. When former soldier Okenu returns home after the end of apartheid he is still struggling with post-traumatic stress disorder, and his wife, Mia, has had a mental breakdown. Their son, Kenti, is left to deal with his parents' mental illnesses and the management of the household. The play ends in chaos, with the mother's implied death and the father's ultimate descent into insanity.

Familial drama similarly characterizes *Phases of Mirah* (2014), Mokgoro's most well-known play. *Phases* may also be her most aesthetically compelling and complex play to date because of its combination of performance forms and storytelling methods, its large cast, and the extensive publicity around it. In the story, a woman struggles with parental abandonment, which leads to drug abuse, intimate partner violence, and eventually murder and imprisonment. In the same way that Athol Fugard, John Kani, and Winston Ntshona's *Sizwe Banzi Is Dead* (1972) and *The Coat* (1973) are associated with the Space Theatre, and Percy Mtwa, Mbongeni Ngema, and Barney Simon's *Woza Albert!* (1981) heralded the new Market Theatre, *Phases of Mirah* is indelibly linked to the launch of Olive Tree Theatre. It is the only one featured on Olive Tree's website, and was the first of Mokgoro's plays to have a run after the theatre's opening in 2013.

The play is partly a character study and partly a coming-of-age story of a Black South African woman, Khalinah, from her teenage years to middle age. She moves through life trying to recuperate from her experiences of sexual assault and parental neglect as a child. The play is told in three phases (rather than three acts), with three actors depicting her at different ages. There is no break in the action to switch to different scenes. Instead, Khalinah narrates the story continuously. Mokgoro's decision to utilize three actors instead of one enables the stages of the character's life to cross, including having teenage Khalinah appear in the same scenes as young adult Khalinah, and having the eldest Khalinah comment on the action occurring in flashbacks. In addition, the distinct differences between the personae of Khalinah at different ages—an innocent child, a troubled young adult, a contemplative and solemn middle-aged woman—are emphasized by the use of three actors. Thus, *Phases* has a chronological structure entirely told in flashback, and time gets collapsed, crossed, and transformed. Besides the characters who inhabit the story, the play features three sets of narrators: the Dream, the Poet, and the Chorus.

The story begins with teenage Khalinah gushing to her mother, Lerna, about the man of her dreams, Oluti, while Lerna warns her to be careful of men at such a young age. Despite her mother's concerns, Khalinah longs for a relationship with this man. However, when she encounters him alone, he is nothing like what she expects, and he rapes her. When her father, Zuri, finds out what happened, he expels her from the house out of shame. Lerna is sympathetic and promises to intervene on her behalf and take care of her in exile. She instructs Khalinah to leave and wait for her at a spot in the community where Lerna will meet her later, hopefully with news that her father has changed his mind and she is now accepted at home. When Lerna doesn't show up, Khalinah assumes that both parents have deserted her, and she runs away. She survives by doing sex work and being dependent on men. Eventually she meets a man, Oreto, who becomes her manager/agent and boyfriend, and with his help she starts a career as a nightclub performer under the stage name Mirah. She also becomes addicted to drugs. Khalinah and Oreto constantly argue, until, in one of these arguments, she stabs and kills him. She goes on the run and decides to return to her family home, but it is too late. She finds her mother nonresponsive and bound to a wheelchair and discovers via a note left by her father that he had had a change of heart and both parents had tried to find her. When their efforts failed, her mother suffered a stroke and her father committed suicide because of the guilt of abandoning his child. After discovering what happened to her parents, Khalinah then carries out a euthanasic killing of her sick mother. Then, while still in mourning over her parents' deaths, she is caught by the police, convicted of her boyfriend's murder, and sent to prison for twenty-five years.

The play ends with her emergence from prison as a middle-aged woman. The ending is melancholic and reflective. It does not allow Khalinah much catharsis or portray the character as tragic. Instead, she contemplates the meaning of life and almost makes peace with the fortuitousness of happiness as she has experienced it. She tells the audience through song in the last line, "The sun is setting. Now journey back to your mother. I have nothing to share with you anymore" (Mokgoro 2014, 16). The ending contrasts sharply with the beginning. When the audience meets Khalinah as a teenager, she is depicted in a highly idealized way as a naive child delirious about her new love interest. Mokgoro's *Paradise Fall* similarly accentuates the protagonist's playfulness, inquisitiveness, and adoration of her father before he is killed and she is kidnapped. Thus, both stories emphasize the idealism and innocence of girlhood, which is interrupted by a breach in a parental relationship. *Phases of Mirah* can be placed into conversation with Gcina Mhlophe's 1985 play *Have You Seen Zandile?*, which was inspired by Mhlophe's childhood. In it, a girl spends her life mourning her separation from her grandmother after her mother kidnapped her, and she tries in vain to recuperate the loss of her relationship with her grandmother. Zandile's memories of her grandmother are decidedly idyllic, in contrast to the experiences of trying to connect with her mother in the present.[8] Commenting on Mhlophe's use of nostalgia in *Have You Seen Zandile?*, Jennifer Delisle (2006, 391) writes, "it encompasses dreams for love, hope, compassion and newness." The same may be said of Mokgoro's *Phases of Mirah*.

The themes of patriarchal power, sexual exploitation, and the cyclical nature of violence are threads that weave the family drama in *Phases* together. However, they are not the central themes conveyed by the play. The emphasis is on the interiority of a woman's life—her thoughts, hopes, dreams, and nightmares—and her connection to her family. The traumatic side of this interiority is also manifested in the violent way in which the characters either are killed by an intimate partner or relative or end their own lives. There is little reference to wider societal structures and their impact on the family in the play, and the decisions Khalinah makes are depicted as deeply personal ones. While the story occurs within the context of racism and apartheid's legacies—of which an audience might be aware—the play does not comment on them.

There has historically been some contention around the function of theatre in South Africa in relation to social protest and commentary. Kathy Perkins (1998, 2) notes that plays that explored aspects of Black life beyond anti-Black racism or urban confrontations with apartheid laws and policies were not usually staged outside of townships during the apartheid era. They also did not attain the international coverage of protest plays, which were mainly focused on male characters. Women's stories were therefore often disparaged as apolitical. Thus, plays like Mhlophe's *Have You Seen Zandile?* received more mainstream respect in the postapartheid period. Miki Flockemann and Thuli Mazibuko (1999, 46) write that such plays act as a "sort of 'counter-discourse' to what has been called 'protest theatre,' because of the way it delves into personal life and experience."

In the early postapartheid era, there was a wider opening for plays that didn't fall neatly into the category of protest theatre. These plays delved deeply into issues of self-identity and told stories about the day-to-day experiences of women and queer people. As South African theatre scholar and artist Mark Fleishman stated in an interview with Awino Okech (2007, 12), in the early postapartheid era, alongside the set of plays that followed the anti-apartheid paradigm, "there were . . . a whole spate of plays that were individualized, in the sense that they were about personal stories and identity issues. So, you got a whole lot of one person shows which were about the history of an Indian family in [Kwa Zulu] Natal for example or issues around women, gay issues, those kinds of things where people suddenly said 'I have a story to tell. My story is important.'" Ntshieng Mokgoro's body of work, including *Phases of Mirah*, benefits from this narrative shift in the early postapartheid era.

While *Phases of Mirah* tells a straightforward story about domestic turmoil, it is highly stylized with strong elements of melodrama. The play features what Mokgoro terms *spiritual realism*, one of her favorite artistic approaches. It contains song, dance, ritual, time overlaps, and spiritual or superhuman characters such as the Chorus. About half the dialogue is written in verse, and Mokgoro emphasizes emotion in the way in which most characters speak. The structure as a whole is that of a ritual-dream through which Khalinah reflects on her life in a chronological series of flashbacks that ultimately end in the present.

As I stated previously, Mokgoro's emphasis on herself as a healer aligns with the self-construct of many other South African women theatre artists, particularly those who are involved in theatre that makes social commentary or primarily focuses on women. This view of theatre as a healing practice is not necessarily influenced by the discourse of national healing and reconciliation in which South Africa was engaged in the early postapartheid years. That discourse was partly employed to assuage white South Africans' and the West's paranoia that Black South Africans would use their new empowerment to discriminate against white people. A myopic emphasis on national and community healing can serve as a pretext for maintaining intragroup hierarchical systems such as racism, classism, patriarchy, heteronormativity, and the oppression of children. Women theatre artists, student activists, and others have moved past superficial tropes of healing and reconciliation by pointing out the shortcomings of the postapartheid state in addressing historical inequalities, including women's and girls' experiences of gender-based violence.

Family stories and stories focused on characters' life histories can highlight marginalized voices, such as those of neglected and abused children, women, and broken families—all subjects explored in Mokgoro's body of work. Younger women artists add to the repertoire of stories that offer complex narratives of marginalized people and topics by drawing from traditions set by elders and cultivating contemporary conversations. Therefore, I want to continue my account of the Olive Tree Women's Theatre Festival in 2015, with which I began this chapter, with a focus on the plays I saw there. In the writing workshop I discussed earlier, participants were asked about the kinds of plays we were tired of seeing onstage. The responses indicated that young people were searching for new ways of telling a multiplicity of stories.

"Without Us There Is No Life": The Fourth Olive Tree Women's Theatre Festival

Globally, the field of directing in mainstream theatre and film is still dominated by men, even though women writers and actors are now numerous.[9] Directing, unlike acting—or, to a lesser extent, playwriting—is a highly specialized professional field. Moreover, the director is the ultimate leader in a theatre production. This expectation of the director's professionalism and leadership has tended historically to align with notions of masculinity. Among women's theatre collectives, the subject of the director's gender is contentious. Sistren Theatre Collective (chapter 1) has worked with male directors in around half of its major plays—albeit some of these men were former students and colleagues of founding artistic director Honor Ford-Smith.[10] In contrast, the Mothertongue Project (the subject of chapter 2) does not hire male directors.

The conflicts around the director's sex, gender, and race don't simply emerge from the discomfort of a (cis) man telling women what to do, especially in plays with all-women casts. There are also ideological stakes involved. Thus, Ellen Donkin and Susan Clement (1993, 2) argue in *Upstaging Big Daddy: Directing Theatre as If Race and Gender Matter*, "because plays are only a blueprint for production, the director moves into a position of enormous responsibility. How the final production 'reads' to an audience is her artistic and political responsibility. . . . In the process of directing a play, she can completely upend the text, encourage her actors to develop subtexts the playwright never dreamed of, enlist her designers in the creation of a destabilizing counterpoint, or cast performers whose very presence throws the text into question."

There should be no assumption that a woman cannot be patriarchal, that a Black person cannot be anti-Black, or that men and white people are incapable of progressive gender and race-consciousness in their direction of plays about Black women. Understanding white supremacy, anti-Blackness, and patriarchy as structures, rather than individualistic traits, means admitting that these are perpetuated by even the people who suffer the most from them. However, it is equally important to acknowledge identity as a critical part of the process. As feminist standpoint theory asserts, those who are most vulnerable within an oppressive system are the best placed to comment on how that system works (see Hartstock 1983; Hekman 1997; Collins 2008; Narayan 2004). This acknowledgment is especially important in a field such as theatre, where subjective life experiences guide the composition of a story. Additionally, the director's awareness of social hierarchies, regardless of their race, gender, or class, is integral to the process.

Importantly as well, the training and mentoring of more Black women directors are part of a process of achieving gender equity in theatre industries. In this respect, Ntshieng Mokgoro's statement on why she founded the Women's Theatre Festival is worthy of detailed quoting:

> I felt there were not many Black female directors, if you had to count it was me, it was Warona [Seane], it was Napo [Masheane]. You couldn't even count up to five. And we started asking, "Where are the female directors and writers?" And when I was doing my developmental work with communities outside the Joburg province, even inside the province, I discovered a lot of young people who were creating magic onstage, but . . . they did not have access to spaces . . . these women were getting discouraged and they were actually leaving the industry to pursue other careers because there was nothing for them because of gatekeeping, which is still pretty much happening even now.

She went on to comment on the differences in job opportunities for white and Black women:

> In this country when we look at other women who were here before, you would realize that these women—especially white women—they got space straight from university. They would get a space to do the job, to

do production, and they would fail dismally, but they would get another turn to keep practicing. So, a person like me would come and get a space one year and I would do this huge production and that's it. Next day you don't go back. You still have to start from scratch to prove yourself, and you have to work twice as hard to prove yourself, like "I'm still here. I'm still existing." But because you don't get space you sort of lose hope and stop practicing. You can only get better once you start practicing what you are doing and that's how men are surviving because they get spaces. . . . So, I thought, "Can we have a space, a safe space for women?" Whether they fail, it's a learning space for them, and if they do good it's a platform to move them to a better level. (pers. comm., 2015)

To address these gender imbalances in the theatre industry, the Olive Tree Women's Theatre Festival is open only to women directors. The emphasis is on women's professional development in the field of directing rather than on women's stories, and so there is no requirement that the plays must be about women. Even so, most plays at the 2015 festival still centered women characters. The stories were not necessarily women's stories/female stories per se, in that not all the plays focused on problems that affect girls and women disproportionately. However, all of them reflected sensitivity to gender differences and dynamics through their portrayals of the relationships between people of different genders. Moreover, viewing young Black women in positions of authority as directors is a breath of fresh air, given the vulnerabilities they face in South Africa and globally. At the 2015 festival there were six plays in total, all of which explored various aspects of life in South Africa. I will discuss the directors/writers of three of these: Lihle Dhlomo, who directed *Last Cow Standing*, which was written and performed by Menzi Mkhwane; Chuma Mapoma, who wrote and directed the collectively devised *Womyn: The Tell Your Truth Movement*; and Gcebile Dlamini, who wrote and directed *Nomzamo*.[11]

Womyn: The Tell Your Truth Movement, directed and scripted by Chuma Mapoma, focuses on gender issues faced by women. The performance is a collage of monologues, in which five characters give testimonies about their lives. Mapoma's initial plan was to adapt Eve Ensler's globally successful 1996 play *The Vagina Monologues*. However, she found that the "words didn't resonate" within the South African context or among the cast. She then decided to create a new play entirely through collaborative creation and devising. She and the cast began by sharing personal stories and improvising, through what she defines as a "conscious support movement" (Mapoma, pers. comm., 2015). Following these improvisations, and conversations, Mapoma scripted scenes and monologues in isiXhosa and English and blended them with sections she wrote on her own. Like Ntozake Shange's choreopoem *for colored girls who have considered suicide / when the rainbow is enuf* (1976) and Ensler's *The Vagina Monologues*, *Womyn* relies on female homosocial bonds as a major cathartic element that links each vignette.

Womyn features different performance techniques and moods, including comedy. In this respect, it—like most plays featured at the festival—contrasts with Swazi director/playwright Gcebile Dlamini's emotional play *Nomzamo*, about a young girl who is sexually abused by an older male relative while her family protects him. Nomzamo only escapes this violence after the man dies toward the end of the story. In its festival performance, the emotional heaviness of the story was amplified by naturalistic casting, with the actor playing fourteen-year-old Nomzamo the same age as the character. This casting choice made the story resonate in a more realistic way than if the actor had been an older teenager or an adult. It was somewhat surprising, considering that I am used to adult actors depicting stories of children who have been sexually assaulted and exploited.[12] Perhaps the casting of an actual teenage girl in the role of the protagonist partly influenced audience members' need to comment on how jarring the story was for them. It was the only play I watched at the festival that led to lengthy audience feedback. This discussion hinged on the painful story, its solemnity, and the question of whether Nomzamo was more of a survivor than a victim (see chapter 2 for more on this postshow discussion).

Gcebile Dlamini started writing *Nomzamo* in 2009, while she was still in university. She stated to me that *Nomzamo* was partly based on her own experiences of childhood sexual abuse as well as the experiences of other girls whom she had met while working on a community outreach project at Hillbrow Theatre in Johannesburg. One girl with whom she was working at the time told her that she was being sexually assaulted by her uncle. This inspired Dlamini to tell a story that represented her and other girls' experiences:

> I felt like I wanted to write that specific story, because for me it is something that was never spoken about. It was just hushed; and the way it came out it felt like I wanted it to. The hardest thing is when it's a family member, and a trusted individual. To know that every time when you go home you're going to face this person. So that was the trigger for me, and that girl actually made me realize and say, "You know what? I don't have to go back home and open that wound and start that conversation, but I can start it inside myself and in the same space that I'm working with because there is so much that is hidden inside." (Dlamini, pers. comm., 2022)

The actor wasn't just the same age as the character, but also the same age that Dlamini had been when she experienced sexual abuse, and the same age as the girl in the community outreach project: a fact that Dlamini reports being "not even conscious of" during the casting. However, she was conscious that girls of this age group (preteens to teenagers) needed to be provided a voice and a space in theatre to represent these experiences.

Dlamini's imperative in *Nomzamo* to voice the experiences of young girls displays an intersectional awareness of age as well as gender and race, particularly the vulnerabilities girls face due to their disempowered status as children. Elaborating on how Black girls usually must suppress their pain and frustration until it boils over into rage, Lashon Daley (2021, 1039) notes that "as a result of their status as children, they lack the authority and autonomy that are afforded to adults. Thus, Black girls experience a doubling of the lack that is experienced by Black women. If the angry Black woman is a representation of doubled lack then the lack experienced by the raging Black girl is doubled again—a quadrupled lack." This rage may be overtly expressed through outbursts of anger, but it is also expressed through critical moments of relaying one's story, regardless of the discomfort it causes those who hear it. The story obviously resonated with the audiences and theatre practitioners for whom it was performed, as Dlamini won the prestigious Naledi Award for Best Community Theatre for *Nomzamo* in 2013. The staging at the Women's Theatre Festival marked the first time that it was performed for a wider audience.

Another play, *Last Cow Standing*, had also been performed several times before it was staged at Olive Tree. In its casting and setting it is unique among the other plays in that it is a fantasy piece with a young boy as the protagonist and is set in the past in a fictional African kingdom. Under his grandmother's instruction, the boy sets out on a quest to save his cow from being sacrificed as part of the king's efforts to appease a deity who cursed the land with a plague. The play takes place over several years while the main character grows from boy to teenager to man. To seamlessly depict all the time and space shifts in the story, the director, Lihle Dhlomo, chose one of the most minimalist sets I have ever seen. The stage was almost bare, and puppetry, light, and shadows were used to depict the boy's epic journey. Dhlomo noted that initially it had more dialogue and included other actors. It was her idea to strip the script down so that the audience's focus would be on the story and Mkhwane's depiction of it. *Last Cow* does not contain explicit messages about women, but it implicitly honors African women's centrality to social and political life—including by making the boy's grandmother the wisest person in the play and making the deity female. *Last Cow* is essentially an allegory about the South African postapartheid state, and the cows symbolize the "wealth of the people to the people" (Dhlomo, pers. comm., 2015), or in other words, the valuable resources that are constantly at risk of being destroyed or appropriated.

The playwright/actor and director are friends who attended the same university and have worked together before (with Mkhwane directing Dhlomo), which explains why Dhlomo states, "After every single fight we had we would grow stronger as a team." In their working relationship, it seems that the fact that a woman was directing a man (in a play written by him, no less) made no difference. Still, when I asked her about her experiences in this role, she spoke of others' perceptions, particularly those of older men, stating, "People look at you and then they assume what you can do. How much information do you know in terms of theatre and you're young on top of that?" She stated that men have been "blown away by the idea that a young female director has directed this" (pers. comm., 2015). Gcebile Dlamini similarly spoke about being underestimated and discriminated against as a young Black woman director, especially after she won the Naledi Award for *Nomzamo*. The reaction from some members of the theatre community was harsh: "I think I got a lot of heads up from females as opposed to males. And there was a lot of talking of 'How did she get it' 'Who is she?' Probably those voices are both males and females, but the ones that I am very clear about were male voices, that were like, 'Who is she?'" (pers. comm., 2022). That experience discouraged her, and made her more discerning about the people she wanted to work with.

All the women had comments about the difficulties of directing in South Africa, but they also underscored the importance of women pursuing the field nonetheless. Chuma Mapoma was the youngest director I interviewed and was at the time of the festival pursuing her MFA in drama and performance at the University of KwaZulu-Natal. She said,

> I feel like men jump at things more than we do. I feel like women step out and they are told to get back in their cage and they quietly get back in their cage. So slowly women are starting to realize that "actually, I want to say something and no one is going to say it the way I'm going to say it; regardless of who's saying I can or cannot." I think we are creating opportunities and other women are creating opportunities—like Ntshieng [Mokgoro] is doing. (pers. comm., 2015)

All three women agreed that the ways that women tell stories are different from the ways that men tell them, especially stories in which exploration of gender hierarchies is central to the narrative. As Mapoma said, there are also certain stories that are so intimately connected to being a woman or girl that were they to be directed by a man, they would come across at best as awkward, or at worst as domineering. She mentioned, for example, a play she worked on that featured women's exploration of their bodies and sex lives.

It is difficult to assume that a male director would have directed the plays featured at the festival differently. For example, much as Dhlomo did with *Last Cow Standing*, Jamaican director Eugene Williams stripped the play *A Vigil for Roxie* (examined in chapter 3) down from its original, multi-actor dramatic form to the monodramatic form in which it now exists. However, there is a tendency to move beyond realism, including through spiritual realism, among women storytellers that is notable in the plays of Sistren, the Mothertongue Project, the Letters from the Dead project, Ntshieng Mokgoro's work, and all the plays at the 2015 Olive Tree Women's Theatre Festival. These forms have always been favored by women's theatre companies, in part because they allow for productions that can travel easily, and an aesthetic that focuses on the actor's body as the source of the story rather than elaborate sets and costuming.

When I asked Dhlomo, Dlamini, and Mapoma which other women directors they admired, they named Lara Foot, Yvette Hardie, Janine Lewis, Lliane Loots, Nondumiso Msimanga, Ntshieng Mokgoro, and Warona Seane.[13] Some of these women have mentored or taught them in university or are artistic directors of companies. The fact that they were able to name them without having to ruminate on the question shows that they have certainly found inspiration and mentorship within South African theatre. It is notable that four of the seven directors named are white, even though South Africa remains a large Black-majority country. This points to a continuing disproportion in the numbers of white women who are able to achieve success as leaders in South African theatre relative to Black women. Nevertheless, with a new generation of Black women theatre directors like those who participated in the fourth Olive Tree Women's Theatre Festival, there is room for optimism about Black women's status as theatre directors and writers in South Africa.

Many years after the 2015 festival, all three women have enjoyed successes in theatre, film, and television and won multiple awards. As of 2022, Gcebile Dlamini is an independent director, actor, and writer, whose projects still include work with young people; Lihle Dhlomo is a film and theatre actress, line producer for feature films, and theatre director, in addition to running a crew agency; and Chuma Mapoma is a writer, actor, and poet who formerly worked as a script supervisor with Durban Motion Pictures.

Figure 9. Beverly Qwabe (*forefront*) and Nipho Hurd (*background*) in *Womyn: The Tell Your Truth Movement*, directed by Chuma Mapoma, Olive Tree Women's Theatre Festival, 2015. Photo by the author.

The number of high-profile Black women directors in South Africa has also expanded. In response to my question about whether she had seen any change in the theatre industry over the years, Gcebile Dlamini responded, "There's a lot of female voices as opposed to when I started myself. . . . Are we making it gender equal? We're pushing towards that. I'll confidently say yes" (pers. comm., 2022). Olive Tree's contribution to mentoring young Black women directors is part of the story of how the theatre industry in South Africa is pushing toward more openings for Black women in theatre. However, its challenges are also part of this narrative.

"We Are Here for a Purpose": Olive Tree's Vision

Olive Tree was able to remain active as a venue for a variety of artistic events and exhibitions until the end of 2019.[14] It also grew in its administration. Mokgoro hired an artistic director, Nondumiso Lwazi Msimanga, to take over for her so that she could concentrate on being the managing director. The theatre also created an award called Ngoro ya Thari (Calabash of the Nation). As Mokgoro explained it, this award recognized Black women who have committed to helping the careers of other women in theatre: "The focus is not on Black excellence . . . but it's more on the time that people contributed, volunteered in trying to develop Black upcoming directors—female directors" (pers. comm., 2018). Her emphasis on mentoring Black women in directing aligns with her continuing emphasis on giving back to her community. She still lives in Alexandra, and expressed disappointment that many famous South Africans who were born or raised in the township have not given back to it. Despite the work she has done to mentor young theatre artists and give back to her community, she does not define herself as an activist because she thinks working in commercial theatre requires a certain level of capitulation or silence, particularly regarding matters of race: "You can't be an activist when you censor yourself" (pers. comm., 2018). When she said this, I countered that all activists censor themselves depending on the context. However, the point she makes about the difficulties working in mainstream theatre while wanting to speak out about its inequities may reveal why there are not more Black women in mainstream theatre leadership positions.

Regarding her ideological perspective on gender justice, Mokgoro chose the word *profeminism* to express her support of feminism, given that so many of the women she works with—including participants in the festival—are feminist (pers. comm., 2018). However, she is uncomfortable with boxing herself into the label of feminism and the responsibilities it comes with. I told her I thought she would be open to accepting womanism, particularly its emphasis on learning from Black women's problem-solving and contributions to society at the grassroots and community level. We spoke about womanist tenets regarding spiritual and artistic worlds, as well as Africa-centered womanism's focus on African culture and philosophies, as part of its social justice philosophy.

Olive Tree's and Mokgoro's commitment to antiracist and antipatriarchal pedagogy focused on resisting the strictures set by mainstream theatre industries. This, coupled with the investment and location in a poor Black community, is emblematic of the radical subjectivity inherent in womanist thought, which Stacey M. Floyd-Thomas (2010, 53) defines as "a process that emerges as Black females in the nascent phase of their identity development come to understand agency as the ability to defy a forced naiveté in an effort to influence the choices made in their life—how Black women's conscientization incites resistance against marginality." Regarding the theatre industry, resistance to the marginalization of Black women directors in South Africa and elsewhere consists not only of entering predominantly white and male spaces but also of creating institutions rooted in the artistic visions and practices of Black people. The business of theatre reflects gender power imbalances within South African society and globally; however, these imbalances can be addressed through art that confronts wider societal problems and claims geographic spaces within the art form and industry for marginalized voices.

After 2015, Olive Tree Theatre hosted only one more theatre festival, in 2016. There was no festival held in 2017 because of the theatre's relocation from Alexandra to Marlboro. Nevertheless, the interest in the festival grew over the years. There were seventeen participants in 2016, up from four in 2013, and 120 applications for the 2018 staging, though it was not held because of inadequate funding (Mokgoro, pers. comm., 2018). Mokgoro emphasized the Pan-African scope of the festival, though it was difficult for people from the African Diaspora and some regions of Africa to participate. Travel was especially expensive for those coming from the Americas. The participants in the festival did not pay to be a part of it, which meant that Olive Tree was completely reliant on external funding, and this funding mostly came from nongovernmental and private organizations.

Olive Tree Theatre is now permanently closed due to financial struggles exacerbated by the COVID-19 pandemic. It stopped operating in 2020 because of a lack of audiences due to social distancing regulations, and it did not reopen. Mokgoro complained about a lack of governmental support and pointed out that it is far easier for white South African theatre practitioners to receive sponsorship from both private funders and the government. Given the lack of state support and inconsistent funding from other sources, Olive Tree relied on having a roster of events to cover the cost of rent and other expenses. Without this stream of income in 2020–21, it could not survive. At one point, Mokgoro had to use her own money to keep the theatre afloat, which was a huge financial burden. Olive Tree is among other cultural initiatives that ended during the beginning of the pandemic. For instance, another, more well-known independent theatre, the Fugard Theatre—named after the playwright Athol Fugard—in Cape Town also closed permanently because of a lack of funding (Ramsay 2021).

The closure of Olive Tree Theatre effectively means the end of the Women's Theatre Festival. Although she has not completely given up on ever having the festival again, Mokgoro is now focusing on other projects, such as her work on community theatre with members of the Khoisan community, making theatre in their own language (pers. comm., 2023). Her individual work as a playwright and director also continues. In 2021, her play *That Night of Trance* (2018), cowritten with Billy Langa, was made into a film, which was shown at theatres throughout South Africa. It was part of an initiative by the South African State Theatre and Ster-Kinekor cinemas to help theatre practitioners deal with the disruptions caused by the COVID-19 pandemic by disseminating their plays to wide audiences in cinemas (Modise 2021). The play focuses on a young woman who discovers her spiritual gift and connection with her ancestors. It reflects Mokgoro's lifelong commitment to exploring spirituality and incorporating it into her artistic work. As a fulfillment of her own spiritual calling, she also got initiated into being a traditional healer in 2022. By pursuing her personal callings and continuing her individual theatre work and work with marginalized communities, she seems to have reconciled with the closure of Olive Tree Theatre and the end of the Women's Theatre Festival. She told me, "It's still in my heart, but . . . what I was supposed to do, I've done it." Now, she wants to "pass on the baton" (pers. comm., 2023). Mokgoro's counterpart, Black woman theatre artist and poet Napo Masheane, founded a women's theatre festival recently: the first HerStory International Theatre Festival was held at the Soweto Theatre in August 2022 and featured fifty works by artists from Africa, the Caribbean, and Europe (Nkosi 2022). Mokgoro also mentioned the Vavasati International Theatre Festival, held by the South African State Theatre since 2013, which focuses on showcasing the work of women theatre artists. There is also the South African Women's Arts Festival (SAWAF), which continues to be held annually. SAWAF is organized by the Playhouse Company, an agency of the Department of Arts and Culture.

It is possible that prospective funders viewed Olive Tree's work as unnecessary given the existence of other festivals and theatres that showcase and mentor young women artists. If so, that outlook would be shortsighted. Olive Tree is distinct from other theatres because of its location in Alexandra, a volatile and poor township, as well as its status as a theatre founded by a Black woman. One of Mokgoro's missions was to bring theatre to her township, allowing residents to experience the art form there rather than having to travel elsewhere. Olive Tree also hosted artists from other places in South Africa and internationally, bringing them into a community they probably would not have ventured to were it not for the theatre. The theatre's closure is alarming and disappointing—even disheartening. However, during the time that it existed, Olive Tree accomplished its goal of providing a space for marginalized voices in theatre; and as my conversations with the artists who participated in the 2015 festival show, it was one of the major influences on their professional development. It also contributed to

Figure 10. Ntshieng Mokgoro at Olive Tree Theatre, 2015. Photo by the author.

creating the international networks in which Mokgoro continues to operate. Essentially, Olive Tree Theatre and its Women's Theatre Festival are emblematic of how Black people valorize their communities through the institutions they build, and consistent activisms dedicated to shaping their own spaces.

Coda

Performing Activism across Space and Time

> Performance space is never empty. Bare, yes,
> open, yes, but never empty. It is always the site of
> physical, social, and psychic forces in society.
> Ngũgĩ wa Thiong'o, "Enactments of Power" (1997, 13)

Neila's Dance: A Reflection

The woman is dressed in black tights, black lipstick, and a purple veil. Without any prompting she enters the circle and begins dancing, moving with such precision and beauty that those not familiar with her techniques would think her dance was completely intuitive. The accompanying drums and tambourines are loud and manage to drown out the sound of the vehicles in the street on this busy, hot Saturday afternoon. She is in a tight circle of people, some of whom are playing instruments and moving their hips and legs lightly as they watch her.

Her dance is a combination of many techniques, and a veritable container for numerous meanings: spirituality, the erotic, Black radicalism, physical and mental endurance. I am seeing so many forms in it that I can't quite define how they work as a whole, but I know they do. Since I am not a trained dancer, I don't know how to categorize her different movements; however, I can discern their resonances in many Jamaican dance forms. At one point her feet shuffle in the style of *dinkimini*; at another point she cuts and clears with the action of someone wielding a machete, a decidedly Revivalist tendency. She uses the stiff shoulder and hip movements that one would see Kumina adherents do at a ceremony, then for a few seconds she performs the shifting foot movements similar to those done

Figure 11. Neila Ebanks performing at the Tambourine Army march, Kingston, 2017. Courtesy of Shasta-Lee Smith, 2017.

in *tambu*. Her body functions as an archive of Jamaican and African Diasporic expression.

My favorite move is when she stoops down and scoops her hands slowly into the asphalt, then rises and stretches them to the sky. This dual bending and stretching to the earth and sky remind me of movements I have seen in some religious and spiritual rituals that acknowledge the presence of the ancestors, the Creator, and divine energies, such as the orishas in Ifa. Then toward the end, she stands to one side of the circle and undulates her torso and hips slowly, like a snake, until she stops and breathes deeply, resting after her five minutes just spent dancing in the sun (Cox 2017).

The dancer's name is Neila Ebanks. She is a well-known choreographer, lecturer at the Jamaica School of Dance at the Edna Manley College of the Visual and Performing Arts, and founding director of eNkompani.E, a dance collective. The venue of her performance is Half Way Tree Square,

Figure 12. Neila Ebanks performing at the Tambourine Army march, Kingston, 2017. Courtesy of Shasta-Lee Smith, 2017.

Kingston, one of the busiest thoroughfares in the country. The event is the Survivor Empowerment March, organized on March 11, 2017, by the Tambourine Army (TA), an activist organization formed by Taitu Heron, Latoya Nugent, and Nadeen Spence. TA represents survivors of sexual violence, in collaboration with numerous other advocacy groups. There were other marches that day throughout the Caribbean, under the theme of supporting victims and survivors of sexual assault and taking a stand against gender-based violence and harassment. Ebanks and eleven members of eNkompani.E participated alongside other groups in the TA march, wearing pants, black blouses with breastplates, and purple chiffon veils "as homage to the mourning femme figures often seen at funerals" (Ebanks, pers. comm., 2022).[1] According to Ebanks they had decided in conversation with Taitu Heron, who led the spiritual aspects of the march, that upon reaching Half Way Tree she would perform the dance encircled by members of

Coda   159

eNkompani.E. When viewed as a whole the dance and the circle constitute a ritual of memorializing, healing, confronting the phenomenon of sexual violence, and generating positive energy against it.

I was writing up my research in the United States, feeling depleted and stressed out, when this march and others were happening. However, seeing Neila's dance via a mobile phone video posted to YouTube by Sherie Cox (2017) energized and empowered me. Her dance communicated with me across national borders. It was a dance that I recognized because its movements were so fundamental to Africana cultures and, in particular, to Jamaican women's audacity through movement. Using the medium of dance in a busy municipal space like Half Way Tree Square, Ebanks and the other demonstrators were making a claim for public space as a site of performance and politics as well as a locale that must be equally claimed by all. Her performance had no didactic elements; neither did it involve verbal exhortation. It was simply a perfect expression of the idea that women must be free to just *be*, with no preconditions. It delighted me and reminded me again of the importance of Black women's performance in their activism. Specifically, it resonated with the conversations I had had over the previous four years, studying the work of Sistren Theatre Collective, the Mothertongue Project, Letters from the Dead, and Olive Tree Theatre. Though not a work of theatre per se, this public performance conversed with the work of other Black women performers across space, time, and national boundaries.

Throughout this book, I have argued in support of theatre that consciously attends to the importance of geographic spaces in producing liberatory ideas about race, gender, sexuality, and class. Africana women–led theatre projects such as those examined in this book teach us lessons about the role of creative expression in grappling with the afterlives of colonialism, apartheid, and racialized slavery; newer structures of racism; and global and nationally specific iterations of patriarchy. Sistren, Mothertongue, Olive Tree, and Letters from the Dead belong to long traditions of Africana women's storytelling and political activism that are finding various means of centering gender and race in conversations about freedom and democracy. There are, however, unavoidable concerns about their economic precarity, especially as organizations started by and comprising mostly Black women.

Sistren, Mothertongue, Letters from the Dead, and Olive Tree: Current Projects and Challenges

External funds from governments, nongovernmental organizations, and private sources, as well as long-term staff and other human resources, are absolutely crucial to the survival of theatre organizations committed to the development of Black communities, and pedagogy on racial and gender justice. With regard to state/government funding one issue that has to also be considered is the extent to which that support might determine the type of engagement these organizations are able to do, specifically if they wish to do productions that explicitly critique the government. Hence, while state funding provides a much-needed lifeline for these and many other organizations, such support is not only usually fleeting but also possibly constricting, forcing them to narrow their activisms in projects tied to socioeconomic developmental goals—though their philosophies and politics are often still reflected in these projects. In order to engage in a range of conversations and advocacy, all of the organizations in this book rely on some form of external funding through artist and development agencies; nongovernmental organizations; intergovernmental organizations like UN Women, which has funded some Sistren projects; academic research organizations like the Social Sciences and Humanities Research Council of Canada, which has been a main funder of Letters from the Dead; and the National Arts Council of South Africa, a government-funded initiative that Mothertongue has benefited from. Even before the COVID-19 pandemic's effects on theatre all of the organizations struggled with funding. For example, as noted in chapter 4, funding issues kept Olive Tree from staging the Women's Theatre Festival in 2017 and 2019, illustrating that theatre events that are not driven by profits need constant and substantial external funding in order to be sustainable.

Amid these challenges, most of these organizations' ability to sustain their work, especially their theatre production, is remarkable. As of 2022, the Mothertongue Project has performed *Walk: South Africa* eleven times since 2014 in South Africa and the Netherlands, with original and newer cast members, who are mostly Black.[2] Alongside *Walk: South Africa* and other smaller projects, Mothertongue also premiered *Womb of Fire* in 2018, written by Rehane Abrahams and directed by Sara Matchett, which continues the group's focus on historical and contemporary violence against Black South African women. *Womb of Fire* has been staged at least once every year since 2018. It is the latest in Mothertongue's catalog of full-length productions, which include the founding play, *What the Water Gave Me* (2000), by Abrahams; *Tseleng: the Baggage of Bags* (2009), by Mbali Kgosidintsi; and *Ngangelizwe* (2013), by Siphumeze Khundayi.[3] Also included is the collectively created performance installation *Breathing Space* (2005), which is based on the life stories of women in the community of Darling and was produced through collaboration between these women and professional artists Jill Levenberg, Mbali Kgosidintsi, Alex Halligey, and Chuma Sopotela (see Mothertongue, n.d.). While the members continue to formulate ideas for plays and other performances, the community theatre company that Mothertongue operated in Langeberg in the Western Cape had to dissolve because its funding stream ended. Prospective funders were preoccupied with providing support for other projects affected by the pandemic. For five years it had been a major fixture in that community, featuring educational initiatives through theatre with schools and community organizations, in addition to training hundreds of young people in theatre techniques. It was the base for the Langeberg Youth Arts Project, which means that project has had to end. Langeberg is a poor community with high levels of unemployment, so the community cannot be called on to provide the resources for the theatre. There was a fundraising initiative in early 2022 via social media, but this did not garner enough support to save it (Makhutshi 2022).

Both Mothertongue's Langeberg theatre project and Olive Tree Theatre exist within the cohort of theatre initiatives whose financial problems were exacerbated by COVID-19. Yet Ntshieng Mokgoro's resolve to create more projects, including her burgeoning work with members of the Khoisan community in the Kalahari region, indicates that she views her past successful work on Olive Tree and the Women's Theatre Festival as part of a large repertoire she is building that is rooted in Black cultural affirmation in South Africa. Since my research began, she has broadened her profile as a theatre artist and mentor. She continues to produce commissioned work, and the plays she has written have been staged by other theatre companies in South Africa as well. Currently she is developing a play on former African National Congress (ANC) president Oliver Tambo, and working with a friend to create a set of African tarot cards accompanied by a site-specific performance, bridging "art and spirituality" (Mokgoro, pers. comm., 2023). She is also building her filmmaking resume with the short film *Shofar*, written by Kingsley Motau, which she directed in 2022. This and other projects join the repertoire of plays she has written, which includes *The Olive Tree* (2009), *Paradise Fall* (2013), *Distant Faces* (2014), *Phases of Mirah* (2015), *Memories and Empty Spaces* (2017), and *That Night of Trance* (cowritten with Billy Langa and first staged in 2019).

Just as Mothertongue and Ntshieng Mokgoro have had to adjust to socioeconomic setbacks and develop projects commensurate with their resources, so too have the creators of the various performances in the Letters from the Dead project. *A Vigil for Roxie* has not been performed since 2015, because of funding difficulties. However, *Song for the Beloved*—the performed exhibition in which *Vigil* was featured in 2015—has been staged five times since then in Chile, Canada, and the United States. These installations were curated by Honor Ford-Smith, Anique J. Jordan, and Kara Springer and featured performances from Chevy Eugene, Camille Turner, Danielle Smith, Nicosia Shakes, and Sanique Walters. As a transnational performance cycle with multiple iterations and collaborators, Letters from the Dead maintains a level of artistic and geographic flexibility that the other projects and groups featured in the book do not have. For example, unlike with Sistren, its success does not get evaluated based on criteria such as its maintenance of a physical headquarters or a membership body.

As the oldest organization featured in this book, Sistren Theatre Collective offers lessons about how activist-oriented and educational theatre collectives experience the ups and downs of funding streams and other challenges. Sistren's theatre production has not continued in recent years, though the collective remains part of a global network of organizations that focus on grassroots engagement and gender equity.[4] Funding problems and limited staffing have led to a reduction in its community-based and theatre projects, as well as its national and international profile. The Hannah Town Cultural Group (HTCG), which has functioned as the main resource for Sistren-produced theatre work, has done several performances since staging *A Slice of Reality* in 2009. HTCG was part of the community-based network for Letters from the Dead, and its members participated in two productions of *A Vigil for Roxie*, performing a Revival ritual prior to the 2014 performance and serving as part of the production team at the 2015 performance analyzed in chapter 3. They also performed their choral antiviolence poem "The Blood" several times up until 2017 at community-based events organized by Sistren. Sistren's work in using performance and other forms of community interface to address gender issues was undertaken through several projects to address violence in urban communities. In addition to participating from 2006 to 2014 in the Ministry of National Security's Citizen Security and Justice Programme (CSJP), the collective organized a wide-ranging community project in 2010–14 titled Tek It to Dem and Rise Up Wi Community.[5] This project consisted of research into violence in the Hannah Town and Rockfort communities in Kingston and contained a strong artistic component that incorporated adults and children. The collective's interrogation of gender included work with men, some of whom were perpetrators of intimate partner and gang violence, as well as targets of state violence. This was Sistren's last major project. More generally, the organization has somewhat devolved, because of funding and human resource problems as well as what founding member Afolashadé and former resource person Hilary Nicholson have referred to as an absence of succession planning (Afolashadé and Nicholson, pers. comm., 2014; and see Ford-Smith 1989; Green 2006; K. Smith 2013).

Notwithstanding these issues, Sistren's impact on Jamaican/Caribbean theatre and the women's/feminist movements over its forty-six years of existence is undeniable. It has managed to outlive other similar organizations founded in the 1960s to early 1980s throughout the world. Furthermore, its early productions are an indispensable part of the repertoire of postcolonial drama in Jamaica. For example, its iconic play *Bellywoman Bangarang* (1978) has been staged many times since the 1970s, including two performances in 2013 and 2019 at the Jamaica School of Drama. It is disappointing that other iconic Sistren plays have not also been restaged in the contemporary period. The list includes *QPH* (1981), which memorialized the destitute women who perished in the Eventide Home Fire in 1980 and was scripted and directed by Hertencer Lindsay with some devising by Sistren members. Also well known are *Nana Yah* (1980) a collectively created play about Jamaican national hero Nanny of the Maroons, which was directed by Jean Small; and *Muffet inna All a Wi* (1986), which was collectively created and directed by Eugene Williams and focused on Jamaican women's various encounters with sexism. Despite the limited staging of its plays, as well as its other logistical problems, Sistren has amassed an incredibly valuable archive of documents, videos, playscripts, letters, and copies of its short-running globally circulated magazine *Sistren*. These documents and videos constitute a veritable resource on the women's movement in Jamaica and the Caribbean from the 1970s to the present.

In 2017, when I was presenting my research on Sistren and Mothertongue, someone asked how the organizations might learn from each other. In my response I stated that Mothertongue seemed to be making inroads into succession planning whereas Sistren has not, particularly through the focus on bringing young people into the organization to lead it into the future, as well as through its emphasis on sexual and gender diversity in its productions, which include queer people's stories. After more thought, I also realized that Mothertongue could learn from Sistren how to collate and maintain a comprehensive archive that decades from now, could be a useful tangible resource for researchers. This would include the demanding work of producing scripts for all its major performances, including those that were devised.

Mothertongue has achieved a major landmark in recording its achievements, even in the absence of a print archive as large as Sistren's. In 2021 it published a book in recognition of its twenty-first anniversary, edited by Alex Halligey and Sara Matchett. I was among the twenty authors who contributed to the volume, titled *Collaborative Conversations: Celebrating Twenty-One Years of the Mothertongue Project* (2021). A similar book, Helen Allison's (1986) *Sistren Song: Popular Theatre in Jamaica*, was written to celebrate as well as catalog Sistren's first nine years, and an edited book that does the same to recognize the collective's five decades of work would be a valuable academic project. A text on Olive Tree Theatre that comprehensively analyzes its contributions and challenges is also absolutely necessary. Honor Ford-Smith continues to produce scholarship on Letters from the Dead, and she has documented, archived, and analyzed the project, though the chapter on *A Vigil for Roxie* in this book is the first writing that focuses solely on that play. Archiving is a difficult but essential task to facilitate future research that will deepen our understandings of theatre as activism and the full range of theatre forms and techniques currently being developed in Africa and the Diaspora.

African Diasporic Underpinnings

The research for this book began before the emergence of several important, well-known women-led movements for gender justice in the world. It has been fascinating and inspiring to observe organizations like the Tambourine Army and Women's Empowerment for Change (WE-Change) in Jamaica; and The Total Shutdown: Intersectional Womin's Movement against GBV as well as the numerous performative and social media campaigns (such as #EndRapeCulture) that have started in South Africa. These well-known platforms and movements have been critical to transnational organizing, and especially to highlighting the voices of younger generations. They operate alongside numerous grassroots-based projects and organizations that rely on Black people's voices, artistic practices, and activism. Many such grassroots-based and national groups came to prominence because of their public demonstrations, like the Marcha das Mulheres Negras (Black Women's March), founded in Brazil in 2013; the Women's March in the United States, which began in 2017; and the Market March Movement in Nigeria, which started in 2019. Other organizations led by Africana women include a focus on gender and sexual justice within a major imperative to sustain their communities and environments. Here, the Green Belt Movement, started by Wangari Maathai in Kenya in the 1970s and still operating today, is one of the most impactful, older woman–led, environmentally focused movements in the world. Another example of environmental activism, though on a smaller scale, is Fondes Amandes in Trinidad, led by a Rastafarian woman, Akilah Jaramogi, which she cofounded with her late husband, Tacuma. Regarding the use of theatre to embody Black women's stories while also creating opportunities for them in that industry, Theatre of Black Women, founded by Bernardine Evaristo, Patricia Hilaire, and

Paulette Randall, comes to mind.[6] Theatre of Black Women is now defunct, but it is still impactful as the first theatre dedicated to Black women in Britain. Also notable is the Black Women Playwrights Group in the United States. In the genre of literature, FEMRITE in Uganda (founded by author Mary Karooro Okurut) and Mbaasem in Ghana (founded by playwright and novelist Ama Ata Aidoo) are two long-standing examples of the link between the creative arts and Black/African women coming to voice in their societies. The spaces for personal testimony provided through social media are also important to this conversation. The list includes #LifeInLeggings, which was started by Ronelle King in Barbados in 2015 and became a pan-Caribbean phenomenon; and #MeToo, which was founded in the United States by Tarana Burke, a Black woman, in 2006 and became more prominent in 2017 when the hashtag arose.[7]

Sistren, Mothertongue, Letters from the Dead, and Olive Tree combine elements of public engagement through community-based grassroots organizing around a multiplicity of issues, creating spaces for women's stories and promoting the work of Black women theatre artists. Their work and that of other organizations that primarily utilize performance or are mainly focused on community interface may not be as famous as that of organizations with better funding, social media presences, or news media coverage. However, attending to them means deepening our understandings of localized activisms by Africana women within and on behalf of marginalized communities, because the local and global spaces that Africana people occupy shape their day-to-day lives, including through oppressive systems like gender-based violence, denial of reproductive justice, economic inequalities, and gang and state violence. As Keisha-Khan Y. Perry (2013, xvi) writes, based on her study of the Gamboa de Baixo neighborhood association in Brazil, a "focus on the gendered dimensions of Black women's activism forces us to rethink Black resistance, as well as reconsider how Blacks offer alternative views on how African diasporic communities operated and should operate." Among Africana women theatre-makers, their work is a main indicator that "Diaspora not only becomes a set of physical movements . . . but also a set of aesthetic and interpretive strategies" (Pinto 2013, 4). The repertoires of Sistren, Mothertongue, Letters from the Dead, Ntshieng Mokgoro, and Olive Tree demonstrate ongoing processes of negotiation, resistance, and struggle, as well as explicit confrontations within local, national, and global contexts. Scholarly approaches that acknowledge these imperatives within a transnational framework address global, national, and local sites in activism and deepen understandings of Africana people's political labor through theatre and performance.

Notes

Introduction

1. A man by the name of Maas Beres (whose last name I don't know) used to train a group of teenage boys in military discipline, including how to stand at attention, march, and salute. Maas Beres himself had participated in this performance as a boy. Dressed in khaki uniforms with wooden rifles, they would march throughout the community on Boxing Day, accompanied by drummers. My yard was one of the stops on the way. Maas Beres would yell orders and target any boy who did not salute properly or stand at attention. This was the most entertaining part of the performance. Later, it occurred to me that this might have been a reenactment of Jamaican soldiers leaving for World War II to fight on the side of the British as colonial subjects. It also fostered homosocial relationships and socialized participants into a traditional view of manhood, marked by a readiness to defend one's community.

2. Among them are theatre director, scholar, and actor Brian Heap, who was staff tutor in drama when I was an undergraduate student and later served as coordinator of the Philip Sherlock Centre for the Creative Arts (PSCCA) at UWI; and poet and playwright Jean Small, former PSCCA coordinator. Others who frequented the center included actor, Sistren member, and founder of Women's Media Watch of Jamaica Hilary Nicholson; actor and writer Carol Lawes; and musician and visual artist Mbala Mbogo.

3. A good example of this is the Universal Negro Improvement Association and African Communities League (UNIA-ACL), the largest Black global movement in history, founded by Marcus Garvey. At the organization's height, in the 1920s and 1930s, UNIA-ACL chapters tended to address local and national problems, including labor rights and anticolonialism, from a global standpoint.

4. For example, in the United States, Black Lives Matter (BLM) protestors, even when abiding by legal strictures, have been subjected to more policing than have anti-BLM protestors, white supremacists, and others who have also occupied public

spaces. The January 6, 2021, violent attack on the US Capitol by a mostly white mob was a blatant reminder to the world of the racially motivated, unequal reactions of the US police forces and military to different forms of protest.

5. Khwezi, who lived with HIV/AIDS for many years, died in October 2016.

6. As a field of study, feminist aesthetics has also been instrumental in connecting philosophical understandings of art to gender, social power, and representation; see Allan 1995; Harker and Farr 2015; Pinto 2013; Reckitt and Phelan 2001; Rosenberg 2009; Ziarek 2012.

7. Canonical white male theatre artists have published the most widely on their methods. For example, I have been in many discussions about theatre and activism in which an interlocutor casually utilized German theatre artist and scholar Bertolt Brecht's dramaturgy as a descriptor of a theatre project I was discussing, simply because it utilized minimalist set design and acting.

8. A large body of scholarship recognizes the pedagogic and expressive role of art created by Africana people (hooks 1990; Jones 2015; Moten 2003; Tate 2009; Wright 1997; Wynter 1992). Much of this scholarship emphasizes the role of the arts in advancing Black radical politics.

9. Conquergood refers to Frederick Douglass's ([1855] 1969) call for a focus on the experiences of enslaved people and the environment of plantations in generating knowledge about slavery, as opposed to relying on texts written about slavery. He states that Douglass anticipated Johannes Fabian's (1990) emphasis on the need for ethnographic approaches that are grounded in experience and performance rather than focused solely on information gathering.

Chapter 1. "Mek Wi Choose fi Wiself"

1. Similarly, in 2013, then minister of youth and culture Lisa Hanna called for a review of Jamaica's anti-choice laws on the grounds that legalizing abortion could decrease crime and violence in the country. She pointed to the cost to the country of taking care of neglected and abused children (Radio Jamaica News 2013).

2. Surveys by other groups that neither utilized nuanced language nor distinguished between reasons for an abortion found that a majority of the public disapproved of abortion. For example, a 2009 study by Mustard Seed Communities, a member of the Ecumenical Pro-Life Council, found that a large majority of respondents were opposed to abortion. Among the questions in the poll were: "Should abortion be used to control family size?" and "How do you feel about the statement: In cases of rape or incest, the crime of the father should not bring about the murder of the child?" (DAWN 2009; *Jamaica Observer* 2009; Maxwell 2012, 111).

3. Carole Pateman (1988), in *The Sexual Contract*, engages in a gendered critique of Enlightenment thinkers, specifically the social contract of John Locke, Thomas Hobbes, and Jean-Jacques Rousseau.

4. Bourne performed an abortion on a fourteen-year-old rape victim in a public hospital and was charged under section 58 of the British OAPA. He was later acquitted, with the defense that the pregnancy was a threat to the girl's life.

5. Tracy Robinson, constitutional lawyer and legal scholar, assisted me with this search.

6. In the case of the sixteen-year-old, the hospital made the report to the police after the girl received medical attention following the abortion. In the other, the police did not reveal how they found out about the abortion.

7. The doctors were investigated not only by the police but also by the Centre for the Investigation of Sexual Offences and Child Abuse and the Office of the Children's Registry (a government agency charged with recording offenses against children).

8. In 2020, a twenty-two-year-old man who allegedly raped a fourteen-year-old girl and impregnated her twice was arrested alongside his mother, who allegedly helped him procure two abortions. The police made the arrests after the girl told her mother about what had happened to her (Radio Jamaica News 2020).

9. The same activists who champion anti-choice laws are central in anti-LGBTQ activism, even as they remain relatively silent on other problems, such as sexual and domestic violence. The most high-profile anti-choice and anti-LGBTQ groups are the Love March Movement, Missionaries of the Poor, Hear the Children's Cry, and the Jamaica Coalition for a Healthy Society. The Tambourine Army, Women's Empowerment for Change (WE-Change), I'm Glad I'm a Girl, Air Me Now, Sistren Theatre Collective, and the Partnership for Women's Health and Well-Being, a pro-choice network, are critical in activism against sexual violence.

10. Two other vocal women who are critical of abortion are Betty Ann Blaine, who cofounded Hear the Children's Cry, and Doreen Brady-West, who was chairperson of the Coalition for the Defence of Life in 2009.

11. According to the APRAG (Jamaica Ministry of Health 2007, 4, 10), 75 percent of women who went to the Victoria Jubilee Hospital in Kingston to be treated after having unsafe abortions were unemployed, and 27 percent were in low-wage jobs. "All had inner-city addresses."

12. A body of scholarship interrogates these tropes in the United States; see Collins 2008; Harris-Perry 2011; Jenkins 2007; Orleck 2006; Roberts 1998.

13. Sistren also formed the Rockfort Cultural Group, from another community on the periphery of downtown Kingston, though HTCG has worked more closely with Sistren.

14. Among these groups were the Caribbean Association of Feminist Research and Action; the Working Committee on Women's Reproductive Health and Rights, under the auspices of Development Alternatives with Women for a New Era (DAWN); Women's Media Watch, Jamaica; and Advocates for Safe Parenthood: Improving Reproductive Equity.

15. This development occurred in the early 2000s to 2010, most notably with the CSJP, geared at addressing gang violence, and the Tek It to Dem (Take It to Them) program, aimed at addressing gender-based violence.

16. The members are Tony Allen, Althea Blackwood, Pauline Blake, Sonia Britton, Karlene Campbell, Cinderella Green, Sandra Hanson, Kadian Jones, Patricia McCrae, Adrian Raphael, Patricia Riley, Joan Stewart, and Marlon Thompson. The skit was devised and performed by Blackwood, Blake-Palmer, Britton, Campbell, Green,

McCrae, Riley, Stewart, and Thompson. HTCG's counterpart, Rockfort Cultural Group, contains a similar mix of women and men.

17. My experience and what I have perceived of other people's experiences are undoubtedly affected by my socioeconomic status as middle class and gender as a woman. There are certain people who may be considered suspicious by the police and security guards and undergo more scrutiny than others.

18. Portia Simpson-Miller served as prime minister in 2006–7 and then in 2012–16.

19. She stated, "If you change the women's voices it's a different play. They've got to speak with their own voice, and in the same way that we watch opera in Italian and everybody is prepared to listen to them sing in Italian, and watch French movies, because they're avant-garde . . . so why should we dilute our thing? And we didn't do it. And it touched everybody" (Lindsay-Sheppard, pers. comm., 2014).

20. One such incident occurred in December 1884. A riot broke out in Kingston because a group of Christmas revelers were harassed by the police who were sent by the mayor. The Riot Act was read and soldiers called in. Hill (1992, 248) accounts, "the regiment opened fire; two people were killed and others seriously injured."

21. "Uptown" is a reference to uptown Kingston, the area where middle-class and rich people normally reside.

22. The submission states, "The real problem of men who are living beyond the reach of the law both in and out of the home, *particularly within the inner-city communities* . . . will continue until these strongholds are dismantled allowing for the law to reach the actions of the predators. We therefore join voices with others in calling for the dismantling of the garrisons to allow for the enforcement of the law in its various forms" (CLDU 2008, 4 [emphasis added]). This statement was made in reference to an article published in the August 3, 2008, issue of the *Jamaica Observer*, which reported on the sexual exploitation of young girls in urban communities (referred to as garrison communities) by dons.

23. Pro-choice submissions to the parliamentary Joint Select Committee on Abortion came from Advocates for Safe Parenthood: Improving Reproductive Equity (ASPIRE) Barbados; ASPIRE Saint Lucia; Woman Inc., Jamaica; Women's Media Watch, Jamaica; the United Church of Jamaica; the Ministry of Health of Guyana; Catholics for Choice; and other smaller organizations and individuals (Heron, Toppin, and Finikin 2009).

24. English translation: "So that you can go in and make decisions on your own. Nobody must make decisions for you. It's your body. You are the one who is feeling it. Those are your feet in the shoes, getting squeezed. They're talking about [allowing an abortion] only in cases of sickness or rape. What kind of nonsense is that?"

25. For example, D'bi Young Anitafrika's repetition and extension of words and use of puns—like her transition of the word *I* into *eye* in her poem "Jazz"—resonate rhythmically and emotively. Another example is the guttural "laaaaaaaawd" that distinguishes the work of Mikey Smith, one of Sistren's contemporaries and cohorts at the Jamaica School of Drama in the 1970s. It was a way of catching back the rhythm of the stanza after it had been interrupted, as well as of voicing pain and frustration.

26. The subject of abortion has arisen multiple times throughout the years, reflected in media coverage; see C. Cooper 2019; Francis 2018; *Gleaner* 2009; Radio Jamaica News 2013; G. Taylor 2019; S. Taylor 2019; Tufton 2018; Virtue 2012.

27. The signatories to the submission were Shawna-Kae Burns, Omar Francis, Jaevion Nelson, Shani Roper, Edward Shakes (my father), Nicosia Shakes, Camilo Thame, and Maziki Thame.

28. I also experienced a sense of unease for multiple reasons, from considering whether to correct how I was titled on my name card (they wrote "Ms." instead of "Dr.") to trying to prioritize which statement against abortion to rebut.

29. The skit's technique is not to be confused with legislative theatre, which Augusto Boal theorized and practiced. Unlike the method utilized by Sistren and HTCG, Boal's (1995) legislative theatre did not require a process of rehearsal and ethnographic research, nor does it require performance within a legislative space.

Chapter 2. "The Wound Is Still There"

Sections of this chapter were previously published in Nicosia Shakes, "Race, the Public Sphere, and Sexual Violence in the Mothertongue Project's *Walk: South Africa*," *Signs: Journal of Women in Culture and Society* 46, no. 3 (2021): 537–60. © 2021 by the University of Chicago.

1. Nina Callaghan, Genna Gardini, Sara Matchett, Koleka Putuma, and Rosa Postlethwaite (five of the six performers of *Walk: South Africa*) all told me in interviews that *Walk: South Africa* is a critique of rape culture.

2. Though men and boys also experience sexual violence and women/girls also perpetrate it (especially in cases of women assaulting children), it is overwhelmingly a crime committed against female-bodied people, especially women and girls. Some feminist writers have associated perpetration of sexual violence with masculinity and victimization with femininity, regardless of the perpetrator's sex. For example, Pumla Gqola (2015), Dianne F. Herman (1984), and Jessica Ringrose and Emma Renold (2011) opine that rape is a crime mostly enacted on people who are feminized, including men and boys, and perpetrated by people who are masculinized.

3. The murderers of Sulnita, Camron, Uyinene, and Hannah received several life sentences each for their crimes. The trial of the two men arrested for murdering Jodene Pieters was postponed in 2018, and I have since then found no update on it. See also Dube 2020.

4. One of the most high-profile cases of sexual violence against a man or boy in South Africa was the rape of an eighteen-year-old Black student by four white teenagers at Jan Kempdorp High School, Northern Cape, in February 2015. While the victim was painted white and then penetrated with a broomstick, other boys of different races watched, laughed, and recorded the act. The rape was allegedly part of a racial initiation ritual. The four attackers, aged fourteen to eighteen, were charged in 2015. The student stayed in school but tragically died of leukemia in 2016 (Evans 2015; Gqola 2015; Malgas 2015; News24 2016).

5. These statistics were gathered from 106 countries, representing every continent.

6. Shireen Hassim (2014, 139–40) notes, "Zuma joined his supporters outside the court everyday defiantly singing liberation songs, including, 'Bring me my machine gun,' a song sung to the action of firing an AK 47 and reinforcing a form of masculine militant politics contrary to the ethos of the 'women-friendly' pretensions of the ANC [African National Congress] government." Some members of workers' unions and other groups thought it politically expedient to side with Zuma, regardless of whether they believed he was guilty (Gqola 2015, 110).

7. Black women playwrights have also focused on rape under authoritarian systems, slavery, and conflict situations. Examples include Robbie McCauley's *Sally's Rape* (1999), Lynn Nottage's *Ruined* (2010), and Sistren's *Nana Yah* (1980).

8. *Jackrolling* was a term coined for frequent gang rapes occurring in and around Pretoria and Johannesburg, while *iintsara* were violent gangs made up of Black youth, mainly from Nyanga township in Cape Town. *Iintsara* activities and jackrolling were pervasive during the latter part of apartheid, in the 1980s–90s. *Ukuthwala* is an older practice that still takes place in some remote rural communities. For more detailed discussions of these practices and their social impact, see Gqola 2007, 123.

9. Homosexuality was explicitly policed under apartheid laws. In 1996 South Africa became the first country in the world to introduce laws to protect lesbians and gay men from discrimination. Though some scholars/activists see the equality clause in the Constitution as inclusive of transgender and intersex people as well (Klein 2009), others find it less specific on these fronts (Livermon 2012).

10. For another example of how racist structures normalize and even encourage gender-based violence among Black people, see Hilary Beckles (2004) for a discussion of how enslaved Black men participated in violence against enslaved Black women in the Caribbean.

11. Booysen stated that up to five or six men had raped her. Prosecutors doubt the number because her statement was given while she was experiencing intense pain and under heavy medication. In giving her account, she mentioned the name Zwai, which was the nickname of one of her friends, Jonathon Davids, who was initially arrested but then released because of lack of evidence. In a media interview, Davids speculated that Booysen might have mentioned his name because she thought that he would know the rapists and might be a source of information for the police. There is also speculation that the name Zwai was that of another young man in the same community (eNCA 2013). Some people have questioned the extent to which the police gave the case enough importance in the early aftermath of Booysen's death.

12. The juvenile served three years and was released in 2015. Ram Singh reportedly committed suicide in jail, though he is rumored to have been murdered by other inmates. The other four—Mukesh Singh, Akshay Thakur, Vinay Sharma, and Pawan Gupta—were sentenced to death and hanged in 2020 (Dorwart 2021).

13. For example, Gqola (2015) discusses two columns written by Ferial Haffajee (2013a, 2013b), "Words Fail Us" and "#WTF Was She Thinking?" Though Haffajee consistently writes against gender-based violence, Gqola identifies in these columns

various features of the female fear factory because the articles imply that Booysen's foster parents were not protective enough of her.

14. For example, after four of Jyoti Singh Pandey's attackers were sentenced to death in 2013, defense lawyer A. P. Singh stated in a post-trial media interview outside the courthouse, "If my sister or daughter . . . disgraced herself or allowed herself to lose face or character . . . I would most certainly take this sister or daughter to the farmhouse and in front of the entire family I would put petrol on her and set her alight" (Udwin 2015).

15. The film is controversial for many reasons, including the fact that it features insensitive interviews with Mukesh Singh, who was not only one of the attackers but was the driver of the bus on which Jyoti was assaulted. Some have raised ethical questions about how the producer acquired permission to interview a man on death row. The interviews with Singh and defense lawyers M. L. Sharma and A. P. Singh are difficult to watch given their violent, remorseless, and misogynistic tones.

16. Had the two women been from the same country, race would have figured much more significantly in these national comparisons. I know of no case of a white woman being raped and murdered in the same way as Booysen, though there are cases of white South African women being raped and murdered. I have not yet come across contemporary data on how South African authorities handle rape cases in which the survivor is a white woman as opposed to a Black South African or other South African woman of color.

17. Among these were the rape and murder of thirty-one-year-old Eudy Simelane in 2008, and the rape and murder of twenty-four-year-old Ngugu "Letty" Wapad in 2010 (this latter resembled in many ways the attack on Anene). Themba Mvubu was sentenced to life in prison for Eudy's murder. Archibald Itumeleng, Moleko Chweu, Thabiso Majama, and a fifteen-year-old were found guilty of Letty's, with the three men sentenced to three life sentences plus ten years and the juvenile to fifteen. Another high-profile case was the rape of Baby Tshepang (a pseudonym) in 2001. Dawid Potse was handed a life sentence for the crime (Evans 2013; *Mail and Guardian* 2013; Ngesi 2002). Baby Tshepang is alive and now in her twenties. Her experience was the basis for Lara Foot Newton's *Tshepang: The Third Testament* (2005).

18. *Walk: South Africa* was performed live five times in 2014, including at a V-Day *One Billion Rising* event at UCT, the Sex Actually festival at the University of Witwatersrand Drama for Life arts center, the Live Art Festival at the Gordon Institute for the Performing and Creative Arts, and the Johannesburg and Cape Town Fringe Festivals.

19. *Vlei* is an Afrikaans word that is pronounced "flay." In size, a *vlei* is larger than a pond but smaller than a lake.

20. Prior to discussing the movement with Khundayi, I had described it as resembling a weakened, more submissive version of the *toyi toyi*, which is iconic in South African anti-apartheid and current street protests and is defined by heavy foot stomping with the knees at waist level and a raised hand.

21. Disebo Gift Makau's body was found on August 15, 2014. The man who murdered her, Stoffel Pule Motlhokwane, was sentenced to two life terms in prison (Igual 2015).

22. Hottentot was a derogatory colonial term for the Khoikhoi people.

23. Her 2015 performance at Stellenbosch University, which was then mired in controversy about racism, received lukewarm applause from its mostly white audience and complaints from members of the audience to the organizers (Mkhabela 2015). It was recorded for TEDx Stellenbosch.

24. The case did not receive much publicity in the media, more than likely because the rapist was an old white man and did not fit the usual profile, or because it did not involve murder as in Anene Booysen's case. Knoetze was sentenced to fifty-two years for nineteen counts related to rape, human trafficking, and sexual abuse of minors; but he will serve only fifteen years. The thirty-five-year-old mother of one of the girls was also convicted for assisting Knoetze in exchange for money. She was sentenced to twenty-two years on twelve counts, but will serve only eleven years in prison. These sentences seem disproportionate to the crimes. I have not named the mother because doing so would identify her daughter (South African Government 2015; South African Police Service 2014).

25. Toni Childs' lyrics, "Mother can you tell me please, 'am I safe?'" from her song, *Death*, also inspired the other sounds that were mixed in. The performance was partly influenced by Sara Matchett's personal struggles with coping with her aging mother's Alzheimer's dementia, and feeling that she can no longer be vulnerable in front of her mother. In her words it was "a last reaching out to mother" (pers. comm., 2015).

26. In addition to Disebo Gift Makau, the list of names included thirty-four-year-old Sizakele Sigasa and twenty-four-year-old Salome Masooa, who were murdered in 2007; twenty-four-year-old Noxolo Nongwaza, who was murdered in 2011; and Mvuleni Fana, who survived being sexually assaulted in 1999. There was also the name Bernadette, listed without a surname, which perhaps was of someone who wished to remain partly anonymous. I have not included other names that probably belong to women who are still alive, in the interest of their privacy. I do not know whether their consent to have their names in the performance or Mothertongue's inclusion of the names based on familiar cases means I have the right to include them here. Masooa's name is included in my recount of the performance because she was a high-profile activist.

27. I asked the question after I critiqued Brechtian epic theatre, which I think has been the dramatic canon most responsible for critiques of emotional performances. I brought up Bertolt Brecht in the discussion because at the time I was having many conversations with other theatre artists in which his methods were constantly idealized. I concede that Brecht's Verfremdungseffekt (V-effekt, alienation effect), which seeks to make the audience think about characters' dilemmas intellectually rather than identifying with them emotionally, has been misinterpreted as *deadpan techniques that offer no space for emotion*. Still, I think Brecht would have had the same critiques of *Nomzamo* as some of the audience members because of his notion of dissociating the audience's emotional connections with characters from their political reaction to the problem depicted in a play.

28. Dlamini was working on an after-school drama project for schoolchildren at Outreach Foundation (Hillbrow Theatre) in Johannesburg in 2009, when one girl in her session told her about her experience. See chapter 4 for more on *Nomzamo*.

29. As I wrote this, I thought of William Shakespeare's play *Hamlet*, with its lengthy soliloquys and excessive performance of young Danish male angst, and I wondered: if we can accept this in *Hamlet* and many European/white male-centered movies and plays, why shouldn't Nomzamo, as a young African girl, also have her thoughts delivered in lengthy angst-filled verse, even if it might be tiresome to some members of the audience?

30. Matchett similarly has problems with Yaël Farber's 2015 play *Nirbhaya*, based on Jyoti Singh Pandey's rape and murder. She feels that the play mythologizes Jyoti and inadvertently downplays the horror of what happened to her (pers. comm., 2015).

Chapter 3. "Mi a go try release yu"

1. It is possible that the name the child meant to write was Omar.

2. The unpublished script for *A Vigil for Roxie* is referenced with permission of the playwrights, Carol Lawes, Eugene Williams, Honor Ford-Smith, and Amba Chevannes. The play was originally completed in 2011 and reworked in 2014 and 2015.

3. The performance was included in the biennial conference of the Hemispheric Institute of Performance and Politics, held at the University of Chile.

4. The conflict has also been referred to less popularly as the West Kingston Incursion, most notably in the name of the committee charged with carrying out the inquiry into the events.

5. Edward Seaga, former prime minister and head of the JLP, oversaw the creation of the community after expelling its original inhabitants, who were not considered loyal to the JLP.

6. Coke inherited his position from his father, Lester Lloyd "Jim Brown" Coke (1969–92), one of Jamaica's most notorious dons.

7. Not all the deaths related to the government's search for Coke took place in West Kingston. For instance, Coke's accountant, Keith Clarke, who lived in a middle-class community many miles from Tivoli Gardens, was murdered when soldiers ransacked his house searching for Coke. The government inquiry exempted Clarke from its official list of civilians who died as a result of the incursion. Therefore, the official number provided is sixty-nine. I did not exclude Clarke from the death toll provided in this chapter. The initial numbers provided by the public defender included seventy-six civilians, forty-four of whom had not engaged the police and soldiers in battle. The deputy superintendent of police testified that six of these deaths were not related to the incursion and should be excluded, and the commission concurred (I did exclude these six from the death toll provided in this chapter). Though the commission's report and other forensic reports state that three members of the security forces were killed, the commission's report only has information on the death of one soldier. Some people in West Kingston have said that up to two hundred people were killed as a result of the incursion. There is still no forensic record supporting this number, and it seems to include those who were

killed during a much longer time period before and after the incursion, which the official figures do not account for. See also Cordner et al., 2017; Jamaica Ministry of Justice 2016, appendix 14.

8. Lundy and Jamain were from Portmore, a town outside Kingston, and had relatives in Tivoli Gardens.

9. Members of the government, especially former prime minister Golding, were exposed and embarrassed, while several lawyers and activists enjoyed the limelight, especially MP and attorney-at-law K. D. Knight, whom the public dubbed "star boy" after a popular dancehall song by an artiste called Mavado.

10. Williams has been engaged in a long legal battle with the Jamaican government to get justice for her son through the conviction of the police officer who killed him. Since no bullets lodged in his body, it was difficult to discern which of the three officers who attacked Jason killed him, which led to a not-guilty verdict in 2005 (Jamaicans for Justice 2010).

11. The exhibition *Bearing Witness: Four Days in West Kingston* (2017–19), which is about the Tivoli Incursion, similarly draws on Revival, as well as Rastafarian and other Jamaican philosophies, cosmologies, and rituals. It was housed at the University of Pennsylvania Museum of Archaeology and Anthropology and curated by Deborah Thomas, Junior "Gabu" Wedderburn, and Deanne M. Bell (see *Tivoli Stories*, n.d.). The documentary *Four Days in May: Kingston 2010*, directed by Thomas, Wedderburn, and Bell, features interviews with residents of Tivoli Gardens.

12. *An Echo in the Bone* uses the ritual of the Nine Night, and *QPH* uses the Kumina ritual of calling on the ancestors to enable a narrative around a traumatic event. Kumina is a religious/spiritual practice with central African origins.

13. Momsen (2002) states that although matrifocality is usually associated with Afro-Caribbean gender relations, most South Asian (predominantly Indian) women who came to the Caribbean in the mid-nineteenth century as indentured laborers were relatively economically independent, in contrast to those women in their countries of origin who did not participate in indentureship.

14. The novel and play were written after the fall of right-wing President Alberto Fujimori's government in 2000, and in the same time frame as the Peruvian Truth and Reconciliation Commission's (2001–3) work to investigate two decades of human rights abuses under the regimes of Fujimori and his predecessors, Fernando Belaúnde and Alan García.

15. The reference to Murray's love for cowboy comics was meant to show his gentle nature. However, it is possible that these comics influenced his fascination with guns, since cowboy comics and movies are usually violent.

16. English translation: "Mama, you know I love you. Sometimes I just talk hard to you because I am under pressure. Ok? How do you think I felt when they killed even Andre? He was just a little youth. And he was so sensible. He deserved better than that. Why do things like this have to happen? Life is just a book of puzzlement. . . . Northside men will feel it because of what they did. They should know they can't cross this border. A lot of them will turn into ghosts tonight, or my name isn't Conqueror.

. . . [to audience] What? Why are you looking at me? You think you are better than me? Look in the mirror and examine yourself. Run along Mr. and Miss Innocent because you are just a vampire. You think you could live if we weren't fighting each other? Open your eyes. I am the master now. None shall escape. That's right."

This monologue is directly inspired by "Doggie's Diary." For example, the sentences, "Run along Mr. and Miss Innocent because you are jus a vampire. You tink you coulda live if we never a fight we one anodder?" are taken from the sentence, "Run along Mr. and Miss perfect because you are just a vampire[;] you are worst than me [sic]" (Lawes et al., 2015, 23; *Gleaner* 2010a).

17. The title "mi general" is also often used as a sign of respect/brotherhood in ordinary conversations among men.

18. Mark Figueroa (2004) argues that male underachievement in schools is ironically an effect of male privileging. Girls perform better than boys in school partly because women need to be more educated than men in order to successfully compete in the economy. In addition, girls are expected to be more disciplined in general, and are given less freedom to pursue recreational activities outside the home than boys. As Keisha Lindsay (2004) points out, girls' and women's better academic performance has not significantly challenged patriarchal structures in Jamaica. The poorest citizens are still mostly female, government is still male dominated, and senior administrators are mostly male (see also Lindsay 2018).

19. In the United States, one academic disagreement is around the term *Black male privilege*, which was popularized by a document called "The Black Male Privilege Checklist" written by Jewel Woods (2008), based on his research with Black men.

20. Among such songs are Dexta Daps's "Grow Rough" (2017), with the lyrics, "If mi gun nah come mi nah go nowhere" (if my gun isn't coming I'm not going anywhere); and Bounti Killa's "Look into My Eyes" (2000), which features, "the only friend I know is this gun I have." Masicka uses female similes for his gun in "Drug Lawd" (2019): "like mi bad bitch so di handle pon mi gun broad" (like my bad bitch that's how broad the handle on my gun is). Gun analogies pervade most popular erotic dancehall songs, including Spice's "Romantic Mood" (2019), "bust it up inna mi belly mac 11 Mackie" (burst it into my belly mac 11 Mackie); Mavado's "Squeeze Breast " (2007), "she say she waah mi squeeze har breast dem like di trigger of my gun" (she says she wants me to squeeze her breasts like the trigger of my gun); and Ishawna's "Mi Belly" (2018), "mek cocky bun mi belly like mi get gunshot" (make the cock burn my belly like I got shot). Hip-hop music similarly features gun content and references, such as Tupac Shakur's personification of his gun as his girlfriend in "Me and My Girlfriend" (1996).

21. The song "'03 Bonnie and Clyde" samples Tupac Shakur's "Me and My Girlfriend" (1996).

22. This analysis is not a complete account of the gender dynamics in hip-hop music. As Kathy Iandoli (2019) points out, women in hip-hop in the early 2000s who depicted themselves in overly sexual ways were partly responding to the industry's sexual exploitation of Black women by seeking to reclaim their sexuality.

23. English translation: "That's how you want to treat me, Roxie? You forgot that I am the one who has your back out there? How many times have I watched the corner for you and told you who was plotting against you and trying to sell you out? You better go take care of your business. Let go of me, boy!"

24. English translation, Roxie: "Come on Shanika. Are you really dealing with me, Roxie, like this?" Shanika: "I said to let go of me!" Roxie: "Shanika! Come on, baby."

25. English translation: "One of them took out a Glock and fired one shot. And Roxie stopped talking. One of them said, 'Shut your mouth. Aren't you a bad girl? Aren't you with a bad man? Bad girls don't cry. Don't make any noise.' He pushed me down, and the one with the Glock turned it on me. The other one drew down his pants. 'Let me see what your man is going to say now.' And they did what they wanted to do. All the while the sun was shining brightly through the holes in the zinc. After they went away everything got quiet. So quiet. Like no shots were fired and everybody was still asleep. Like nobody heard anything."

26. I have avoided more details about this incident because of the legal stakes involved and because I do not have permission from the man's family to detail what allegedly happened to him.

27. Sexual relationships and sexual violence by men against men in crime networks are even more suppressed in public discourse. For instance, it is alleged that some influential gang leaders, such as the now deceased Donald "Zeeks" Phipps, have forced their male enemies to perform sex acts on them (*Gay Jamaica Watch* 2005). The novel *A Brief History of Seven Killings* by Marlon James (2014), which won the Man Booker Prize in 2015, addresses this topic, albeit in a spectacularized way.

28. Most of the prime beachfront properties in Jamaica have been sold or leased to private hoteliers and other companies. There is currently a movement to prevent the government from leasing sections of the Cockpit Country to Noranda, a North American aluminum company, for bauxite mining. The Cockpit Country is a major watershed in western Jamaica and home to the Leeward Maroons, a community formed by people who escaped slavery during the seventeenth and eighteenth centuries (see *Save Cockpit Country*, n.d.; Spence 2021).

29. English translation: "No. I don't want to come to any memorial. Right now, I don't want to remember all that took place."

30. English translation: "All of the men are already dead. Living men are at the dance, and it is living men I want."

31. English translation: "God bless the man who invented DNA. That's what we need. They need to bring DNA to Jamaica. Maybe then Miss Iris will stop building memorials."

32. Like Ford-Smith, Afolashadé is a cofounder of Sistren Theatre Collective. Many people who have worked on the Letters from the Dead project are affiliated with Sistren. However, Letters from the Dead is distinct from Sistren.

33. In the popular theatre industry, the roots play emerged in the 1980s as a theatre form that is mainly marketed to working-class Jamaicans. It utilizes farce, stock

characters, and racial, class, and gender caricatures like other popular theatre forms in other parts of the world. Types of theatre that are geared at primarily middle-class audiences contain similar tendencies, though without the more explicit farcical elements and challenges to middle-class social norms found in roots theatre.

Chapter 4. Alternative Spaces

1. A large part of the support that Mhlophe and Dike received in publishing their plays came from outside South Africa, including from the Open University in the United Kingdom.

2. Later, the 1936 Native Trust and Land Act of South Africa increased the quota to 13 percent (South African Government 2013).

3. The two plays were *How Long?* (1973) and *Too Late!* (1975). Unlike Kente's larger repertoire the plays contained explicit anti-apartheid critiques (Kruger 1999; Duval Smith 2004).

4. The Market Theatre, founded in 1976 by white artists Mannie Manim and Barney Simon, staked its reputation on being a "nonracial" theatre, and committed to hosting anti-apartheid plays. The Market Theatre Laboratory, founded in 1989 by Simon and Black actor/writer John Kani, is now a major training ground for new theatre artists throughout the African continent.

5. A shebeen sells primarily liquor, usually without a license.

6. Abrahams was commenting on the techniques that she applied in her play *What the Water Gave Me*, first produced in 2000. For some discussion of how personhood is constructed in African and African Diasporic philosophical systems and cosmologies, see P. Henry 2000; Mawere 2011; Washington 2014.

7. *Sleepwalking Land* (*Terra Sonâmbula*) was first published in Portuguese and then translated into English by David Brookshaw in 2006. The novel is set during the Mozambican civil war of the 1980s and focuses on the human effects of war.

8. *Have You Seen Zandile?* and *Paradise Fall* share with *Phases* a cathartic scene in which the main character learns via letters that though the parent she longed for has passed away, that parent's love for her is still intact.

9. The quotation in the section title is from Chuma Mapoma (pers. comm., 2015). These lines were also said by a character in *Womyn: The Tell Your Truth Movement*, scripted and directed by Mapoma at the Olive Tree Women's Theatre Festival in 2015.

10. Sistren members received some training in theatre techniques through the Jamaica School of Drama and other relationships with theatre artists, but besides Honor Ford-Smith, the collective was not able to produce a unit of members to direct major productions. For an analysis of some of Sistren's problems regarding division of labor and internal hierarchies, see Ford-Smith 1989. The use of external male and female directors for most of its plays was necessary but could be problematized through a feminist lens.

11. I interviewed another director as well, but I was unable to get her permission to include the interview in the book due to communication problems.

12. For instance, Sistren's 1978 play *Bellywoman Bangarang*, which focuses on teenage pregnancy, is always performed with adult women in the cast. Another example is the 2015 Broadway production of Danai Gurira's *Eclipsed*, in which most of the characters are teenagers. The production featured actors in their early to midthirties.

13. Msimanga is the former artistic director of Olive Tree Theatre and cofounder of the theatre company Clockwork HeART. She performs and writes as an independent artist and has taught theatre-making at the University of the Witwatersrand (Wits University) and the National School of the Arts. Seane is the former artistic manager of Soweto Theatre, and continues to direct, act, and teach at institutions such as the Market Theatre Laboratory. Hardie is founder of Freevoice Productions and executive director of the International Association of Theatre for Children and Young People (ASSITEJ). Foot is a playwright and director, as well as CEO and artistic director of the Baxter Theatre in Cape Town. Lewis is currently associate professor and head of the Department of Performing Arts at Tshwane University of Technology. Loots is not a theatre artist per se. She is a dancer-choreographer who lectures in the Drama and Performance Studies program at the University of KwaZulu-Natal (UKZN) and is also artistic director of the UKZN Centre for Creative Arts and founder of Flatfoot Dance Company. She taught Mapoma at UKZN.

14. The quotation in the section title is taken from a statement by Ntshieng Mokgoro in my interview with her in 2015. She said, "I just love women who believe in themselves and who say, 'Nothing can stop us from living. We are here for a purpose and we want to push that purpose.'"

Coda

1. The breastplates were designed by sculptor extraordinaire Stefan Clarke, who lectures at the School of Visual Arts at Edna Manley College.

2. The only member of the original cast who is no longer involved is Rosa Postlethwaite.

3. Sara Matchett directed *What the Water Gave Me*, *Tseleng*, and *Ngangelizwe*.

4. Within this global network is GROOTS: Grassroots Organizations Operating Together in Sisterhood.

5. A loose translation into English may be Take It to Them (Show Them) and Elevate Our Community.

6. Theatre of Black Women was founded in 1982. It lasted until 1988, when it no longer received funding from the Arts Council of Great Britain (see Goodman 1993).

7. #LifeInLeggings was a hashtag used mostly on Facebook and Twitter by women to speak about their experiences with sexual violence and harassment as well as share stories of other women they knew. One early controversies around #MeToo is that when Hollywood actor Alyssa Milano publicized the hashtag on social media she did not accord credit to Tarana Burke and/or did not know that Tarana Burke had started the movement. It was another example of Black women's labor being appropriated by white women.

References

ABC13 (KTRK-TV Houston). 2010. "Jamaican Doctor Accused of Abortion on 13-Year-Old." February 19, 2010. https://abc13.com/archive/7287577/.

Abrahams, Rehane. 2006. "What the Water Gave Me." In *New South African Plays*, edited by Charles J. Fourie, 16–33. London: Aurora Metro Press.

Abrahams, Yvette. 1996. "Was Eva Raped? An Exercise in Speculative History." *Kronos: Journal of Cape History* 23 (1): 3–21.

Ackroyd, Judith. 2007. "Applied Theatre: An Exclusionary Discourse?" *Applied Theatre Researcher* 8. Griffith University.

Africa Check. 2015. "British Paper Mangles SA Rape Statistics." Posted May 28, 2015. https://africacheck.org/reports/british-paper-mangles-sa-rape-statistics/.

Ajayi, Omofolabo. 2002. "Who Can Silence Her Drums? An Analysis of the Plays of Tess Onwueme." In *African Theatre*, vol. 2, *Women*, edited by Martin Banham, James Gibbs, and Femi Osofisan, 109–21. London: James Currey.

Alexander, M. Jacqui. 2005. *Pedagogies of Crossing: Meditations on Feminism, Sexual Politics, Memory, and the Sacred*. Durham, NC: Duke University Press.

Allan, Tuzyline Jita. 1995. *Womanist and Feminist Aesthetics: A Comparative Review*. Athens: Ohio University Press.

Allen, Jafari S. 2011. *¡Venceremos? The Erotics of Black Self-Making in Cuba*. Durham, NC: Duke University Press.

Allison, Helen. 1986. *Sistren Song: Popular Theatre in Jamaica*. London: War on Want.

Altbeker, Antony. 2007. *A Country at War with Itself: South Africa's Crisis of Crime*. Jeppestown, South Africa: Jonathan Ball.

Anthony, Trey. 2005. *"Da Kink in My Hair": Voices of Black Womyn*. Toronto: Playwrights Canada Press.

Armstrong, Sue. 1994. "Rape in South Africa: An Invisible Part of Apartheid's Legacy." *Focus on Gender* 2 (2): 35–39.

Ayiera, Eve. 2010. "Sexual Violence in Conflict: A Problematic International Discourse." *Feminist Africa* 10:7–20.

Bailey, Barbara, and Elsa Leo-Rhynie, eds. 2004. *Gender in the 21st Century: Caribbean Perspectives*. Kingston: Ian Randle

Barajas, Joshua. 2018. "New Study Gives Broader Look into How Police Killings Affect Black Americans' Mental Health." *PBS NewsHour*, June 21, 2018.

Barrett, Kaymara. 2019. "Jherane Patmore: Bloodclaat Feminist, Sister Rebel." *BASHY Magazine*, February 25, 2019.

Barrett, Livern. 2019. "'I Had an Abortion at 19': Parliamentary Committee Continues Hearing Arguments on Thorny Issue." *Jamaica Observer*, April 11, 2019.

Barriteau, Eudine. 2004. "Constructing Feminist Knowledge in the Commonwealth Caribbean in the Era of Globalization." In Bailey and Leo-Rhynie 2004, 437–65.

Batra, Kanika. 2011. *Feminist Visions and Queer Futures in Postcolonial Drama: Community, Kinship, Citizenship*. New York: Routledge.

Beauboeuf-Lafontant, Tamara. 2009. *Behind the Mask of the Strong Black Woman: Voice and the Embodiment of a Costly Performance*. Philadelphia: Temple University Press.

Beckles, Hilary. 2004. "Black Masculinity in Caribbean Slavery." In Reddock 2004, 225–44.

Berkman, Michael, and Robert E. O'Connor. 1993. "Do Women Legislators Matter? Female Legislators and State Abortion Policy." *American Politics Quarterly* 21:102–24.

Bhalla, Nita, and Humphrey Malalo. 2019. "Kenya's Rape Survivors Win Right to Abortion in Landmark Court Ruling." *Reuters*, June 12, 2019.

Birch, Anna, and Joanne Tompkins, eds. 2012. *Performing Site-Specific Theatre: Politics, Place, Practice*. London: Palgrave Macmillan.

Bloch, Susana. 2017. *Alba Emoting: A Scientific Method for Emotional Induction* N.p.: CreateSpace.

Boal, Augusto. 1995. *Legislative Theatre: Using Performance to Make Politics*. Translated by Adrian Jackson. London: Routledge.

Bonner, P. L., and Noor Nieftagodien. 2008. *Alexandra: A History*. Johannesburg: Wits University Press.

Boyce Davies, Carole. 1994. *Black Women, Writing and Identity: Migrations of the Subject*. New York: Taylor and Francis.

Boyne, Ian. 2010. "That Doggie Diary." *Gleaner*, September 12, 2010.

Bozzoli, Belinda. 2004. *Theatres of Struggle and the End of Apartheid*. Athens: Ohio University Press.

Braithwaite, Kamau. 1984. *History of the Voice: The Development of National Language in Anglophone Caribbean Poetry*. London: New Beacon Books.

Branche, Raphaëlle, and Fabrice Virgili. 2012. *Rape in Wartime*. Houndmills, Basingstoke: Palgrave Macmillan.

Brantley, Ben. 2015. "'Nirbhaya,' a Lamentation and a Rallying Cry for Indian Women." Review of *Nibhaya*, directed by Yaël Farber. *New York Times*, May 17, 2015.

Bridger, Emily. 2018. "Soweto's Female Comrades: Gender, Youth and Violence in South Africa's Township Uprisings, 1984–1990." *Journal of Southern African Studies* 44 (4): 559–74.

Britton, Hannah Evelyn. 2005. *Women in the South African Parliament: From Resistance to Governance*. Urbana: University of Illinois Press.

———. 2020. *Ending Gender-Based Violence: Justice and Community in South Africa*. Urbana: University of Illinois Press.

Brown, Jacqueline Nassy. 2005. *Dropping Anchor, Setting Sail: Geographies of Race in Black Liverpool*. Princeton, NJ: Princeton University Press.

Buchwald, Emilie, Pamela R. Fletcher, and Martha Roth. 1993. *Transforming a Rape Culture*. Minneapolis, MN: Milkweed Editions.

Buiten, Denise, and Kammila Naidoo. 2016. "Framing the Problem of Rape in South Africa: Gender, Race, Class and State Histories." *Current Sociology* 64 (4): 535–50.

Campbell, Edmond. 2009. "Parliament Drama—Theatre Director Checks In on Abortion Debate in Historic Fashion." *Gleaner*, March 13, 2009.

Campbell, Gwyn, and Elizabeth Elbourne. 2014. *Sex, Power, and Slavery*. Athens: Ohio University Press.

Carr, Robert. 2002. *Black Nationalism in the New World: Reading the African-American and West Indian Experience*. Durham, NC: Duke University Press.

Chase-Riboud, Barbara. 2004. *Hottentot Venus: A Novel*. New York: Anchor.

Chevannes, Barry. 2001. *Learning to Be a Man: Culture, Socialization, and Gender Identity in Five Caribbean Communities*. Kingston: University of the West Indies Press.

Christian, Barbara. 1988. "The Race for Theory." *Feminist Studies* 14:67–79.

CLDU (Coalition of Lawyers for the Defence of the Unborn). 2008. "Submissions to the Joint-Select Committee of Parliament Considering Abortion from the Coalition of Lawyers for the Defence of the Unborn." Kingston.

Clifford, Cayley. 2021. "Highest in the World? Social Media Post Gets South Africa's Rape Rate Wrong." Africa Check. Posted January 21, 2021. http://africacheck.org/fact-checks/fbchecks/highest-world-social-media-post-gets-south-africas-rape-rate-wrong.

Cock, Jacklyn. 1989. "Keeping the Fires Burning: Militarisation and the Politics of Gender in South Africa." *Review of African Political Economy* 16:50–65.

Collins, Patricia Hill. 2008. *Black Feminist Thought: Knowledge, Consciousness, and the Politics of Empowerment*. New York: Routledge.

Coly, Ayo A. 2019. *Postcolonial Hauntologies: African Women's Discourses of the Female Body*. Lincoln: University of Nebraska Press.

Connerton, Paul. 1989. *How Societies Remember*. Cambridge: Cambridge University Press.

Conquergood, Dwight. 2002. "Performance Studies: Interventions and Radical Research." *TDR: The Drama Review* 46 (2): 145–56.

Cooper, Adam, and Don Foster. 2008. "Democracy's Children? Masculinities of Coloured Adolescents Awaiting Trial in Post-Apartheid Cape Town, South Africa." *Boyhood Studies* 2 (1): 3–25.

Cooper, Afua. 1999. *Utterances and Incantations: Women, Poetry and Dub*. Toronto: Sister Vision Press.

———. 2007. *The Hanging of Angélique: The Untold Story of Canadian Slavery and the Burning of Old Montréal*. Athens: University of Georgia Press.

Cooper, Carolyn. 2009. "Aborting Women's Rights." *Gleaner*, September 27, 2009.

———. 2019. "Putting Obeah on Andrew Holness." *Gleaner*, July 7, 2019.

Cordner, Stephen, Michael S. Pollanen, Maria Cristina Mendonca, and Maria Dolores Morcillo-Mendez. 2017. "The West Kingston/Tivoli Gardens Incursion in Kingston, Jamaica." *Academic Forensic Pathology* 7 (3): 390–414.

Cox, Sherie. 2017. "Neila Ebanks (Taitu Heron at End)—Dancing in HWT Tambourine Army." YouTube video, uploaded March 13, 2017, 5:27. https://www.youtube.com/watch?v=lN1F0LgjS6g.

Crawford-Brown, Claudette. 2010. *Children in the Line of Fire: The Impact of Violence and Trauma on Families in Jamaica and Trinidad and Tobago*. New ed. Kingston: Arawak.

Cross, Jason. 2019. "MLK's Niece Urges Ja Not to Go Down Abortion Road—Warns against America's 'Mistake' during Tour of Kingston Homes." *Gleaner*, May 23, 2019.

Cunningham, Anastasia. 2014. "Jamaicans Say No to Abortion: Gleaner Poll Shows 69% in Favour of Retaining the Law." *Gleaner*, October 7, 2014.

Curry, Tommy J. 2017. *The Man-Not: Race, Class, Genre, and the Dilemmas of Black Manhood*. Philadelphia: Temple University Press.

Daley, Lashon. 2021. "Coming of (R)Age: A New Genre for Contemporary Narratives about Black Girlhood." *Signs: Journal of Women in Culture and Society* 46 (4): 1035–56.

Danielsson, Sarah Kristina. 2019. *War and Sexual Violence: New Perspectives in a New Era*. Leiden: Ferdinand Schöningh.

DAWN Caribbean Working Group on Women's Reproductive Health and Rights. 2009. "Church Interference in the Abortion Debate?" *Gay Jamaica Watch* (blog), October 3, 2009. http://gayjamaicawatch.blogspot.com/2009/10/church-interferance-in-abortion-debate.html.

De Beer, Diane. 2018. "Birthing a Country: 'Womb of Fire.'" Review of *Womb of Fire*, directed by Sara Matchett. *Theatre Times*, May 17, 2018. https://thetheatretimes.com/birthing-country-womb-fire/.

Delisle, Jennifer. 2006. "Finding the Future in the Past: Nostalgia and Community-Building in Mhlophe's Have You Seen Zandile?" *Journal of Southern African Studies* 32 (2): 387–401.

Devonish, Hubert. 2007. *Language and Liberation: Creole Language Politics in the Caribbean*. Kingston: Arawak.

Dlamini, Penwell. 2019. "Marlboro Gautrain Station Hit by #AlexTotalShutdown Protest." *TimesLIVE* (Johannesburg), April 3, 2019. https://www.timeslive.co.za/news/south-africa/2019-04-03-marlboro-gautrain-station-hit-by-alextotalshutdown-protest/.

Donkin, Ellen, and Susan Clement. 1993. *Upstaging Big Daddy: Directing Theater as If Gender and Race Matter*. Ann Arbor: University of Michigan Press.

Dorwart, Laura. 2021. "How a Gang Rape Case in Delhi Stunned the World." *A&E True Crime* (blog), August 27, 2021. https://www.aetv.com/real-crime/delhi-gang-rape-case-nirbhaya-crime-jyoti-singh.

Dosekun, Simidele. 2007. "'We Live in Fear, We Feel Very Unsafe': Imagining and Fearing Rape in South Africa." *Agenda: Empowering Women for Gender Equity* 21 (74): 89–99.

Douglass, Frederick. (1855) 1969. *My Bondage and My Freedom*. New York: Dover.

Downs, Kenya. 2016. "When Black Death Goes Viral, It Can Trigger PTSD-like Trauma." *PBS NewsHour*, July 22, 2016.

Dube, Casper. 2020. "Fallen Angels List of South African Murdered Women and Girls." *Savanna News* (blog), June 11, 2020. https://savannanews.com/fallen-angels-list-of-south-african-murdered-women-and-girls/.

Duncan, Nancy. 1996. *BodySpace: Destabilizing Geographies of Gender and Sexuality*. London: Routledge.

Du Plessis, Charl. 2007. "Globalization and the Threat to Women's Progress from Poor Men of the South." *African Journal of Business Ethics* 2 (1): 10–19.

Du Toit, Louise. 2014. "Shifting Meanings of Postconflict Sexual Violence in South Africa." *Signs: Journal of Women in Culture and Society* 40: 101–23.

Duval Smith, Alex. 2004. "Gibson Kente: Founding Father of Township Theatre." *Independent* (UK), November 15, 2004.

EIGE (European Institute for Gender Equality). 2020. "Gender Equality Index 2020: Sweden." Posted October 28, 2020. https://eige.europa.eu/publications/gender-equality-index-2020-sweden.

El-Bushra, Judy, and Ibrahim Sahl. 2005. *Cycles of Violence: Gender Relations and Armed Conflict*. Nairobi: ACORD.

eNCA (eNews Channel Africa). 2013. "Davids Sets Record Straight on Booysen Case." Posted May 23, 2013. http://www.enca.com/south-africa/jonathan-davids-speaks-out-about-anene-booysens-case.

Epskamp, Kees. 2006. *Theatre for Development: An Introduction to Context, Applications and Training*. London: Zed Books.

Evans, Sarah. 2013. "Letty Wapad: The Rape That Didn't Shake a Nation." *Mail and Guardian* (Johannesburg), October 30, 2013.

———. 2015. "Video Shows Boy Being Raped in 'Race Attack.'" *Mail and Guardian* (Johannesburg), February 6, 2015.

Fabian, Johannes. 1990. *Power and Performance: Ethnographic Explorations through Proverbial Wisdom and Theater in Shaba, Zaire*. Madison: University of Wisconsin Press.

Figueroa, Mark. 2004. "Male Privileging and Male 'Academic Underpeformance' in Jamaica." In Reddock 2004, 137–66.

Flockemann, Miki, and Thuli Mazibuko. 1999. "Between Women—An Interview with Gcina Mhlophe." *Contemporary Theatre Review* 9 (1): 41–51.

Floyd-Thomas, Stacey M. 2010. "Womanist Theology." In *Liberation Theologies in the United States: An Introduction*, edited by Stacey M. Floyd-Thomas and Anthony B. Pinn, 37–61. New York: New York University Press.

Foot Newton, Lara. 2005. *Tshepang: The Third Testament*. London: Oberon Books.

Ford-Smith, Honor. 1986. "Sistren: Exploring Women's Problems through Drama." *Jamaica Journal* 19:2–12.

———. 1989. *Ring Ding in a Tight Corner: A Case Study of Funding and Organizational Democracy in Sistren, 1977–1988*. Toronto: Women's Program.

———. 1990. "Notes towards a New Aesthetic." *Melus* 16:27–34.

———. 1995. "An Experiment in Popular Theatre and Women's History: 'Ida Revolt inna Jonkonnu Stylee.'" In *Subversive Women: Women's Movements in Africa, Asia, Latin America and the Caribbean*, edited by Saskia Weiringa, 147–64. London: Zed Books.

———. 1997. "Ring Ding in a Tight Corner: Sistren, Collective Democracy and the Organisation of Cultural Production." In *Feminist Genealogies, Colonial Legacies, Democratic Futures*, edited by M. Jacqui Alexander and Chandra Talpade Monanty, 213–58. New York: Routledge.

———. 2011. "Local and Transnational Dialogues on Memory and Violence in Jamaica and Toronto: Staging Letters from the Dead among the Living." *Canadian Theatre Review* 148:10–17.

———. 2014. "Gone but Not Forgotten: Memorial Murals, Vigils, and the Politics of Popular Commemoration in Jamaica." In Perera and Razack 2014, 263–88.

———. n.d. *Memory, Urban Violence and Performance* (website). Accessed October 20, 2022. https://forevermissed.wordpress.com/.

Francis, Kimone. 2018. "Experts Urge Repeal of Century-Old Law." *Jamaica Observer*, April 10, 2018.

Gabbatt, Adam. 2012. "Jamaican Doctor Arrested for Performing Abortion on 12 Year-Old." *Guardian* (UK), July 13, 2012.

Gardini, Genna. 2015. *Matric Rage*. Cape Town: Uhlanga Press.

Gay Jamaica Watch (blog). 2005. "Zekes Trial Shocker—Court Told of Oral Sex Act with Man." October 25, 2005. http://gayjamaicawatch.blogspot.com/2005/10/zekes-trial-shocker-court-told-of-oral.html.

Giokos, Eleni, and Thabeli Vilakazi. 2016. "Four South African Women Who Shook the Nation." CNN, August 17, 2016.

Gleaner. 2009. "Coalition's Voice on Abortion Gets Louder." July 24, 2009.

———. 2010a. "Crushed Stone." September 5, 2010.

———. 2010b. "Doggie Was Full of Manners." September 20, 2010.

———. 2019. "Ho Lung: I'd Rather Die Than Support Abortion." January 31, 2019.

Gordon, Edmund T. 2007. "The Austin School Manifesto: An Approach to the Black or African Diaspora." *Cultural Dynamics* 19:93–97.

Gordon, Margaret T., and Stephanie Riger. 1991. *The Female Fear: The Social Cost of Rape*. Urbana: University of Illinois Press.

Gottesdiener, Laura. 2021. "'Feeling Free': Women Criminalized by Mexico's Abortion Bans Celebrate Ruling." *Reuters*, September 9, 2021.

Gouws, Amanda. 2022. "Rape Is Endemic in South Africa: Why the ANC Government Keeps Missing the Mark." *Conversation* (blog), April 4, 2022. http://theconversation.com/rape-is-endemic-in-south-africa-why-the-anc-government-keeps-missing-the-mark-188235.

Gqola, Pumla Dineo. 2007. "How the 'Cult of Femininity' and Violent Masculinities Support Endemic Gender Based Violence in Contemporary South Africa." *African Identities* 5 (1): 111–24.

———. 2015. *Rape: A South African Nightmare*. Johannesburg: Jacana Media.

Gray, Obika. 1990. *Radicalism and Social Change in Jamaica, 1960–1972*. Knoxville: University of Tennessee Press.

———. 2004. *Demeaned but Empowered: The Social Power of the Urban Poor of Jamaica*. Kingston: University of the West Indies Press.

Green, Sharon L. 2006. "On a Knife Edge: Sistren Theatre Collective, Grassroots Theatre, and Globalization." *Small Axe* 11:105–8.

Gregg, Veronica Marie. 2005. *Caribbean Women: An Anthology of Non-Fiction Writing, 1890–1980*. Notre Dame, IN: University of Notre Dame Press.

Gunne, Sorcha, and Zoë Brigley. 2010. *Feminism, Literature and Rape Narratives: Violence and Violation*. New York: Routledge.

Haffajee, Ferial. 2013a. "Words Fail Us." News24 (Capetown), February 10, 2013. http://www.news24.com/Archives/City-Press/Editors-note-Words-fail-us-20150429.

———. 2013b. "#WTF Was She Thinking?" News24 (Capetown), February 11, 2013. http://www.news24.com/Columnists/Ferial-Haffajee/WTF-was-she-thinking-20130211.

Hall, Arthur. 2018. "Her Body, Her Choice | Poll Finds Massive Support for a Woman's Right to Have an Abortion." *Gleaner*, May 13, 2019.

Halliday, Aria. 2020. "'Twerk Sumn!': Theorizing Black Girl Epistemology in the Body." *Cultural Studies* 34 (6): 874–91.

Halligey, Alex, and Sara Matchett, eds. 2021. *Collaborative Conversations: Celebrating Twenty-One Years of the Mothertongue Project*. Cape Town: Modjaji Books.

Hamber, Brandon. 2007. "Masculinity and Transitional Justice: An Exploratory Essay." *International Journal of Transitional Justice* 1 (3): 375–90.

Hansberry, Lorraine. 1996. *A Raisin in the Sun*. In *Black Theatre USA*, edited by James V. Hatch and Ted Shine, 104–46. New York: Free Press.

Harker, Jaime, and Cecilia Konchar Farr, eds. 2015. *This Book Is an Action: Feminist Print Culture and Activist Aesthetics*. Urbana: University of Illinois Press.

Harrison, Paul Carter, Victor Leo Walker, and Gus Edwards. 2002. *Black Theatre: Ritual Performance in the African Diaspora*. Philadelphia: Temple University Press.

Harris-Perry, Melissa V. 2011. *Sister Citizen: Shame, Stereotypes, and Black Women in America*. New Haven, CT: Yale University Press.

Hartman, Saidiya V. 1997. *Scenes of Subjection: Terror, Slavery, and Self-Making in Nineteenth-Century America*. New York: Oxford University Press.

Hartsock, Nancy. 1983. "The Feminist Standpoint: Developing the Ground for a Specifically Feminist Historical Materialism." In *Discovering Reality: Feminist Perspectives on Epistemology, Metaphysics, Methodology, and the Philosophy of Science*, edited by Sandra Harding and Merrill Hintikka, 283–310. Dordrecht: Reidel.

Harvey, David. 2007. *A Brief History of Neoliberalism*. Oxford: Oxford University Press.

Hassim, Shireen. 2014. *The ANC Women's League: Sex, Gender and Politics*. Athens: Ohio University Press.

Hekman, Susan. 1997. "Truth and Method: Feminist Standpoint Theory Revisited." *Signs: Journal of Women in Culture and Society* 22 (2): 341–65.

Henry, Balford. 2020. "House Committee Recommends Conscience Vote on Abortion." *Jamaica Observer*, March 28, 2020.

Henry, Paget. 2000. *Caliban's Reason: Introducing Afro-Caribbean Philosophy*. New York: Routledge.

Herman, Dianne F. 1984. "The Rape Culture." In *Women: A Feminist Perspective*, edited by Jo Freeman, 45–53. Palo Alto, CA: Mayfield.

Heron, Taitu [stawberry tea]. 2009a. "Sistren Drama to JSC Prt 1." YouTube video, uploaded March 19, 2009, 4:20. https://www.youtube.com/watch?v=W5luMWew8rU.

———. 2009b. "Sistren Drama to JSC Prt2." YouTube video, uploaded March 19, 2009, 9:10. https://www.youtube.com/watch?v=CMi4d6z6g-A.

Heron, Taitu, Danielle Toppin, and Lana Finikin. 2009. "Sistren in Parliament: Addressing Abortion and Women's Rights through Popular Theatre." *MaComere: Journal of the Association of Caribbean Women Writers and Scholars* 11:45–60.

Hickling, Frederick. 2004. "From Explainations and Madnificent Irations to de Culcha Clash: Popular Theatre as Psychotherapy." *Interventions: International Journal of Post-Colonial Studies* 6:45–66.

Hill, Errol. 1992. *The Jamaican Stage, 1655–1900: Profile of a Colonial Theatre*. Amherst: University of Massachusetts Press.

Ho Lung, Richard. 2008. "Killing with Kindness." *Gleaner*, May 22, 2008.

hooks, bell. 1990. *Yearning: Race, Gender, and Cultural Politics*. Boston: South End Press.

Hope Enterprises. 2006. *Final Report of Public Opinion Survey on the Legalization of Abortion*. Prepared for the Jamaican Family Planning Board. Kingston, July 2006.

Hudson-Weems, Clenora. 2000. "Africana Womanism: An Overview." In *Out of the Revolution: The Development of Africana Studies*, edited by Delores P. Aldridge and Carlene Young, 205–18. New York: Lexington Books.

Hunter, Margaret, and Kathleen Soto. 2009. "Women of Color in Hip Hop: The Pornographic Gaze." *Race, Gender and Class* 16 (1/2): 170–91.

Hutchison, Yvette. 2013. *South African Performance and Archives of Memory*. Manchester: Manchester University Press.

Iandoli, Kathy. 2019. *God Save the Queens: The Essential History of Women in Hip-Hop*. New York: Dey Street Books.

Igual, Roberto. 2015. "Justice Served! Killer Gets Two Life Sentences for Horror Lesbian Murder." MambaOnline.com, May 27, 2015. https://www.mambaonline.com/2015/05/27/justice-served-killer-gets-two-life-sentences-horror-lesbian-murder/.

Irish, Jenni. 1993. "Massacres, Muti and Misery." *Agenda: Empowering Women for Gender Equity* 16:5–9.

Irish-Bramble, Ken. 2012. *Bricks, Ballots and Bullets: Political and Communal Violence in Jamaica*. Saarbrücken, Germany: LAP Lambert Academic.

Jamaica Ministry of Health. 2007. *Final Report of the Abortion Policy Review Advisory Group*. Kingston, February 2007.

Jamaica Ministry of Justice. 2016. *Report: Western Kingston Commission of Enquiry.* June 2016.
Jamaica Observer. 2009. "Pro-Lifers Continue Campaign against Abortion." June 30, 2009.
———. 2014. "Dr. Lloyd Cole Acquitted in Abortion Case." March 11, 2014.
———. 2018. "$190m Paid to Victims of West Kingston Incursion." May 22, 2018.
Jamaicans for Justice. 2010. "Victims' Voices: Monica Williams." YouTube video, uploaded December 5, 2010, 9:58. https://www.youtube.com/watch?v=JCKLLlSjfic.
Jamaica Star. 2010. "Tivoli Girls Fight for Soldiers." June 15, 2010.
James, Marlon. 2014. *A Brief History of Seven Killings: A Novel.* New York: Riverhead Books.
Jenkins, Candice Marie. 2007. *Private Lives, Proper Relations: Regulating Black Intimacy.* Minneapolis: University of Minnesota Press.
Johnson, T. Hassan. 2018. "Challenging the Myth of Black Male Privilege." *Spectrum: A Journal for Black Men* 6 (2): 21–42.
Jones, Omi Osun Joni L. 1997. "'Sista Docta': Performance as Critique of the Academy." *TDR: The Drama Review* 41:51–67.
———. 2015. *Theatrical Jazz: Performance, Àse, and the Power of the Present Moment.* Columbus: Ohio State University Press.
Jones, Omi Osun Joni L., Lisa L. Moore, and Sharon Bridgforth, eds. 2010. *Experiments in a Jazz Aesthetic.* Austin: University of Texas Press.
Klein, Thamar. 2009. "Intersex and Transgender Activism in South Africa." *Liminalis: Journal for Sex/Gender Emancipation and Resistance* 3:15–41.
Kruger, Loren. 1999. *The Drama of South Africa: Plays, Pageants and Publics since 1910.* London: Routledge.
Lahiri, Madhumita. 2011. "Crimes and Corrections: Bride Burners, Corrective Rapists, and Other Black Misogynists." *Feminist Africa* 15:121–34.
Lane, Linda, and Birgitta Jordansson. 2020. "How Gender Equal Is Sweden? An Analysis of the Shift in Focus under Neoliberalism." *Social Change* 50 (1): 28–43.
Larasati, Rachmi Diyah. 2012. "Desiring the Stage: The Interplay of Mobility and Resistance." In Nielsen and Ybarra 2012, 253–65.
Lawes, Carol, Eugene Williams, Honor Ford-Smith, and Amba Chevannes. 2015. "*A Vigil for Roxie.*" Unpublished playscript, in author's possession.
Lawrence, Rebekah. 2009. "Sistren's Intervention." Letter to the editor. *Gleaner*, March 16, 2009.
Lewis, Desiree. 2009. "Gendered Spectacle: New Terrains of Struggle in South Africa." In *Body Politics and Women Citizens: African Experiences*, edited by Ann Schlyter, 127–35. Stockholm: Swedish International Development Cooperation Agency.
Lindsay, Keisha. 2004. "Is the Caribbean Male an Endangered Species?" In Reddock 2004, 56–82.
———. 2018. *In a Classroom of Their Own: The Intersection of Race and Feminist Politics in All-Black Male Schools.* Urbana: University of Illinois Press.

Little, Becky. 2020. "When the 'Capitol Crawl' Dramatized the Need for Americans with Disabilities Act." History Channel (website). Posted July 24, 2020. https://www.history.com/news/americans-with-disabilities-act-1990-capitol-crawl.

Livermon, Xavier. 2012. "Queer(y)ing Freedom: Black Queer Visibilities in Post-apartheid South Africa." *GLQ: A Journal of Lesbian and Queer Studies* 18:297–323.

Lodhia, Sharmila. 2015. "From 'Living Corpse' to India's Daughter: Exploring the Social, Political, and Legal Landscape of the 2012 Delhi Gang Rape." *Women's Studies International Forum* 50:89–101.

Loomba, Ania. 2005. *Colonialism/Postcolonialism*. 2nd ed. London: Routledge.

MacKinnon, Catharine A. 1991. *Toward a Feminist Theory of the State*. Cambridge, MA: Harvard University Press.

———. 2005. *Women's Lives, Men's Laws*. Cambridge, MA: Belknap Press of Harvard University Press.

Madison, D. Soyini. 2007. "Co-Performative Witnessing." *Cultural Studies* 21 (6): 826–31.

———. 2010. *Acts of Activism: Human Rights as Radical Performance*. Cambridge: Cambridge University Press.

Magubane, Zine. 2001. "Which Bodies Matter? Feminism, Poststructuralism, Race, and the Curious Theoretical Odyssey of the 'Hottentot Venus.'" *Gender and Society* 15:816–34.

———. 2004. *Bringing the Empire Home: Race, Class, and Gender in Britain and Colonial South Africa*. Chicago: University of Chicago Press.

Mahdawi, Arwa. 2022. "Outrage in South Africa as Charges Dropped in Gang Rape Case." *Guardian*, October 27, 2022.

Mail and Guardian (Johannesburg). 2013. "Kana Given Double Life Sentence for Booysen's Rape, Murder." November 1, 2013.

———. 2014. "In Marlboro, Living Is No Life at All." April 10, 2014.

Majola, Bongani. 2007. "New Deal for Declining Marlboro South." JoBurg: Johannesburg News Agency, November 14, 2007.

Makhutshi, Ntomboxolo. 2022. "The Mothertongue Project Fundraiser: Champion Page." Backabuddy. Created March 4, 2022. https://www.backabuddy.co.za/champion/project/mothertongue-fundraiser.

Malgas, Nathalie. 2015. "Jan Kempdorp Rape Victim to Remain in School." Eyewitness News (Johannesburg), February 15, 2015. http://ewn.co.za/2015/02/15/Jan-Kempdorp-rape-victim-to-remain-in-school.

Mama, Amina. 1995. *Beyond the Masks: Race, Gender, and Subjectivity*. New York: Routledge.

Maparyan, Layli. 2008. *The Womanist Idea*. New York: Routledge.

Marzette, DeLinda. 2013. *Africana Women Writers: Performing Diaspora, Staging Healing*. New York: Peter Lang.

Matchett, Sara. 2009. *Breathing Space: Cross-Community Professional Theatre as a Means of Dissolving Fixed Geographical Landscapes*. Cologne: LAP Lambert Academic.

———. 2012. "Breath as Impulse, Breath as Thread: Breath as Catalyst for Making an Autobiographical Performance in Response to 'Corrective Rape' and Hate Crimes against Lesbians." *South African Theatre Journal* 26 (3): 280–91.

Matchett, Sara, and Nicola Cloete. 2015. "Performativities as Activism: Addressing Gender-Based Violence and Rape Culture in South Africa and Beyond." In Plastow, Hutchison, Matzke, and Banham 2015, 17–29.

Matchett, Sara, and Makgathi Mokwena. 2014. "Washa Mollo: Theatre as a Milieu for Conversations and Healing." In *Arts Activism, Education, and Therapies: Transforming Communities across Africa*, edited by Hazel Barnes, 107–25. Amsterdam: Rodopi.

Mawere, Munyaradzi. 2011. *African Belief and Knowledge Systems: A Critical Perspective*. Bamenda, Cameroon: Langaa RPCIG.

Maxwell, Shakira. 2012. "Fighting a Losing Battle? Defending Women's Reproductive Rights in Twenty-First Century Jamaica." *Social and Economic Studies* 61 (3): 95–115.

McCauley, Robbie. 1999. *Sally's Rape*. In *A Sourcebook of African-American Performance: Plays, People, Movements*, edited by Annmarie Beane, 246–64. London: Routledge.

McDowell, Linda. 1996. "Spatializing Feminism." In *BodySpace: Destabilizing Geographies of Gender and Sexuality*, 28–44. London: Routledge.

———. 1999. *Gender, Identity and Place: Understanding Feminist Geographies*. Minneapolis: University of Minnesota Press.

McIntosh, Douglas. 2021. "More Than 1.2 Million Jamaicans in Jobs." Jamaica Information Service, July 16, 2021. https://jis.gov.jm/more-than-1-2-million-jamaicans-in-jobs/.

McKittrick, Katherine. 2006. *Demonic Grounds: Black Women and the Cartographies of Struggle*. Minneapolis: University of Minnesota Press.

McKoy's News. 2017. "OBGYN Performing Abortion on 12-Year-Old Found Not Guilty." March 3, 2017. https://mckoysnews.com/obgyn-performing-abortion-12-year-old-found-not-guilty/.

McLachlan, Fiona. 1987. "The Apartheid Laws in Brief." In *The Anti-Apartheid Reader: The Struggle against White Racist Rule in South Africa*, edited by David Mermelstein, 76–78. New York: Grove Press.

Migraine-George, Thérèse. 2008. *African Women and Representation: From Performance to Politics*. Trenton, NJ: Africa World Press.

Miller, Errol. 1991. *Men at Risk*. Kingston: Jamaica Publishing House.

———. 2004. "Male Marginalization Revisited." In Bailey and Leo-Rhynie 2004, 99–133.

Minto, Jevon. 2015. "Soldier Sentenced for Soliciting Sex #WKgnCOE." Nationwide 90FM (Kingston). Posted October 22, 2015. https://nationwideradiojm.com/soldier-sentenced-for-soliciting-sex-wkgncoe/.

Mitchell, Robin. 2018. "Shaking the Racial and Gender Foundations of France: The Influences of 'Sarah Baartman' in the Production of Frenchness." In *Black French*

Women and the Struggle for Equality, 1848–2016, edited by Félix Germain, Silyane Larcher, and T. Denean Sharpley-Whiting, 185–97. Lincoln: University of Nebraska Press.

Mkhabela, Sabelo. 2015. "Cape Town Poet and Playwright Koleka Putuma Is not Afraid of Awkward Silences." OkayAfrica (website). Posted October 29, 2015. http://www.okayafrica.com/culture-2/cape-town-poet-playwright-koleka-putuma/.

Modise, Kedibone. 2021. "New Film 'That Night of Trance' Interrogates Issues of Identity." IOL (Independent Online). Posted August 25, 2021. https://www.iol.co.za/entertainment/movies/news/new-film-that-night-of-trance-interrogates-issues-of-identity-e27a61b0-e614-45d9-b2b7-daed41d20c04.

Moffett, Helen. 2006. "'These Women, They Force Us to Rape Them': Rape as Narrative of Social Control in Post-Apartheid South Africa." *Journal of Southern African Studies* 32 (1): 129–44.

Mokgoro, Ntshieng. 2014. *Phases of Mirah*. Unpublished playscript, in author's possession.

Momsen, Janet. 2002. "The Double Paradox." In *Gendered Realities: Essays in Caribbean Feminist Thought*, edited by Patricia Mohammed, 44–55. Kingston: University of the West Indies Press.

Morgan, L. 1989. "When Does Life Begin? A Cross-Cultural Perspective on the Personhood of Fetuses and Young Children." In *Abortion Rights and Fetal "Personhood,"* edited by Edd Doerr and James W. Prescott, 97–114. Long Beach, CA: Centerline Press.

Moten, Fred. 2003. *In the Break: The Aesthetics of the Black Radical Tradition*. Minneapolis: University of Minnesota Press.

Mothertongue (website). n.d. "Past Productions." Accessed October 20, 2022. https://www.mothertongue.co.za/index.php/productions/past-productions.

Mothertongue Project. 2013. "Walk: South Africa." YouTube video, filmed 2013, uploaded April 16, 2014, 6:39. https://www.youtube.com/watch?v=SbEXlhtl_cU&t=64s.

———. 2014. "Walk: South Africa—Cape Town Fringe 2014." YouTube video, filmed 2014, uploaded July 11, 2015, 24:47. https://www.youtube.com/watch?v=V7JgPV8nflo.

Motsemme, Thabiseng. 2004. "'The Mute Always Speak': On Women's Silences at the Truth and Reconciliation Commission." *Current Sociology* 52:909–32.

Munroe, Michelle A., and Damion K. Blake. 2017. "Governance and Disorder: Neoliberalism and Violent Change in Jamaica." *Third World Quarterly* 38 (3): 580–603.

Nagar, Richa. 2002. "Women's Theater and the Redefinitions of Public, Private, and Politics in North India." *ACME: An International E-Journal for Critical Geographies* 1 (1): 55–72.

———. 2014. *Muddying the Waters: Coauthoring Feminisms across Scholarship and Activism*. Urbana: University of Illinois Press.

Narayan, Uma. 2004. "The Project of Feminist Epistemology: Perspectives from a Nonwestern Feminist." In *The Feminist Standpoint Theory Reader: Intellectual and Political Controversies*, edited by Sandra Harding, 213–24. New York: Routledge.

Ndashe, Sibongile. 2006. "Can I Speak Please!" *Pambazuka News* (website). Posted May 11, 2006. https://www.pambazuka.org/governance/can-i-speak-please.

Ndlovu, Malika. 2014. "Walk: South Africa: A Narrative Reflection on the Significance and Impact of This Mothertongue Production." Unpublished paper, in author's possession.

Nettleford, Rex M. 2002. "Jamaican Dance Theatre: Celebrating the Caribbean Heritage." In *Caribbean Dance from Abakua to Zouk: How Movement Shapes Identity*, edited by Susanna Sloat, 81–94. Gainesville: University Press of Florida.

News24 (Capetown). 2016. "Jan Kempdorp Sexual-Assault Pupil Dies." April 22, 2016. https://www.news24.com/News24/jan-kempdorp-sexual-assault-pupil-dies-20160422.

Ngesi, Vuyusile. 2002. "Unrepentant Rapist of Baby Tshepang Gets Life." IOL (Independent Online). Posted July 26, 2002. https://www.iol.co.za/news/south-africa/unrepentant-rapist-of-baby-tshepang-gets-life-90451.

Ngũgĩ wa Thiong'o. 1997. "Enactments of Power: The Politics of Performance Space." *TDR: The Drama Review* 41 (3): 11–30.

Nicholson, Greg. 2016. "How South African Anti-Rape Protesters Disrupted Zuma's Speech." *Guardian* (UK), August 9, 2016.

Nielsen, Lara D., and Patricia A. Ybarra, eds. 2012. *Neoliberalism and Global Theatres: Performance Permutations*. Houndmills, Basingstoke: Palgrave Macmillan.

Nkosi, Ntombifuthi Junerose. 2022. "Herstory International Theatre Festival Celebrates Women across Borders and Barriers." JoBurg, August 8, 2022. https://www.joburg.org.za/media_/Newsroom/Pages/2022%20News%20Articles/August/Herstory.aspx.

Norwood, Carolette. 2021. "Misrepresenting Reproductive Justice: A Black Feminist Critique of 'Protecting Black Life.'" *Signs: Journal of Women in Culture and Society* 46 (3): 715–41.

Nottage, Lynn. 2010. *Ruined*. New York: Dramatist's Play Service.

Ntshidi, Edwin. 2021. "Alex Business Owners Close Shop amid Violence Linked to Calls for Zuma's Release." Eyewitness News (Johannesburg), July 11, 2021. https://ewn.co.za/2021/07/11/Alex-business-owners-close-shop-amid-violence-linked-to-calls-for-zuma-s-release.

Nwachukwu, John Owen. 2021. "LGBTQ, Abortion: Jamaican Betty Blaine Leads Nigeria, Others against President Biden, Other World Leaders." *Daily Post Nigeria*, March 28, 2021.

Oberhauser, Ann M., Jennifer L. Fluri, Risa Whitson, and Sharlene Mollett. 2017. *Feminist Spaces: Gender and Geography in a Global Context*. London: Routledge.

Ogmundson, Richard. 2005. "Does It Matter If Women, Minorities and Gays Govern? New Data Concerning an Old Question." *Canadian Journal of Sociology / Cahiers Canadiens de Sociologie* 30 (3): 315–24.

Ogunyemi, Chikwenye Okonjo. 1985. "Womanism: The Dynamics of the Contemporary Black Female Novel in English." *Signs: Journal of Women in Culture and Society* 11 (1): 63–80.

Okagbue, Osita A. 2009. *Culture and Identity in African and Caribbean Theatre*. London: Adonis and Abbey.

Okech, Awino. 2007. "'She Is Also Playing: She Is Also Wearing the Mask That I Am Wearing': Investigating the Gendered Dynamics of Implementing a Forum Theatre Project for Young Women in Manenberg." Master's thesis, University of Cape Town.

Ongiri, Amy Abugo. 2010. *Spectacular Blackness: The Cultural Politics of the Black Power Movement and the Search for a Black Aesthetic*. Charlottesville: University of Virginia Press.

Orentlicher, David. 2015. "Abortion and the Fetal Personhood Fallacy." *Bill of Health* (blog), Harvard Law, August 11, 2015. https://blog.petrieflom.law.harvard.edu/2015/08/11/.

Orleck, Annelise. 2006. *Storming Caesar's Palace: How Black Mothers Fought Their Own War on Poverty*. Boston: Beacon Press.

Parker, Faranaaz. 2012. "'Illegal' JMPD Evictions Shatter Marlboro Community." *Mail and Guardian* (Johannesburg), August 22, 2012.

Parks, Suzan-Lori. 1997. *Venus*. New York: Theatre Communications Group.

Pateman, Carole. 1988. *The Sexual Contract*. Stanford, CA: Stanford University Press.

Patton, Stacey. 2017. *Spare the Kids: Why Whupping Children Won't Save Black America*. Boston: Beacon Press.

Paul, Annie. 2015. "Class Shaming in Jamaica: The West Kingston Commission of Enquiry." *Active Voice* (blog), June 28, 2015. https://anniepaul.net/2015/06/28/class-shaming-in-jamaica-the-west-kingston-commission-of-enquiry/.

Paxton, Pamela Marie. 2014. *Women, Politics, and Power: A Global Perspective*. 2nd ed. Thousand Oaks, CA: Sage.

PBC Jamaica. 2019a. "Human Resources and Social Development Committee—July 17, 2019." YouTube video, streamed live July 17, 2019, 1:56:07. http://www.youtube.com/watch?v=N8Eyn12ZI2I&t=4426s.

PBC Jamaica. 2019b. "Human Resources and Social Development Committee—July 25, 2019." YouTube video, streamed live July 25, 2019, 2:32:37. https://www.youtube.com/watch?v=KORGMXJRldw.

Pearson, Mike, and Michael Shanks. 2001. *Theatre/Archaeology*. London: Routledge.

Perera, Suvendrini, and Sherene Razack, eds. 2014. *At the Limits of Justice: Women of Colour on Terror*. Toronto: University of Toronto Press.

Pérez, Elizabeth. 2016. "The Ontology of Twerk: From 'Sexy' Black Movement Style to Afro-Diasporic Sacred Dance." *African and Black Diaspora: An International Journal* 9 (1): 16–31.

Perkins, Kathy A., ed. 1998. *Black South African Women: An Anthology of Plays*. London: Routledge.

———. 2009. *African Women Playwrights*. Urbana: University of Illinois Press.

Perry, Keisha-Khan Y. 2013. *Black Women against the Land Grab: The Fight for Racial Justice in Brazil*. Minneapolis: University of Minnesota Press.

Pinto, Samantha. 2013. *Difficult Diasporas: The Transnational Feminist Aesthetic of the Black Atlantic*. New York: New York University Press.

Planning Institute of Jamaica. 2019. *Economic and Social Survey 2018*. Kingston.

———. n.d. *Vision 2030 Jamaica*. Accessed October 20, 2022. https://www.vision2030.gov.jm.

Plastow, Jane, Yvette Hutchison, Christine Matzke, and Martin Banham, eds. 2015. *African Theatre*. Vol 14, *Contemporary Women*. Suffolk, UK: James Currey.

Radio Jamaica News. 2012. "Dr Lloyd Cole Charged in Alleged Case of Procuring Abortion." April 1, 2012. http://rjrnewsonline.com/local/dr-lloyd-cole-charged-in-alleged-case-of-procuring-abortion.

———. 2013. "Hanna Wants Abortion Law Reviewed." June 19, 2013. http://rjrnewsonline.com/local/hanna-wants-abortion-law-reviewed.

———. 2019. "Seventy-Five Per Cent Oppose Legalising Abortion in Jamaica, Poll Reveals." March 17, 2019. http://rjrnewsonline.com/local/seventy-five-per-cent-oppose-legalising-abortion-in-jamaica-poll-reveals.

———. 2020. "Mother and Son Arrested in Relation to Alleged Rape of 14 Year Old Girl." September 23, 2020. http://rjrnewsonline.com/local/mother-and-son-arrested-in-relation-to-alleged-rape-of-14-year-old-girl.

Ramsay, Fiona. 2021. "The Closing of South Africa's Fugard Theatre Points to Systemic Failures." *Conversation* (blog), March 18, 2021. https://theconversation.com/the-closing-of-south-africas-fugard-theatre-points-to-systemic-failures-157433.

Rao, Maya Krishna. 2013. "Walk—Maya Krishna Rao." YouTube video, uploaded February 8, 2013, 8:59. https://www.youtube.com/watch?v=msUvCWKcCVQ.

Reckitt, Helena, and Peggy Phelan, eds. 2001. *Art and Feminism*. London: Phaidon.

Reddock, Rhoda, ed. 2004. *Interrogating Caribbean Masculinities: Theoretical and Empirical Analyses*. Kingston: University of the West Indies Press.

Reid, Tyrone. 2010. "Psychopath? Forensic Psychiatrist Says Slain Gangster . . . Would Never Have Been Fully Rehabilitated." *Gleaner*, September 19, 2010.

Reynolds, Dee, and Matthew Reason. 2012. *Kinesthetic Empathy in Creative and Cultural Practices*. Bristol, UK: Intellect.

Richie, Beth E. 2012. *Arrested Justice: Black Women, Violence, and America's Prison Nation*. New York: New York University Press.

Ringrose, Jessica, and Emma Renold. 2011. "Slut-Shaming, Girl Power and 'Sexualisation': Thinking through the Politics of the International Slutwalks with Teen Girls." *Gender and Education* 24:333–43.

Roach, Joseph R. 1996. *Cities of the Dead: Circum-Atlantic Performance*. New York: Columbia University Press.

Roberts, Dorothy. 1998. *Killing the Black Body: Race, Reproduction, and the Meaning of Liberty*. New York: Vintage.

Robinson, Corey. 2011. "Eventide Fire Remembered: Torrington Park Marks Anniversary with Demand for an End to Political Rivalry." *Jamaica Observer*, May 23, 2011.

Robinson, Tracy. 2003. "Beyond the Bill of Rights: Sexing the Citizen." In *Confronting Power, Theorizing Gender: Interdisciplinary Perspectives from the Caribbean*, edited by V. Eudine Barriteau, 231–61. Kingston: University of the West Indies Press.

Rosenberg, Tina. 2009. "On Feminist Activist Aesthetics." *Journal of Aesthetics and Culture* 1 (1): article 4619. https://doi.org/10.3402/jac.v1i0.4619.

Rowley, Michelle V. 2011. *Feminist Advocacy and Gender Equity in the Anglophone Caribbean: Envisioning a Politics of Coalition*. New York: Routledge.

Sajnani, Nisha, and Maitri Gopalakrishna. 2017. "Rasa: Exploring the Influence of Indian Performance Theory in Drama Therapy." *Drama Therapy Review* 3 (2): 225–40.

Salo, Elaine. 2009. "Coconuts Do not Live in Townships: Cosmopolitanism and Its Failures in the Urban Peripheries of Cape Town." *Feminist Africa* 13:11–21.

Sandner, Philipp. 2018. "Queen Muhumuza: Fighting Colonialism in East Africa." DW (Deutsche Welle), September 2, 2018. https://www.dw.com/en/queen-muhumuza-fighting-colonialism-in-east-africa/a-42522227.

Save Cockpit Country (website). n.d. Accessed October 20, 2022. https://savecockpitcountry.org/.

Savory Fido, Elaine. 2005. "Strategies for Survival: Anti-Imperialist Theatrical Forms in the Caribbean." In *Imperialism and Theatre: Essays on World Theatre, Drama, and Performance*, edited by J. Ellen Gainor, 243–56. London: Routledge.

Sawer, Marian, Manon Tremblay, and Linda J. Trimble. 2006. *Representing Women in Parliament: A Comparative Study*. Abingdon, Oxon: Routledge.

Sayej, Nadja. 2018. "'It's My Ass and My Instagram': Amber Rose Is Over Your Slut-Shaming." *Harper's Bazaar*, September 25, 2018.

Scarry, Elaine. 1985. *The Body in Pain: The Making and Unmaking of the World*. New York: Oxford University Press.

Schauffer, Dennis. 2011. "In Memoriam: Gibson Kente." *South African Theatre Journal* 20 (1): 302–22.

Scott, Dennis C. 1974. *An Echo in the Bone*. Alexandria, VA: Alexander Street Press.

Sedgwick, Eve Kosofsky. 2003. *Touching Feeling: Affect, Pedagogy, Performativity*. Durham, NC: Duke University Press.

Segal, Lotte Buch. 2016. *No Place for Grief: Martyrs, Prisoners, and Mourning in Contemporary Palestine*. Philadelphia: University of Pennsylvania Press.

Segall, Kimberly Wedeven. 2013. *Performing Democracy in Iraq and South Africa: Gender, Media, and Resistance*. Syracuse, NY: Syracuse University Press.

Shakes, Nicosia. 2018. "The Radical Aesthetic of Sistren Theatre Collective." In *Caribbean Reasonings: Rupert Lewis and the Black Intellectual Tradition*, edited by Clinton A. Hutton, Maziki Thame, and Jermaine McCalpin, 311–37. Kingston: Ian Randle.

———. 2019. "Laws Must Protect Citizens." Letter to the editor. *Gleaner*, May 28, 2019.

———. 2021. "Activist Aesthetics and the Work of the Mothertongue Project." In Halligey and Matchett 2021, 40–61.

Shalhoub-Kevorkian, Nadera. 2014. "Terrorism and the Birthing Body in Jerusalem." In Perera and Razack, 2014, 38–56.

Shandilya, Krupa. 2015. "Nirbhaya's Body: The Politics of Protest in the Aftermath of the 2012 Delhi Gang Rape." *Gender and History* 27 (2): 465–86.

Shen, Aviva. 2013. "One Year after Horrific New Delhi Gang Rape, India Still Struggles with Rape Culture." *ThinkProgress*, December 29, 2013. https://archive.think

progress.org/one-year-after-horrific-new-delhi-gang-rape-india-still-struggles-with-rape-culture-5d0d0f1ff404/.

Simon-Kumar, Rachel. 2014. "Sexual Violence in India: The Discourses of Rape and the Discourses of Justice." *Indian Journal of Gender Studies* 21 (3): 451–60.

Sistren. 1980. *Nana Yah*. Unpublished playscript, in author's possession.

———. 1990. *Miss Amy and Miss May*. Kingston: Sistren Theatre Collective and Video for Change. DVD.

Small, Jean. 2001. *A Black Woman's Tale*. In *Contemporary Drama of the Caribbean*, edited by Erika J. Waters and David Edgecombe, 135–54. Kingshill, Saint Croix: University of the Virgin Islands.

Smith, Christen. 2008. "Scenarios of Racial Contact: Police Violence and the Politics of Performance and Racial Formation in Brazil." *Emisférica* 5 (2). http://www.hemisphericinstitute.org/eng/publications/emisferica/5.2/.

———. 2015. *Afro-Paradise: Blackness, Violence, and Performance in Brazil*. Springfield: University of Illinois Press.

———. 2016. "Sorrow as Artifact: Radical Black Mothering in Times of Terror—A Prologue." *Transforming Anthropology* 24 (1): 5–7.

———. 2018. "The Fallout of Police Violence Is Killing Black Women like Erica Garner." *PBS NewsHour*, January 5, 2018.

Smith, Karina. 2013. "From Politics to Therapy: Sistren Theatre Collective's Theatre and Outreach Work in Jamaica." *New Theatre Quarterly* 29 (1): 87–97.

Smith, Raymond T. 1956. *The Negro Family in British Guiana: Family Structure and Social Status in the Villages*. London: Routledge.

Sobo, Elisa J. 1996. "Abortion Traditions in Rural Jamaica." *Social Science and Medicine* 42 (4): 495–508.

South African Government (website). "1913 Natives Land Act Centenary." June 2013. https://www.gov.za/1913-natives-land-act-centenary.

———. 2015. "Police Welcomes Human Trafficking Conviction." May 11, 2015. https://www.gov.za/speeches/hawks-welcome-human-trafficking-conviction-11-may-2015-0000.

South African Police Service (website). 2014. "Eastern Cape Duo in Court for Sexually Exploiting Three Girls." August 13, 2014. https://www.saps.gov.za/newsroom/selnewsdetailsm.php?nid=89.

———. n.d. "South African Police Service Crime Statistics." South African Police Service. Accessed January 20, 2023. https://www.saps.gov.za/services/older_crimestats.php.

South Coast Herald. 2018. "Surge in Sexual Assault and Violence Has Led to South Africa Being Dubbed 'the Rape Capital of the World.'" September 7, 2018.

Soyinka, Wole. (1975) 1994. *Death and the King's Horseman*. New York: W. W. Norton.

Spence, Chanel. 2021. "Government Revises Agreement for Mining in Cockpit Country." Jamaica Information Service. Posted May 27, 2021. https://jis.gov.jm/government-revises-agreement-for-mining-in-cockpit-country/.

Springer, Jennifer Thorington. 2008. "'Roll It Gal': Alison Hinds, Female Empowerment, and Calypso." *Meridians* 8 (1): 93–129.

Statista. 2022. "Homicide Rates in Selected Latin American and Caribbean Countries in 2021." Data released January 2022. https://www.statista.com/statistics/947781/.

Stone, Carl. 1983. *Democracy and Clientelism in Jamaica*. New Brunswick, NJ: Transaction.

Swart, Heidi. 2013. "Will Anene Booysen's Brutal Rape and Murder Shake the Nation into Action?" *Mail and Guardian*, February 15, 2013.

Tafari-Ama, Imani M. 2006. *Blood, Bullets and Bodies: Sexual Politics below Jamaica's Poverty Line*. Lancashire, UK: Beaten Track.

Tallbear, Kim. 2014. "Standing with and Speaking as Faith: A Feminist Indigenous Approach to Inquiry." *Journal of Research Practice* 10 (2). https://jrp.icaap.org/index.php/jrp/article/view/405.

Tate, Shirley Anne. 2009. *Black Beauty: Aesthetics, Stylization, Politics*. Farnham, Surrey: Ashgate.

Taylor, Diana. 2003. *The Archive and the Repertoire: Performing Cultural Memory in the Americas*. Durham, NC: Duke University Press.

Taylor, Gladstone. 2019. "PM Brushes aside Debate on Obeah, Sexuality and Abortion." *Gleaner*, June 17, 2019.

Taylor, Sharine. 2019. "Not a 'Cayliss Gyal': Telling the Stories of Jamaicans Who've Had Abortions." Rewire News, March 6, 2019. https://rewire.news/article/2019/03/06/not-a-cayliss-gyal/.

Taylor-Robinson, Michelle M., and Roseanna Michelle Heath. 2003. "Do Women Legislators Have Different Policy Priorities Than Their Male Colleagues? A Critical Case Test." *Women in Politics* 24 (4): 77–101.

Theobald, Anne. 2012. *The Role of Women in Making and Building Peace in Liberia: Gender Sensitivity versus Masculinity*. Stuttgart: Ibidem-Verlag.

Thomas, Deborah A. 2011. *Exceptional Violence: Embodied Citizenship in Transnational Jamaica*. Durham, NC: Duke University Press.

———. 2019. *Political Life in the Wake of the Plantation: Sovereignty, Witnessing, Repair*. Durham, NC: Duke University Press.

Thomas, Greg. 2005. "Man and Woman, Slavery and Empire: Deconstructing 'Gender' in Plantation America." *JENdA: A Journal of Culture and African Women's Studies* 7. https://www.africaknowledgeproject.org/index.php/jenda/issue/view/11.

Thompson, James. 2009. *Performance Affects: Applied Theatre and the End of Effect*. Basingstoke: Palgrave Macmillan.

Thompson, Leonard. 2014. *A History of South Africa*. 4th ed. Edited by Lynn Berat. New Haven, CT: Yale University Press.

Tivoli Stories (website). n.d. "Bearing Witness: Four Days in West Kingston." Accessed October 20, 2022. http://www.tivolistories.com/bearing-witness.html.

Tufton, Christopher. 2018. "Abortion War Needs Dose of Compassion." *Gleaner*, October 26, 2018.

Turner, Sasha. 2019. *Contested Bodies: Pregnancy, Childrearing, and Slavery in Jamaica*. Philadelphia: University of Pennsylvania Press.

Turner, Victor W. (1969) 1995. *The Ritual Process: Structure and Anti-Structure*. New York: Aldine Transaction.

Udwin, Leslee. 2015. *India's Daughter*. British Broadcasting Corporation. Film, 63 min.

Ukaegbu, Victor. 2004. "The Problem with Definitions: An Examination of Applied Theatre in Traditional African Context(s)." *National Drama* 3:45–54.

Ulysse, Gina Athena. 2007. *Downtown Ladies: Informal Commercial Importers, a Haitian Anthropologist, and Self-Making in Jamaica*. Chicago: University of Chicago Press.

UN News. 2013. "'South Africa Must Do More to Tackle 'Pandemic of Sexual Violence'—UN Rights Chief." February 8, 2013. https://news.un.org/en/story/2013/02/431602.

UN Women. 2022. "Facts and Figures: Ending Violence against Women." Last updated February 2022. https://www.unwomen.org/en/what-we-do/ending-violence-against-women/facts-and-figures.

Upham, Mansell. 2022. "Respectability Regained—Moeder Jagt's Triumphant Reversal of Her Slave Past." *Muatze* (blog), May 21, 2022. https://mansellupham.wordpress.com/2022/05/21/.

Valenti, Jessica. 2014. "When You Call a Rape Anything but Rape, You Are Just Making Excuses for Rapists." *Guardian* (UK), April 24, 2014.

Van Erven, Eugène. 2001. *Community Theatre: Global Perspectives*. London: Routledge.

Virtue, Erica. 2012. "Stop This Pregnancy, Please!" *Gleaner*, May 6, 2012.

Walker, Alice. 1983. *In Search of Our Mothers' Gardens: Womanist Prose*. San Diego, CA: Harcourt Brace Jovanovich.

Walsh, Denise M. 2010. *Women's Rights in Democratizing States: Just Debate and Gender Justice in the Public Sphere*. New York: Cambridge University Press.

Washington, Teresa N. 2014. *The Architects of Existence: Aje in Yoruba Cosmology, Ontology, and Orature*. N.p.: Oya's Tornado.

Waterson, Roxana. 2010. "Testimony, Trauma and Performance: Some Examples from Southeast Asian Theatre." *Journal of Southeast Asian Studies* 41 (3): 509–28.

Woods, Clyde, and Katherine McKittrick. 2007. *Black Geographies and the Politics of Place*. Toronto: Between the Lines.

Woods, Jewel. 2008. "The Black Male Privileges Checklist." *Jewel Woods* (blog), August 11, 2008. http://jewelwoods.com/node/9 (website discontinued but post is accessible through https://archive.org)

WorldAtlas. 2020. "Murder Rate by Country." Posted January 9, 2020. https://www.worldatlas.com/articles/murder-rates-by-country.html.

World Population Review. n.d. "Rape Statistics by Country 2022." Accessed October 20, 2022. https://worldpopulationreview.com/country-rankings/rape-statistics-by-country.

Wright, William D. 1997. *Black Intellectuals, Black Cognition, and a Black Aesthetic.* Westport, CT: Praeger.

Wynter, Sylvia. 1992. "Rethinking 'Aesthetics': Notes towards a Deciphering Practice." In *Ex-Iles: Essays on Caribbean Cinema*, edited by Mbye Cham, 237–79. Trenton, NJ: Africa World Press.

———. 1993. "Beyond Miranda's Meanings: Un/Silencing the 'Demonic Grounds' of Caliban's 'Woman.'" In *The Routledge Reader in Caribbean Literature*, edited by Alison Donnell and Sarah Welsh, 476–82. New York: Routledge.

Ziarek, Ewa Płonowska. 2012. *Feminist Aesthetics and the Politics of Modernism.* New York: Columbia University Press.

Index

Page numbers in *italics* denote figures.

Aboriginal Peoples, 95
abortion, 12, 140–41, 168n4, 168nn1–2, 169nn6–11, 170n24, 171n26, 171n28; decriminalization of, 24, 31–32; performance activism around, 21–58. *See also* anti-choice laws; pro-choice movement
Abortion Policy Review Advisory Group (APRAG), 26, 30, 32–34, 55, 169n11
Abortion Public Forum, *42*
Abrahams, Rehane, 11, 140; *What the Water Gave Me,* 161, 179n6, 180n3
Ackroyd, Judith, 15
activist aesthetics, 13
activist performance, 12, 47
activist theatre, definition, 13, 15
Adisa, Opal Palmer, 55
Adishakti Laboratory for Theatre Arts and Research, 82
Advocates for Safe Parenthood: Improving Reproductive Equity (ASPIRE), 169n14, 170n23
Afolashadé, 124–25, 163, 178n32
Africana studies, 3, 127
African Diaspora, 8, 17, 19, 41–43, 114, 138, 140; motherhood in, 27, 105, 109; personhood in, 179n6; ritual performance in, 49–50, 94, 124; self-making in, 130; theatre in, 154, 165–66; and women's theatre collectives, 4, 6, 28. *See also* Black Diaspora; Jamaican Diaspora

African National Congress (ANC), 11, 134, 141, 172n6
Afrocentrism, 102
Afroz, Mohammed, 69
Aidoo, Ama Ata, 166
Air Me Now, 169n9
Ajayi, Omofolabo, 49
Alba Emoting, 82–83
Alexander, M. Jacqui, 31
Alexandra (Alex), South Africa, 10; and Olive Tree Theatre, 4, 7, 13, 19, 130–38, *138*, 153–55
Alexandra Youth Congress, 134
#AlexTotalShutDown, 135
Allen, Jafari S., 131
Allen, Lillian, 48
Allen, Tony, 169n16
Allison, Helen: *Sistren Song,* 164
Americans with Disabilities Act, 23
#AmINext, 60
Anene Booysen Skills Development Centre, 70
Angélique, Marie-Joseph, 10–11
Anglophone Caribbean, 6, 28
Anitafrika, D'bi Young, 48, 170n25
Anthony, Trey: *Da Kink in My Hair,* 51
anti-apartheid movement, 7, 67, 132, 134–36, 144, 173n20, 179nn3–4
anti-Blackness, 54, 119, 143, 146, 167n4
anti-choice laws, 169n9; activism against, 13, 17–18, 21–58, 168n1
anticolonialism, 9, 41, 167n3

anti-imperialism, 25, 34, 50, 54
Antigua and Barbuda, 31
antilesbian/antiqueer punitive rape, 66, 78
antiqueerness, 66, 78, 80
antiracism, 153
Apache: "Gangsta Bitch," 114
apartheid, 9–10, 88, 160, 172n9, 173n20, 179nn3–4; and Mothertongue Project, 6; and Olive Tree Theatre, 7, 127–50; and racialization, 73, 132–37, 140, 143; and sexual violence, 65–68, 77, 127, 172n8. *See also* anti-apartheid movement; post-apartheid period (South Africa); white supremacy
applied theatre, 15
archiving, 16, 23, 38, 78, 93, 104–5, 158, 164–65
Argentina, 56, 95
Armstrong, Sue, 67
artist-scholars, 15, 94
artivists/artivisms, 15
Arts Council of Great Britain, 180n6
ASPIRE Saint Lucia, 170n23
Australia, 64

Baartman, Sara (Saartjie), 78–79
Baby Tshepang, 173n17
badness-honour, 97
Bailey, Amy, 3
Barbados, 31, 166, 170n23
Barriteau, Eudine, 24
Batra, Kanika, 51
Baxter Theatre, 129, 138, 180n13
Beckles, Hilary, 172n10
Belaúnde, Fernando, 176n14
Bell, Deanne M.: *Bearing Witness*, 176n11; *Four Days in May*, 176n11
Bellevue Garden Theatre, 41
Belly, 115
Bellywoman Bangarang, 51, 164, 180n12
Bennett, Hyacinth, 52
Besterspruit, South Africa, 132
Beyoncé, 114
Black Diaspora, 17, 50, 55; musical forms in, 136; performance forms in, 28; self-making in, 130. *See also* African Diaspora; Jamaican Diaspora
Black Lives Matter (BLM), 5, 96, 167n4
Black-majority communities, 7–8, 10, 28, 125, 151
Black male privilege, 177n19
Black radical movements, 114, 157, 168n8
Black uplift, 102

Black Women Playwrights Group, 166
Blackwood, Althea, 37, 39, *42*, 46, 169n16
Blaine, Betty Ann, 50, 169n10
Blake, Damion K., 98
Blake, Pauline, 37, 39, *42*, 45, 169n16
Bloch, Susana, 82
Boal, Augusto, 103, 171n29
Booysen, Anene, 5, 59–61, 69–73, 86–87, 172n11, 172n13, 173n16, 174n24
Bounti Killa: "Look into My Eyes," 177n20
Boyne, Ian, 110
Brady-West, Doreen, 169n10
Brazil, 94, 165–66
Brecht, Bertolt, 168n7, 174n27
Bredasdorp, South Africa, 69–71
Breeze, Jean "Binta," 48
British Broadcasting Corporation, 70
Britton, Hannah Evelyn, 66, 133
Britton, Sonia, 38–39, *42*, 169n16
Britz, Camron, 61, 171n3
Brookshaw, David, 179n7
Brown University, 8, 127; International Advanced Research Institutes, 3
Buchwald, Emilie, 61
Burke, Tarana, 166, 180n7
Burns, Shawna-Kae, 171n27

Caliban, 9
Callaghan, Nina, 8, 59, 73, 83–84, 86, 171n1
Camissa, 73
Campbell, Karlene, 39, *42*, 169n16
Canada, 10, 96, 161–62; Montreal, 10; Toronto, 16, 94–95
Cape Town, South Africa, 11, 63, 127, 129, 132, 138–39, 154, 172n8, 173n18, 180n13; cosmopolitanism in, 9; and Mothertongue Project, 59, 72–73, 87, 89. *See also* University of Cape Town (UCT)
Cape Town Fringe Festival, 73, 89, 173n18
Capitol Crawl, 23
Caribbean Association of Feminist Research and Action, 169n14
Catholicism, 25, 33, 35, 45, 54, 170n23
Catholics for Choice, 33, 170n23
Central Africa, 41, 176n12
Central Intelligence Agency, 97
Centre for the Investigation of Sexual Offences and Child Abuse, 169n7
Chevannes, Amba, 103, 106, 175n2. See also *Vigil for Roxie, A*
Chevannes, Barry, 112
Child, Toni: "Death," 174n25

202   Index

child abuse, 24, 51, 120, 169n7. *See also* domestic violence; gender-based violence; sexual violence
Chile, 17, 96, 162, 175n3
Chirwa, Naledi, 11
Christianity, 40, 77, 96; and abortion activism, 31, 33–40, 50, 54–56; evangelism, 55. *See also* Catholicism; Revival
Citizen Security and Justice Programme (CSJP), 6, 37, 163, 169n15
citizenship, 8, 27, 51
Civil Rights for the Unborn, 54
Clarke, Keith, 175n7
Clarke, Stefan, 180n1
classism, 3, 5, 72, 85, 105, 125, 130, 145; and anti-choice laws, 29, 33–34, 43, 45, 47–48; racialized, 10, 28
Clement, Susan, 145
Clockwork HeART, 180n13
Coalition for the Defence of Life, 169n10
Coalition of Lawyers for the Defence of the Unborn (CLDU), 33–36, 45
Cockpit Country, Jamaica, 178n28
Coke, Christopher "Dudus," 99–100, 109, 112, 175nn6–7
Coke, Lester Lloyd "Jim Brown," 175n6
Colchado, Oscar, 107
Cole, Lloyd, 30
Collins, Patricia Hill, 76
Colombia, 96, 123; Bogotá, 122
colonialism/imperialism, 27, 41, 93–94, 105, 109, 140, 160, 174n22; and anti-choice laws, 28–31, 34–35, 50; British, 29–31, 35, 101, 167, 167n1; European, 5, 66, 75–76; and racialized gender, 8–10; and sexual violence, 59, 65–67, 75–80. *See also* anti-imperialism; decoloniality; postcolonialism
Coly, Ayo A., 78–79
commercial theatre, 6, 101, 122, 124, 128–29, 136–37, 153
Commission of Enquiry into the Extradition Request for Christopher Coke (Manatt Commission of Enquiry), 100
communism, 97, 134
community theatre, 2, 43, 149, 154, 162
Congress of South African Students, 134
Conquergood, Dwight, 17, 168n9
contraception, 2–3, 44
conventional/elite theatre spaces, 12–13, 16
Cooper, Afua, 10, 48
Cooper, Carolyn, 28
co-performative witnessing, 17

Cornelius, Hannah, 61, 171n3
Correa, Anna: *Rosa Cuchillo*, 107
Couto, Mia: *Sleepwalking Land*, 141, 179n7
COVID-19 pandemic, 19, 56, 93, 135, 154–55, 161–62
Cox, Sherie, 160
Crawford-Brown, Claudette, 118
Cuba, 97, 131
Cullors, Patrisse, 96
culturalism, 25, 50, 78
cultural workers, 14–15
curation/curators, 16, 124, 163, 176n11
Cuthbert-Flynn, Juliet, 53–54
Cuvier, Georges, 79

Daily Post Nigeria, 50
Daley, Lashon, 149
dancehall music, 48, 50, 108, 115, 121, 176n9, 177n20
Davids, Jonathon, 172n11
DAWN, 169n14
death penalty, 67–68
decoloniality, 5–6, 19, 78
decriminalization of abortion, 24, 31–32
Delisle, Jennifer, 143
Democratic Republic of the Congo, 67, 116
democratic socialism, 32, 97
demonic grounds, 9
Department of Homeland Security (US), 99
development, 8, 13, 15, 24, 39, 52, 130, 146, 161; theatre for, 2, 15; UN goals for, 45
Development Alternatives with Women for a New Era (DAWN), 169n14
devised theatre, 3, 23, 37–38, 61, 72, 103, 117, 147, 164, 169n16
Dexta Daps: "Grow Rough," 177n20
Dhlomo, Lihle, 147, 149–51. *See also Last Cow Standing*
Dike, Fatima, 179n1; *The Sacrifice of Kreli*, 128
Diradeng, Michael, 134
disability, 23, 31, 33, 53
District Six, South Africa, 132
Dlakavu, Simamkele, 11
Dlamini, Bathabile, 11
Dlamini, Gcebile, 84–85, 147–52, 174nn27–28, 175n29. *See also Nomzamo*
domestic violence, 24. *See also* child abuse; gender-based violence; sexual violence
Dominica, 31
Donkin, Ellen, 145
Dosekun, Simidele, 63
Douglass, Frederick, 168n9

Index   203

Dragon Room, 73, 83, 86–87
drums, 21, 39, 41–42, 47, 49, 103, 157, 167n1
Durban Motion Pictures, 151
Dutch East India Company (Vereenigde Oostindische Compagnie), 11
du Toit, Louise, 62–63, 68–69, 78

Eaton Centre, 95
Ebanks, Neila, *158*, 158–160
Ecumenical Pro-Life Council, 33, 168n2
Edna Manley College of Visual and Performing Arts, 158, 180n1
Ellington, Owen, 98
Emancipation Day (Jamaica), 42
#EndRapeCulture, 165
England, 29–30, 31, 35, 79. *See also* Great Britain; United Kingdom
eNkompani.E, 158–60
Ensler, Eve: *The Vagina Monologues*, 147–48
ethnography, 3–4, 16, 22, 39, 117, 168n9, 171n29; auto-, 75; multisited, 17. *See also* co-performative witnessing
Eugene, Chevy, 163
European Enlightenment, 28, 168n3
Evaristo, Bernardine, 165
Eventide Home Fire, 97, 164

Fabian, Johannes, 168n9
Facebook, 180n7
Fana, Mvuleni, 174n26
Farber, Yaël, 129; *Nirbhaya*, 70, 175n30
Farquaharson, May, 3
Farr, Cecilia Konchar, 13
femininity, 77, 171
feminism, 8, 113, 164, 169n14, 179n10; and aesthetics, 13, 168n6; and anti-sexual violence activism, 71–72, 78, 81, 85, 171n2; Black, 6, 48; Caribbean, 6; feminist geography, 9; Global South, 6; Indian, 71; Jamaican, 3; and motherhood, 27; and pro-choice activism, 33, 48, 53; and profeminism, 153; standpoint theory, 146; and theatre performance, 19; transnational, 6, 81. *See also* womanism
FEMRITE, 166
Ferguson, Fenton, 52
Fido, Elaine Savory, 41
Figueroa, Mark, 177n18
Finikin, Lana, *42*, 51
First Nations Peoples, 95
Flatfoot Dance Company, 180n13
Fleishman, Mark, 144

Fletcher, Pamela R., 61
Flockermann, Miki, 144
Florida: Orlando, 96
Floyd-Thomas, Stacey M., 153
Fondes Amandes, 165
Foot Newton, Lara, 129, 151, 180n13; *Tshepang*, 173n17
Ford-Smith, Honor, 14–16, 103, 106, 116, 118, 123, 163, 165, 175n2, 178n32, 179n10; "Memory, Urban Violence and Performance in Jamaican Communities," 4, 6, 94–95, 117. *See also* Letters from the Dead, *Song for the Beloved*; *Vigil for Roxie, A*
Fortuin, Nicole, 80
France, 79
Francis, Omar, 171n27
freehold townships, 132, 135
Freevoice Productions, 180n13
French, Joan, 14
Friends of Liberty Hall Foundation, 102
Fugard, Athol, 128, 154; *The Coat*, 141; *Sizwe Banzi Is Dead*, 141
Fugard Theatre, 154
Fujimori, Alberto, 176n14

Gandhi, Sonia, 70
gang violence, 13, 24, 37, 67, 135, 163, 166, 169n15, 178n27; and Letters from the Dead, 4–5, 7, 19, 92–93, 96–101, 104–6, 109–15, 118, 123
García, Alan, 176n14
Gardini, Genna, 72, *74*, 80–84, 87–88, 171n1
Garvey, Marcus, 102, 167n3. *See also* Liberty Hall: The Legacy of Marcus Garvey
Garza, Alicia, 96
gender-based violence, 7, 13, 38, 145, 159, 166, 169n15, 172n10, 172n13; and Mothertongue, 59–89; and Sistren/HTCG, 37, 39. *See also* child abuse; domestic violence; sexual violence
gender justice, 7–8, 24, 87, 129, 136, 153, 161, 165; and pro-choice activism, 18, 25, 50, 56–57
gentrification, 9–10
George William Gordon House, 39
Ghana, 166
ghettoization, 9
Gleaner, 25, 28, 52–54, 110
Glen Vincent Health Centre, 32
Global Majority, 5, 7, 34

204   Index

Global North, 128
Global South, 6, 63, 128, 133
Golding, Bruce, 100, 176n9
Goldson, Lloyd, 30
Gordon, Edmund T., 130
Gordon Institute for the Performing and Creative Arts, 173n18
Gqola, Pumla, 62–63, 69–70, 171n2, 172n13
Gray, Obika, 97
Great Britain, 40, 50, 71, 76, 96, 166, 168n4, 180n6; British colonialism, 29–31, 35, 101, 167, 167n1. *See also* England; United Kingdom
Green, Cinderella, 39, 57, 169n16
Green Belt Movement, 165
Gregg, Veronica Marie, 35
GROOTS: Grassroots Organizations Operating Together in Sisterhood, 180n4
Group Areas Act (1950), 133
Gupta, Pawan, 69, 172n12
Gurira, Danai: *Eclipsed*, 180n12
Guyana, 31–32, 170n23
gynecology and obstetrics, 30–35, 46

Haffajee, Ferial, 172n13
Haiti, 67
Halligey, Alex, 162; *Collaborative Conversations,* 164
Hanna, Lisa, 52, 168n1
Hannah Town Cultural Group (HTCG), 104, 169n13, 169n16, 171n29; and *A Slice of Reality,* 17–18, 21–58, 73, 87, 95, 163. See also *Slice of Reality, A*
Hansberry, Lorraine: *A Raisin in the Sun*, 108
Hanson, Sandra, 169n16
Hardie, Julian, 39, *42*
Hardie, Yvette, 151, 180n13
Harker, Jaime, 13
Hartman, Saidiya V., 10
Harvey, David, 119
Hassim, Shireen, 172n6
Have You Seen Zandile?, 128, 143–44, 179n8
Heap, Brian, 167n2
Hear the Children's Cry, 169nn9–10
Hemispheric Institute of Performance and Politics, 17, 122
Herman, Dianne F., 171n2
Heron, Taitu, 22–23, 51, 159
heteronormativity, 3, 67, 74, 145
heteropatriarchy, 31, 67, 77
heterosexuality, 29, 67

Hilaire, Patricia, 165
Hill, Errol, 41, 170n20
Hillbrow Theatre, 148, 174n28
hip-hop, 48, 114–15, 177n20, 177n22
HIV/AIDS, 34, 168n5
Holocaust, 67
Ho Lung, Richard, 25, 36
homelands/land reserves/Bantustans, 129, 133–34
homophobia. *See* antiqueerness
homosexuality, 172n9. *See also* LGBTQ rights; queerness
homosociality, 148, 167n1
Hunter, Margaret, 115
Hurd, Nipho, *152*

Iandoli, Kathy, 177n22
iintsara gangsters, 67, 172n8
I'm Glad I'm a Girl, 169n9
India, 5, 28, 82, 133, 135, 144, 176n13; Delhi, 69, 70–71; sexual violence in, 59–60, 69–72
Indian National Congress, 70
Indigenous Peoples, 9
Industrial Revolution, 35
Influx Control Law (1923), 133
Institute for Crime Prevention and Rehabilitation of Offenders, 67
International Association of Theatre for Children and Young People (ASSITEJ), 180n13
International Women's Day, 24
Iraq, 67
Irvin, Kerryn, 137
Ishawna: "Mi Belly," 177n20
isiXhosa, 77, 147
Israel, 67

jackrolling, 67, 172n8
Jamaica CAUSE, 54
Jamaica Coalition for a Healthy Society, 169n9
Jamaica Defence Force, 98–99
Jamaica Family Planning Board, 2
Jamaica Information Service, 23
Jamaica Labour Party (JLP), 54, 97–98, 100, 175n5
Jamaica Ministry of Culture, 42
Jamaica Ministry of Health, 32, 38
Jamaica Ministry of National Security, 37, 163. *See also* Citizen Security and Justice Programme (CSJP)
Jamaican Constitution, 12, 29, 56

Jamaican Diaspora, 16, 18, 41, 120, 123; dance forms in, 49–50; and testimony, 43. *See also* African Diaspora; Black Diaspora
Jamaican Family Court, 32
Jamaican Office of the Children's Registry, 30, 169n7
Jamaican Parliament, 56–57, 99, 113, 175n5; Human Resources and Social Development Committee, 54; Joint Select Committee on Abortion, 33, 52, 170n23; *A Slice of Reality* in, 12–13, 18, 21–24, 28–29, 36–52, 55
Jamaican Patwa, 18, 40–42, 47–50
Jamaicans for Justice, 100
Jamaica School of Dance, 158, 170n25
Jamaica School of Drama, 14, 41, 95, 158, 164, 170n25, 179n10
Jamaica Star, 118
James, Marlon, 178n27
Jaramogi, Akilah, 165
Jaramogi, Tacuma, 165
Jay-Z: "'03 Bonnie and Clyde," 114, 177n21
Jöb, Jacki, 88
Joburg Theatre, 137–38
Johannesburg, South Africa, 4, 10, 62, 84, 88, 132, 134, 138–39, 148, 172n8
Johannesburg Fringe Festival, 173n18
Jones, Kadian, 169n16
Jordan, Anique, 124, 163. *See also* Letters from the Dead, Song for the Beloved
Joy Town Community Development Foundation, 55

Kabwe, Mwenya, 127
Kana, Johannes, 69
Kani, John, 128, 179n4; *The Coat*, 141; *Sizwe Banzi Is Dead*, 141
Kente, Gibson "Bra Gib" Mthuthuzeli, 128, 136–37; *How Long?*, 179n3; *Too Late!*, 179n3
Kenya, 36, 165
Kenyan High Court, 36
Kgosidintsi, Mbali: *Tseleng*, 161, 180n3
Khoekhoe People, 11, 75, 79
Khoisan community, 154, 162
Khundayi, Siphumeze, 72, 74, 77–80, 83, 88, 173n20; *Ngangelizwe*, 161, 180n3
Khwezi (Fezekile Ntsukela Kuzwayo), 11, 65, 168n5
King, Alveda, 54
King, Martin Luther, Jr., 54
King, Ronelle, 166

Kingston, Jamaica, 10, 21, 32, 91, 95, 103, 117, *158–59*, 169n11, 170nn20–21, 176n8; Hannah Town, 18, 102; Rockfort, 163, 169n13, 169n16; Spanish Town, 104; West Kingston/Tivoli Incursion, 96–102, 109–10, 113, 118, 175n4, 175n7, 176n11
Knight, K. D., 176n9
Knoetze, Martin Tindle, 82, 174n24
Koodiyattam breath performance, 82–83

Lahiri, Madhumita, 78
Langa, Billy: *That Night of Trance*, 155, 162
Langeberg, South Africa, 6, 162
Langeberg Youth Arts Project, 6, 162
Last Cow Standing, 147, 149–51
Lawes, Carol, 103, 105–7, *107*, 116–17, 124, 167n2, 175n2. *See also Vigil for Roxie, A*
Lawrence, Rebekah, 52
Lawyers' Christian Fellowship, 33
Leeward Maroons, 178n28
legislative theatre, 171n29
Lennox, Annie, 71
lesbians, 66, 77–78, 80, 172. *See also* LGBTQ rights; queerness
Letters from the Dead, 5–7, 15–17, 129, 140, 151, 160–61, 166, 178n32; and *Song for the Beloved*, 4, 91–93, 96, 101–3, 123, 162; and *A Vigil for Roxie*, 13, 19, 91–126, 162–63, 165. *See also Song for the Beloved; Vigil for Roxie, A*
Levenberg, Jill, 162
Lewin, Hardley, 98
Lewis, Desiree, 66
Lewis, Janine, 151, 180n13
LGBTQ rights, 4, 59, 78, 96, 169n9. *See also* homosexuality; lesbians; queerness
liberalism, 97
Liberty Hall: The Legacy of Marcus Garvey, 91–92, *92*, 99, 102
#LifeInLeggings, 60, 166, 180n7
Lindsay, Keisha, 177n18
Lindsay-Sheppard, Hertencer, 41, 164
Live Art Festival, 173
Livermon, Xavier, 78
Loots, Lliane, 151, 180n13
Love March Movement, 33, 169n9

Maas Beres, 167n1
Maathai, Wangari, 165
Mabiletsa, Deborah, 136
Madison, D. Soyini, 12
Madres de la Plaza de Mayo, 95
Makau, Disebo Gift, 78, 173n21, 174n26

Manenberg, South Africa, 9
Manganye, Marjorie, 136
Manho, Sulnita, 61, 171n3
Manim, Mannie, 179n4
Manatt, Phelps and Phillips, 100
Maparyan, Layli, 104
Mapoma, Chuma, 147–48, 150–52, *152*, 179n9, 180n13. See also *Womyn Marcha das Mulheres Negras*, 165
Market March Movement, 165
Market Theatre, 128, 138–39, 141, 179n4
Market Theatre Laboratory, 179n4, 180n13
Marlboro, South Africa, 7, 13, 130, 132, 135–38, 154
Marlboro Gardens, 135
Marlboro Industrial, 135
Mary's Child, 35
masculinity, 65, 68, 145, 171n2, 172n6
Masheane, Napo, 129, 146, 155
Masicka: "Drug Lawd," 177n20
Masooa, Salome, 174n26
Matchett, Sara, 3, 14, 175n30, 180n3; and *Collaborative Conversations*, 164; and Mothertongue Project, 7–8, 11, 15, 59–60; and *Walk: South Africa*, 59–60, 71–74, *74*, 82–83, 86, 171n1, 174n25; and *Womb of Fire*, 11, 161. See also *Walk: South Africa*
matrifiliation, 108
matrifocality, 106, 176n13
matrilocality, 106
matrix of domination, 76
Mavado: "Squeeze Breast," 177n20; "Star Boy," 176n9
Mavuso, Amanda, 11
Mazibuko, Lindiwe, 71
Mazibuko, Thuli, 144
Mbaasem, 166
Mbogo, Mbala, 167n2
McCauley, Robbie: *Sally's Rape*, 172n7
McCrae, Patricia, 39, *42*, 46, 169n16
McGann, Roy, 97
McKittrick, Katherine, 9
McLachlan, Fiona, 133
McNeill, Ken, 32
Mda, Zakes, 128
memorialization, 4, 7, 16, 19, 73, 92–93, 96, 160, 164; in *A Vigil for Roxie*, 19, 92–93, 119, 123, 125–26; in *Walk: South Africa*, 73
methodology of book, 3–8, 16–18. See also co-performative witnessing; ethnography
#MeToo, 60, 166, 180n7

Mexico, 36, 56
Mhlophe, Gcina, 128, 143–44, 179n8. See also *Have You Seen Zandile?*
Migraine-George, Thérèse, 14
Milano, Alyssa, 180n7
Milford, Christina, 55
Ministry of Health of Guyana, 170n23
MINUSTAH, 67
Miss Amy and Miss May, 3
Missionaries of the Poor, 25, 33, 54, 169n9
Mkhwane, Menzi, 147, 149–51. See also *Last Cow Standing*
mobile prompting, 75
Mokgoro, Ntshieng, 4, 7, 13, 16, 18–19, 84, 128–30, 142, 145–46, 150–54, *156*, 166, 180n14; Alexandra's importance for, 131, 136–39, 155; *The Anger*, 140; *Distant Faces*, 140–41, 162; *Memories and Empty Spaces*, 140, 162; *The Olive Tree*, 137, 140, 162; and *Paradise Fall*, 140–41, 143, 162, 179n8; *Phases of Mirah*, 140–44, 162, 179n8; *Shofar*, 162; *That Night of Trance*, 155, 162. See also Olive Tree Theatre
Mokonyane, Nomvula, 11
Momsen, Janet, 106
Montego Bay, Jamaica, 2, 38
Montego Bay High School, 2
Moore, Marlon, 113
morality posturing, 25, 29, 33–36
Mothertongue Project, 3–4, 6–7, 14–16, 129, 140, 145, 151, 160, 162, 166, 174n26; *Breathing Space*, 161–62; *Collaborative Conversations*, 164; *Rite of Being*, 8; *Walk: South Africa*, 5, 13, 18–19, 46, 59–89, 103, 161, 171n1, 173n18; *Womb of Fire*, 11, 161. See also Langeberg Youth Arts Project
Motlhokwane, Stoffel Pule, 173n21
Mozambique, 141, 179n7
Mrwetyana, Uyinene, 61–62, 171n3
Msimanga, Nondumiso Lwazi, 151–52, 180n13
Mthembu, Sarah, 136
Mtwa, Percy: *Woza Albert!*, 141
Muhumuza, Queen (Uganda), 47
Munroe, Michelle A., 98
Murphy, Jamain, 99
Murphy, Lundy, 99
Murray, Cedric "Doggie," 109–10, 113, 176n15
Musée de l'Homme, 79
Muséum National d'Histoire Naturelle, 79
Mustard Seed Communities, 168n2
Mvubu, Themba, 173n17

Index   207

Nagar, Richa, 28
Nanny of the Maroons, 164
National Arts Council of South Africa, 161
National Black Theatre of Harlem, 138
National School of the Arts, 180n13
Nationwide 90FM, 118
Natives Land Act (1913), 132
Native Trust and Land Act (1936), 179n2
Ndlovu, Malika, 8, 82, 87
Nelson, Dwight, 52
Nelson, Jaevion, 171n27
neoliberalism, 8–9, 24, 93, 98, 119–20, 122, 125
Netherlands, 161
New France, 10
New Jersey, 123
Ngema, Mbongeni: *Woza Albert!*, 141
Nicholson, Hilary, 163, 167n2
Nigeria, 50, 165
Nodlayiya, Vathiswa, 88
Nongwaza, Noxolo, 174n26
Noranda, 178n28
Northern Ireland, 31
Norwood, Carolette, 54
#NotInMyName, 60
Nottage, Lynn: *Ruined*, 116, 172n7
Nomzamo, 84–85, 147–50, 174n27, 175n29
Ntshona, Winston: *The Coat*, 141; *Sizwe Banzi Is Dead*, 141
Nugent, Latoya, 159

Offences against the Person Act (OAPA), 29–30
Okech, Awino, 8, 144
Okurut, Mary Karooro, 166
Olive Tree Theatre, 5, 13, 15–16, 135, 160, 165–66, 180n13; founding of, 136–39, 141; and *The Olive Tree*, 140; vision of, 152–56; Women's Theatre Festival, 4, 7, 17–19, 84, 127–31, 137, 146–56, 161–62, 179n9
One in Nine Campaign, 65
ontological violence, 59–89
Onuora, Oku, 48
Open University, 179n1
Orange Free State, South Africa, 133
Orange Street Fire, 97
Orthous, Pedro, 82
Outreach Foundation, 174n28

Palestine, 67, 76, 95
Pan-Africanism, 7, 50, 91, 102, 154
Pandey, Avnindra, 69
Papenfus, H. B., 132

Paradise Fall, 140–41, 143, 162, 179n8
Partnership for Women's Health and Well-Being, 56–57, 169n9
Pashe, Patience, 136
Pateman, Carole, 168n3
Patmore, Jherane: *Abortion Monologues*, 53
patriarchy, 5, 23, 85, 108, 113–14, 127, 143, 145, 160, 177n18; and anti-choice laws, 25–26, 28–31, 50, 54; and the double paradox, 106; in government, 13, 40, 50; hetero-, 31, 67, 77; patriarchal violence, 65, 68; and sexual violence, 65–68; as structure, 146. *See also* sexism
Payne, Abbebe, 103
Peace Management Initiative, 113
Pearson, Mike, 13
pedagogy, 5, 13, 18–19, 21, 139, 161, 168n8; antipatriarchal, 153; antiracist, 153; theatre as, 3, 15, 57, 103, 123–24
People's National Party (PNP), 97
People's National Party Women's Movement, 24
performance installations, 73, 75, 88, 96, 102–3, 105, 161, 162–63
performance studies, 12–13, 127, 180n13
performativity, 5, 17, 26, 43, 74, 83, 87, 165
peri-urban communities, 7, 9–10, 131–32
Perkins, Kathy, 143
Perry, Keisha-Khan Y., 166
Peru, 107
Peruvian Truth and Reconciliation Commission, 176n14
Phases of Mirah, 140–44, 162, 179n8
Philip Sherlock Centre for the Creative Arts (PSCCA), 167n2
Phipps, Donald "Zeeks," 178n27
Pieters, Jodene, 61, 171n3
Pillay, Navi, 71
Pinochet, Augusto, 96
Pistorius, Oscar, 70
placemaking, 7
plantocracy, 35
Playhouse Company, 155
plays v. skits, 22
poetry, 22, 23, 43, 47–48, 50; dub, 48
police violence, 10, 41, 71, 93–94, 104–6, 134–35, 167n4, 170n20, 176n10; West Kingston/Tivoli Incursion, 96–102, 109–10, 113, 118, 175n4, 175n7, 176n11. *See also* state violence
polyrhythms, 50
population control, 2
Population Registration Act (1950), 133

208   Index

pornographic gaze, 115
postapartheid period (South Africa), 6, 9, 66, 88, 129–30, 139, 144–45, 150
postcolonialism, 6, 9, 41, 51, 66, 79, 97
Postlethwaite, Rosa, 72, *74*, 74–78, 80, 83, 88, 171n1, 180n2
Potse, Dawid, 173n17
Pregnancy Resource Centre, 55
Pretoria, South Africa, 11, 23, 172n8
pro-choice movement, 170n23; and race, 27–28, 50; and *A Slice of Reality*, 13, 17–18, 21–58, 87
Protecting Black Life, 54
Public Broadcasting Corporation of Jamaica (PBCJ), 23
public space, 10–12, 28–29, 61, 72, 160
Pulse nightclub shooting (2016), 96
Putuma, Koleka, 72, *74*, 80–83, 86, 171n1

queerness, 3, 74, 77–78, 80, 85, 88, 96, 144, 164, 172n9. *See also* lesbians; LGBTQ rights
Qwabe, Beverly, *152*

racial justice, 7, 135
racial segregation, 9, 27, 67, 133. *See also* apartheid
racism, 11, 92, 127, 143, 145, 160, 174n23; and anti-choice laws, 34, 54–55; and Black male precarity, 112–13; challenging, 5, 7, 13; classed, 28, 125; and gender-based violence, 172n10; and sexual violence, 66–67, 75, 79–80, 85; and space-making, 130–31. *See also* antiracism; apartheid; police violence; racial segregation; state violence; white supremacy
Randall, Paulette, 165
Rao, Maya Krishna: *Walk*, 5, 59, 72, 81–82, 88
rape culture, 60–61, 63, 69, 80, 88, 165, 171n1
rape trauma syndrome, 84
Raphael, Adrian, 169n16
Rastafari, 47, 103, 165, 176n11
Reganass, Heather, 67
reggae music, 48, 108
Renold, Emma, 171n2
reproductive freedom, 2
reproductive justice, 18, 21, 55, 57, 166
research-to-performance methodology, 46, 57, 103
respectability politics, 34, 50, 73, 105
Revival, 96, 103–4, 121, 157, 163, 176n11
Rhone, Trevor: *Old Story Time*, 105

Richards, Kenneth, 35
Richards, Shirley, 33
ride-or-die chick figure, 114–15
Riley, Patricia, 39, *42*, 169n16
Ringrose, Jessica, 171n2
Rites and Reason Theatre, 127
ritual, 5, 7, 41, 140, 158–60, 176nn11–12; and *Phases of Mirah*, 144; ritual performance, 16, 49–50, 94, 124; and *A Slice of Reality*, 49–51; and *A Vigil for Roxie*, 93–95, 104–8, 118, 123–25, 163; and *Walk: South Africa*, 77, 83
Robinson, Tracy, 51, 169n5
Rockfort Cultural Group, 169n13, 169n16
roots theatre, 178n33
Roper, Shani, 171n27
Rose, Amber, 87
Rose, Tracey, 80
Roth, Martha, 61
Rutgers University, 123
R. v. Bourne (1938), 30, 168n4

Saint Kitts and Nevis, 31
Salo, Elaine, 9
Sandton, South Africa, 10, 132
Santibáñez, Guy, 83
Scarry, Elaine, 63
scenes of subjection, 10
Scotland, 31
Scott, Dennis C.: *An Echo in the Bone*, 105
Seaford Town, Jamaica, 1–2
Seaga, Edward, 175n5
Seane, Warona, 129, 146, 151, 180
Sedgwick, Eve Kosofsky, 88
Segall, Kimberly Wedeven, 65–66, 88
self-making, 127–56
Serote, Alinah, 136
Sex Actually, 89, 173n18
sexism, 43, 47, 79–80, 112, 130, 164. *See also* patriarchy
sexual agency, 25, 27, 35–36, 50, 68
sexual justice, 6, 24, 165
sexually transmitted infections, 2
sexual violence, 10, 52, 159, 171nn3–4, 172nn11–13, 173n21, 173nn14–17, 174n24; and anti-choice laws, 25–26, 31–32, 36, 44–46, 51, 55, 168n2, 168n4, 169nn8–9, 170n24; antilesbian/antiqueer punitive rape, 66, 78; anti-sexual violence activism, 18–19, 60, 71–72, 78, 81, 85, 165–66, 171n2; and apartheid, 65–68, 77, 127, 172n8; and colonialism, 59, 65–67, 75–80; definitions of, 63–64;

Index 209

sexual violence (*continued*): by Jacob Zuma, 11, 23, 172n6; and *Nirbhaya*, 175n30; and *Nomzamo*, 148–49; and *Phases of Mirah*, 141–42; racialized, 66–67, 75, 79–80, 85; and slavery, 59, 65–67, 141, 172n7; trauma of, 19, 60, 76, 80–86; and *A Vigil for Roxie*, 104–6, 114–18; and *Walk: South Africa*, 5, 59–89, 171n1, 174n26. *See also* child abuse; domestic violence; gender-based violence; jackrolling; rape culture
Shakes, Edward, 171n27
Shakes, Elaine, 1–2
Shakes, Nicosia, 163, 171n27; *Afiba and Her Daughters*, 127
Shakespeare, William: *Hamlet*, 117, 175n29; *The Tempest*, 9
Shakur, Tupac: "Me and My Girlfriend," 177nn20–21
Shandilya, Krupa, 71
Shange, Ntozake: *for colored girls who have considered suicide / when the rainbow is enuf*, 148
Shanks, Michael, 13
Sharma, M. L., 173n15
Sharma, Vinay, 69
Shikwambane, Tinyiko, 11
Shottas, 115
Sibanda, Stembiso, 88
Sigasa, Sizakele, 174n26
Simelane, Eudy, 173n17
Simon, Barney, 128, 179n4; *Woza Albert!*, 141
Simpson-Miller, Portia, 39, 170n18
Singapore, 69–70
Singh, A. P., 173nn14–15
Singh, Manmohan, 70
Singh, Mukesh, 69, 172n12, 173n15
Singh, Ram, 69, 172n12
Singh Pandey, Jyoti, 5, 59–60, 69–72, 87, 173nn14–15, 175n30
Sistren (magazine), 164
Sistren Theatre Collective, 3–5, 7–8, 14–15, 129, 140, 145, 151, 160–61, 165–66, 167n2, 169n9, 169n13, 170n25, 171n29; *Bellywoman Bangarang*, 51, 164, 180n12; and labor divisions, 179n10; and Letters from the Dead, 178n32; *Muffet inna All a Wi*, 164; *Nana Yah*, 164, 172n7; *QPH*, 41, 105, 164, 176n12; Rise Up Wi Community, 6, 163; and *A Slice of Reality*, 13, 17–18, 21–58, 73, 87, 95, 163; Tek It to Dem, 6, 163, 169n15. *See also* Rockfort Cultural Group; *Slice of Reality, A*

site-specific performance, 7, 12–13, 73, 95, 162
Six-Day War (1986), 134
Skosana, Lukhanyiso, 88–89
slavery, 41, 94, 127, 168n9, 172n10, 178n28; and anti-choice laws, 28, 35; and Black death, 109; legacies of, 8–10, 35, 59, 93, 140, 160; and motherhood, 27; and sexual violence, 59, 65–67, 141, 172n7
Slice of Reality, A, 95, 163; and class, 47–48; legacies of, 51–53, 56–58; making of, 37–43; and pro-choice activism, 17–18, 21–27, 29–36, 53–56, 87; and racially gendered sexuality, 27–29; and ritual movement, 49–51; as site-specific theatre, 13, 73; and testimony, 43–47
slow death, 94
SlutWalk, 87
Small, Jean, 164, 167n2; *A Black Woman's Tale*, 51
Smith, Alex Duval, 139
Smith, Christen, 94
Smith, Danielle, 163
Smith, Jason, 104
Smith, Mikey, 170n25
Smith, Raymond T., 108
Sobo, Elisa J., 26
social change, 1, 3, 14–15, 123
social justice, 5–7, 19, 22, 58, 91, 93, 96, 136, 153
social media, 4, 12, 53, 60, 100, 110, 162, 165–66, 180n7. *See also individual hashtags and platforms*
Social Sciences and Humanities Research Council of Canada, 161
Song for the Beloved, 4, 91–93, 96, 101–3, 123, 162. *See also* Letters from the Dead
Sophiatown, South Africa, 132
Sopotela, Chuma, 162
Soto, Kathleen, 115
South African Constitution, 66, 172n9
South African Department of Arts and Culture, 155
South African Police Service, 63
South African State Theatre, 155
South African Women's Arts Festival (SAWAF), 155
Soviet Union, 97
Soweto, South Africa, 134–35, 138, 155, 180n13
Soweto student protests (1976), 134
Soweto Theatre, 129, 138, 155, 180n13

Soyinka, Wole: *Death and the King's Horseman*, 117
space-making, 8, 19, 127–56
Space Theatre, 141
Spence, Nadeen, 159
Spencer, Rudyard, 52
Spice: "Romantic Mood," 177n20
spiritual realism, 144, 151
Springer, Kara, 163
Standpipe, Jamaica, 10
state violence, 4–5, 7, 13, 19, 37, 66–67, 94, 97, 118–19, 123, 163, 166. *See also* police violence
Steenkamp, Reeva, 70
Stellenbosch University, 174n23
Stephens, Tanya: "Gangsta Gal," 115; "These Streets Don't Love You Like I Do," 115
Ster-Kinekor cinemas, 155
Stewart, Anita (Anilia Soyinka), 48
Stewart, Joan, 39, *42*, 169n16
Stone Crusher gang, 109
storytelling, 5, 19, 38, 48, 75, 103, 141, 151, 160
street performances, 2, 16, 19, 95
street theatre, 38
succession planning, 163–64
surveillance: racialized, 10
survivor (term), 60
Survivor Empowerment March, *158–59*
survivor-/victim-blaming, 65, 70, 73, 86
Sweden, 64
Syria, 67

Tafari-Ama, Imani M., 113, 118
TallBear, Kim, 17
Tambo, Oliver, 162
Tambourine Army, *158*, 158–59, 165, 169n9
Teer, Barbara Ann, 138
Termination of Pregnancy Act (Jamaica), 18, 22, 32–33, 39, 51, 54–55, 57
testimony, 28, 43–44, 46, 88, 96, 99–101, 118, 147, 166
Thailand, 56
Thakur, Akshay, 69, 172n12
Thame, Camilo, 171n27
Thame, Maziki, 55, 171n27
theatre, definition, 5
theatre as pedagogy, 3, 15, 57, 103, 123–24
theatre as therapy, 15
theatre-based activism, 4, 15, 18
theatre education institutions, 37
theatre for development, 2, 15
Theatre of Black Women, 165–66, 180n6

theatre studies, 12–13
Thiong'o Ngũgĩ wa, 157
Thomas, Deborah: *Bearing Witness*, 176n11; *Four Days in May*, 176n11
Thompson, James, 58
Thompson, Marlon, *42*, 169n16
Tometi, Ayọ, 96
Toppin, Danielle, 51
#TotalShutDown, 60, 65, 135, 165
Transvaal, South Africa, 132
trauma, 43, 68, 104, 109, 140–43, 176n12; and applied theatre, 15; past perpetrator, 68; of pregnancy, 45, 65; secondary, 65; of sexual violence, 19, 60, 76, 80–86; of state violence, 92, 99
Trinidad and Tobago, 31, 118, 165
Tshabalala, Lillian, 136
Tshwane University of Technology, 180n13
Tumblr, 53
Turner, Camille, 163
Turner, Sasha, 35
Twala, Annie, 136
Twitter, 180n7

Udwin, Leslee: *India's Daughter-The Nirbhaya*, 70
Uganda, 47, 166
Ukaegbu, Victor, 15
ukuthwala, 67, 172n8
Ulysse, Gina Athena, 130–31
uMkhonto we Sizwe, 141
umxhentso, 77
United Church of Jamaica, 33, 170n23
United Kingdom, 179n1. *See also* England; Great Britain; Northern Ireland; Scotland; Wales
United Nations, 24, 64, 71; Convention on the Elimination of All Forms of Discrimination against Women, 45; MINUSTAH, 67; UN Women, 161
United States, 3, 23, 98, 99–100, 102, 115, 122, 138, 160, 162, 167n4, 177n19; and aesthetic norms, 15; and anti-choice activism, 34, 54–55; anti-sexual violence activism in, 60, 165–66; hip-hop in, 48; migrants to, 105, 109, 119–22; police violence in, 94, 96, 167n4; US imperialism, 5, 97
Universal Negro Improvement Association and African Communities League (UNIA-ACL), 102, 167n3
University of Cape Town (UCT), 63, 72, 76, 127, 173n18

Index 211

University of Chile, 175n3
University of KwaZulu-Natal, 150; Centre for Creative Arts, 180n13
University of Pennsylvania Museum of Archaeology and Anthropology, 176n11
University of the West Indies (UWI), Mona, 3, 167n2; Institute for Gender and Development Studies, 55
University of Witwatersrand, 88–89, 180n13
University of Witwatersrand Drama for Life Centre, 173n18
unmuting, 82
unstageable plays, 127–28
US Capitol attack (2021), 167n4

V-Day One Billion Rising, 173n18
victim (term), 60
Vigil for Roxie, A, 4–5, 18–19, 91–92, 151, 162, 165, 175n2; and Black male precarity, 109–14; and Black women's love, 114–19; and economic survival, 119–22; and Letters from the Dead, 94–96; and maternal grief, 107–9; performance of, 104–7; as political event, 122–26; and ritual, 93–95, 104–8, 118, 123–25, 163; situating, 101–4; and West Kingston Incursion, 96–101
Vlei, Princess, 75–78

Wales, 31
Walk, 5, 59, 72, 81–82, 88. See also Rao, Maya Krishna; sexual violence; Singh Pandey, Jyoti; *Walk: South Africa*
Walk: South Africa, 13, 18–19, 46, 103; creation of, 69–73; performance of, 73–97, 161, 173n18; resonances of, 87–89; and ritual, 77, 83; and sexual violence context, 5, 59–69, 171n1. See also Booysen, Anene; Mothertongue Project; ontological violence; sexual violence; Singh Pandey, Jyoti
Walters, Sanique, 163
Wapad, Ngugu "Letty," 173n17
Waterson, Roxana, 43
Wedderburn, Junior "Gabu": *Bearing Witness,* 176n11; *Four Days in May,* 176n11
West Africa, 41

West Kingston Commission of Enquiry, 96, 100
West Kingston/Tivoli Incursion, 96–102, 109–10, 113, 118, 175n4, 175n7, 176n11
white supremacy, 5, 67, 140, 146, 167n4. See also apartheid
Williams, Eugene, 101–4, 122–23, 151, 164, 175n2; *Muffet inna All a Wi,* 164. See also *Vigil for Roxie, A*
Williams, Monica, 104, 176n10
"Wi Oun Laif," 49
Woman Inc., 170n23
womanism, 6, 8, 13, 19, 48, 104, 153. See also feminism
Women and Men for Women's Reproductive Freedom and Autonomy, 55
Women in Black, 95
Women's Empowerment for Change (WE-Change), 165, 169n9
women's liberation, 8, 13
Women's March, 165
Women's Media Watch of Jamaica, 26, 167n2, 169n14, 170n23
Womyn, 147–48, *152,* 179n9
Woods, Jewel, 177n19
Working Committee on Women's Reproductive Health and Rights, 169n14
Working Group for Reproductive Health, 38
World Health Organization, 2, 46, 64
World Population Review, 63–65
World War I, 101
World War II, 101, 167n1
Wynter, Sylvia, 9

Xaba, Nelisiwe, 80
xenophobia, 120, 132

Yarona Mall, 137–38, *138*
York University, 94
Yoruba Ifa cosmology, 140
youth uprising (1986–87), 134–35
YouTube, 22, 61, 72, 80, 160
"Yu Nuh Seet," 47–48

Zara, 11
Zulu, Lindiwe, 11
Zuma, Jacob, 11, 23, 65, 71, 135, 172n6

NICOSIA SHAKES is an assistant professor of history and critical race and ethnic studies at the University of California, Merced.

National Women's Studies Association /
University of Illinois Press First Book Prize

Sex Tourism in Bahia: Ambiguous Entanglements   *Erica Lorraine Williams*
Ecological Borderlands: Body, Nature, and Spirit
    in Chicana Feminism   *Christina Holmes*
Women's Political Activism in Palestine: Peacebuilding, Resistance,
    and Survival   *Sophie Richter-Devroe*
The Sexual Politics of Empire: Postcolonial Homophobia in Haiti   *Erin L. Durban*
Women's Activist Theatre in Jamaica and South Africa: Gender, Race,
    and Performance Space   *Nicosia Shakes*

The University of Illinois Press
is a founding member of the
Association of University Presses.

———————————————

University of Illinois Press
1325 South Oak Street
Champaign, IL 61820-6903
www.press.uillinois.edu